A

You are the brand.

$23.95

DATE		

DISCARDED

"Steve Adubato is a pro! My hat goes off to him because there are only a few great communicators around . . . and he is one of the best!" — **Suze Orman,** financial guru and *New York Times* bestselling author

"In this confusing and ever-changing world of marketing and branding, Steve's book *You Are the Brand* will help you make the connections you need to make." — **Neal Shapiro,** president and CEO, Thirteen/WNET (PBS)

"Steve is a great guy. We're kind of one in the same in that we're both Jersey boys and grew up that way—Italian families. We understand each other. . . . His new book *You Are the Brand* is a must-read." — TLC's "Cake Boss," **Buddy Valastro**

"*You Are the Brand* takes you behind the scenes and reveals surprising approaches to building a personal or business brand. Steve is a true media expert with real-world experience. His advice is spot on. I highly recommend this book." — **Michael Port,** *New York Times* bestselling author of *The Think Big Manifesto*

"Steve always has a refreshing take on the events of the day. His voice brings clarity to confusion and his passion produces more light than heat." — **Jim Bell,** executive producer, The *TODAY* show

"*You Are the Brand* renews the high position in which Steve Adubato is held by top professionals. He is one of the best around when it comes to communicating a message." — **Marty Appel,** long-time New York Yankees PR director

"Steve is one of the best in the business." — **Jonathan Alter,** *New York Times* bestselling author of *The Promise: President Obama, Year One*

"Steve Adubato has written a book that is super important and timed perfectly. *You Are the Brand* is a must-read for all in this ever-changing world, both business and personal." — **Jack Mitchell,** author of *Hug Your Customers* and *Hug Your People*

"I love working with Steve Adubato because he's informative and so knowledgeable. The world of broadcasting simply can't live without him." — **Rosanna Scotto,** co-host FOX 5's *Good Day New York*

"In *You Are the Brand* Steve continues his role as the perpetual teacher by reinforcing that there are lessons to be learned from every circumstance." — **Thomas Marino,** CPA, JH Cohn partner and CEO

"As the country's foremost media expert, Steve Adubato has made himself the go-to brand for radio and television producers across the nation. Follow the advice Steve lays out in this book. You won't be disappointed!" — **Scott Lakefield,** program director, WOR Radio/New York

"*You Are the Brand* is a great book. It should be required reading for every CEO and executive responsible for shaping and executing their organization's reputation and brand in the marketplace. Steve Adubato has hit a home run." — **Ronald J. Del Mauro,** CEO, Saint Barnabas Health Care System

"I have long known and respected Steve Adubato and his work; it's the reason I've always enjoyed working with him." — **Dan Abrams,** former president of MSNBC and founder of Abrams Media Network

"Steve's book leaves out one very important chapter—the Adubato brand. Built from hard work combined with intellect, inventiveness, and insight, he is a case study all need to examine and learn from. He has affected more people and businesses in a positive manner than I can count." — **Nick Matarazzo,** CEO, Jumpstart Automotive Group

"We live in a message-filled world, and the trick is to cut through the noise. In *You Are the Brand*, Steve tells us how to do that by creating a concept—a brand—that captures the hearts and minds of your target audience." — **Fran Durst,** Northeast communications manager, Wells Fargo

"Quite simply, Steve Adubato gets it . . . he has the unique capacity to bridge Wall Street and Main Street and his perspectives and insights are right on target and useful in dealing with everyday challenges." — **Robb Sansone,** executive vice president and CFO, Fedway Associates, Inc.

"Steve's number should be automatically programmed into the cell phones of every executive, celebrity, athlete, and politician in America. His intelligent, no-nonsense advice offers a strategic way to contain, control, and condense any PR crisis." — **Rafe Gomez**/The Rehirement Coach, author of *What's in It for Me?*

"If you are interested in developing a slogan, this book is not for you. Success requires brand consideration, and Steve provides you with the blueprint to get there!"

— **Fred Graziano,** head of Retail Banking, TD Bank

"Steve Adubato's realistic and to-the-point approach in *You Are the Brand* will prove to be an invaluable tool for those navigating their way through the process of achieving their 'branding' dream!"

— **Caroline Manzo,** *Real Housewives of New Jersey*

"Steve Adubato has the uncanny ability to drill down to the messages that matter most when building, growing, or defending a brand— whether delivered in an intimate conversation or a broad public forum. This is why so many successful organizations seek his unique style of counsel." — **Stephen K. Jones,** F.A.C.H.E., president and CEO of Robert Wood Johnson University Hospital

"Steve has tremendous energy. . . . It's quite remarkable. He's bright, he gets right to the point, he cuts through the clutter, and keeps it interesting." — **AJ Kubani,** founder "As Seen on TV," CEO, Telebrands of Fairfield

"*You Are the Brand* provides an in-depth look at the brands that are standing strong, as well as ones that could use an image boost. The case studies, coupled with Steve's insight from years of experience in this arena, give readers the tools necessary to successfully define and further develop their brands. I recommend this book to corporate leaders who are looking to differentiate their companies in a crowded marketplace." — **Patrick C. Dunican Jr.,** chairman and managing director, Gibbons P.C.

"Steve has a way of getting to the essence of the subject matter."

— **Richard Vezza,** publisher, *The Star-Ledger*

"Steve Adubato is one of my favorites. He has a clear point of view and isn't afraid to share it, particularly when it comes to media coverage of important stories."

— **Joe Scarborough,** host of *Morning Joe*, MSNBC

"The heart of speaking and communicating is doing it from the heart, and Steve has mastered this important art form and shares with you its mighty secrets."

— **Mark Victor Hansen,** co-creator of the #1 *New York Times* bestselling series Chicken Soup for the Soul®

You
Are
the
Brand

You Are the Brand

STEVE ADUBATO, PH.D.

R RUTGERS UNIVERSITY PRESS
New Brunswick, New Jersey, and London

LIBRARY OF CONGRESS CATALOGING-IN-PUBLICATION DATA

Adubato, Steve.
You are the brand / Steve Adubato.
    p. cm.
   Includes bibliographical references.
   ISBN 978-0-8135-5042-8 (hardcover : alk. paper)
   1. Branding (Marketing)—Case studies. 2. Branding (Marketing) I.
Title.
   HF5415.1255.A38 2011
   658.8'27—dc22

                                 2010045437

A British Cataloging-in-Publication record for this book is available from the
British Library.

Visit our Web site: http://rutgerspress.rutgers.edu

Manufactured in the United States of America

This book is dedicated to all the passionate and persistent entrepreneurs (many, but not all of whom, are featured in this book) of every stripe who go out in the marketplace every day to build, promote, and protect their brands and reputations in spite of tremendous odds—including a difficult and unpredictable economy. As entrepreneurs, we all deal with rejection, but it never stops us from moving forward. That's a bond that entrepreneurs share, which makes us a special and unique brand of professional. I hope this book will help all of us in our journey and make the effort just a little bit more manageable.

CONTENTS

ACKNOWLEDGEMENTS

I'd like to acknowledge a team of professionals without whom this book would never have been completed. Stand & Deliver vice president of marketing, Mary Gamba, and this book's editor, Theresa Foy DiGeronimo, are undoubtedly a dynamic duo. Their ability to collaborate, challenge, and push me to be a more concise, clear, and compelling writer is unquestionable. Consistently, both Mary and Theresa not only recommended, but insisted, that certain case studies and chapters in this book be included, while others be taken out. Their decision making was guided by what would be most valuable to the readers of this book so that those readers could take this information and more effectively brand themselves and their organizations. *You Are the Brand* is a much better book because of Mary and Theresa's contributions.

In addition, I was blessed to have a terrific group of researchers lead by my associate, Jacqui Cooke, who was a former student of mine in college and has grown to be a smart, resourceful, and dedicated staff person. Further, while on high school and college breaks, interns including Brian McHugh, Victoria Eisenstein, and my own son Stephen, also contributed to this research effort. I am confident that Brian at Michigan State, Victoria at the University of Delaware, and Stephen at Fordham University have all grown from the experience of working on this book.

I would also like to acknowledge and thank the many professionals who took the time to talk with me and explain their brand—how it works and when it doesn't work, what they've done to fix or adjust it. All of these professionals have demanding and busy schedules, but they took the time to share their stories with me and my readers. For that, I will be forever indebted.

I also want to thank my colleagues in public television, where I have worked as an anchor for nearly two decades, particularly those at Thirteen/WNET (PBS) in New York, as well as my editors at *The Star-Ledger* of Newark, for which I write a weekly column, and NJBiz, a respected publication for which I've written multiple columns on the subjects of branding, communication, and marketing.

I also want to acknowledge my family, particularly my wife, Jennifer, who in spite of having our third child together at the time of writing this book, did her best to listen (or at least make believe she was listening) as I read through constant drafts of the case studies. I want to thank my three sons, Stephen, Nick, and Chris. Chris, who is only six, works consistently with me in our home "bookstore" organizing my books and packing them in boxes for upcoming events and seminars. He is already working on building his own brand and is quite entrepreneurial in spite of his tender age. Our littlest one, Olivia, who was born at the time I finished this book, is too young to really know what "branding" is all about, but I'm confident that one day her personal and professional brand will make the rest of the family proud.

Finally, I want to thank Marlie Wasserman at Rutgers University Press, who once again demonstrated her belief that as an author I have something to contribute to the larger community that is interested and concerned about communication, leadership, media, and branding.

You
Are
the
Brand

Introduction

You are the brand. Yes—you.

Sure, as a business person, you probably have a basic marketing plan that focuses on ways to reach your target audience. But what about a *branding* plan that focuses on you—your reputation and your unique position in a highly competitive market? You know branding is a big deal for organizations and celebrities such as BP, Coca-Cola, Nike, Starbucks, Oprah, the New York Yankees, Tiger Woods, Martha Stewart, Lebron James, and Trump. But, it's not just Tiger who needs to work on his personal image (and I mean *really* work on his image). Branding is important for you, too—that is, if you want to be more successful than you are right now. *You Are the Brand* is your case-study guidebook to making yourself stand out and above all others in your field of business.

What's in It for You?

Branding is important for you no matter where you are in your professional life—whether you have a job or are looking for a job, whether you are a veteran in your field or a newbie, whether you are working in a company or working on your own, whether you are already quite successful or are still hanging on to a shoestring budget. The tips, strategies, methods, and advice you are about to read are sound, proven, and effective and will help you reach your business goals.

Who says so? The thirty-eight people and companies whose stories of branding you're about to explore in this book say so. Flip back to the table of contents, and you'll see lots of notable names. Celebrities like Tiger Woods, Howard Stern, Martha Stewart, Bobbi Brown, and Oprah Winfrey sure know the value of branding. And you'll see the brands everybody knows about, such as Starbucks, Coke, BlackBerry, Toyota, BP Oil, and E*TRADE. You'll also see political brands from Obama to Chris Christie, Sarah Palin and the Kennedys.

Personally and professionally, I find it fascinating to analyze and dissect the branding strategies of famous people and companies—How does Coke make the stupid mistake of rebranding a "new" Coke? How has the Oprah Winfrey brand managed to stay strong for so long on so many media and communication platforms? Can BP ever regain its reputation? How do two banks effectively merge into one organization with one name? Why does a powerful institution like the Catholic Church keep making the same egregious branding and public relations mistakes again and again, expecting a different outcome each time? What was Tiger thinking? Why does a law firm like Gibbons or an accounting firm like JH Cohn undertake multi-tiered branding and "out of the box" marketing initiatives in industries not known for either? And, how does the TODAY show endure in an ever-changing media landscape?

When I face similar issues in my own work, these cases serve as illustrative models. Even when the facts of the cases are far removed from my business life, I've got to say that they still make for entertaining reading!

Another look at the table of contents will show you names of people who are not so notable at all. Looking at these chapter titles, you may say to yourself, "Why do I care about Daniela Costanzo, or Nick Matarazzo, or TJ Nelligan, or Michael Port, or Buddy Valastro?" Believe me—you should care. It's folks like Daniela, Nick, TJ, Michael, and Buddy who often have a whole lot to teach about creating a buzz in the world of the average guy—the world where you live, the world where professional PR agencies aren't in charge of molding a client's reputation, the world in which you can look at yourself and say, "I can do that!"

Consider the case of Buddy Valastro, otherwise known as the "Cake Boss" on the TLC hit reality series. Before the wider public knew his name, Hoboken-based Buddy worked hard to develop a solid reputation as a customer-service-obsessed chef with a big personality. Those tools and a savvy business sense helped Buddy parlay his success into a national cable TV career and a series of spinoff products and business opportunities. Those same tools can also enhance your brand and success immensely.

While you're learning important lessons from this big-time celebrity chef (that have nothing to do with cake frosting!), you may also be surprised to find out how much can be gained from a look at a small-town fitness and spin instructor. I met Daniela Costanzo at the New York Sports Club where my wife and I work out. I was looking for a new exercise routine and heard through word of mouth that Daniela ran the best spin class in the area. This brand reputation gave her a loyal following among men and women, and I later found out that that reputation was supported by an exciting and highly interactive Web site (SpinWithD.com) and slick promotional postcards designed and then distributed at key locations in the area. You'll quickly see how these and Daniela's other branding efforts are transferable to any professional arena.

In the same way, Michael Port's experiences offer branding strategies that have helped him stand out in a crowded and competitive field as an actor, motivational speaker, and author. His story and others like it will show you how to brand in a variety of real-life circumstances that influence the process of building a reputation for all of us who do not have professional image-makers on the payroll. *You Are the Brand* will reinforce the message that everyone and everything must brand effectively or pay a hefty price in the marketplace.

In the end, you'll find that effective branding is not about being the only one who does what you do—obviously, there are lots of people who take up real estate in your competitive marketplace. Instead, you'll see that effective branding—whether on the celebrity or real-world level—is all about doing what you do with a unique flair that creates a buzz among existing customers and potential prospects and makes you the indispensable go-to person.

So . . . what is your brand in the marketplace you are trying to reach? How can you position yourself? How would key prospects and customers describe you? What can you do to make yourself and your product/services stand out? The answers to these questions will be yours after you read the case studies and the follow-up analyses that give you relevant tips and lessons you can use immediately in your own branding campaign.

Why This Book?

You might be saying, "Who is this guy Steve Adubato to talk about branding, and what's he got to say that's new and different on the subject?"

Let's be honest here. My face is on the cover of not only this book, but also the three previous books I've written. I admit it. I am a self-promoter, guilty as charged. And I'll also admit that I'm good at it.

That's exactly why this book on branding is so different from others on the same shelf of the bookstore. My entire professional life has been about branding. Learning it, living it, making mistakes at it, and now teaching it at several universities including NYU, Seton Hall University, and Montclair State University. In the process, I've usually managed to find the fine line between shameless self-promotion and smart, strategic branding—first for myself, then for others, and now for you.

My lessons in branding began in 1983, when, as a twenty-five-year-old, I ran for the state legislature in a community I had just moved into. I had no money and virtually no name recognition. I was a very long shot. I understood from the start that I'd better be dammed good at selling myself if I wanted to survive this daunting political test. I not only survived, I won the seat with 32,000 votes by beating the incumbent, a prominent bank president who was more than twice my age. However, I didn't do this just by slapping my name on bumper stickers.

I learned quickly that successful branding requires not only a strong visual logo and slogan that grab people's attention, but also a very direct and personal connection. During my legislative campaign, I knocked on hundreds of doors with a terrific advance team of volunteers who knocked on those doors ahead of me to either pave the way, push me away, or simply leave a small, handwritten note if nobody was at home.

By doing this and following up with a computer-generated letter with a handwritten personal note, I increased the odds that voters would have a more positive image of "my brand" when they received direct mail from my campaign or saw posters or TV spots promoting my candidacy. I learned in 1983, and again when I ran for reelection in 1985, that whether you are a neophyte political candidate or a struggling but energetic entrepreneur, you are the brand and the brand is you.

After I lost my reelection effort in '85, I was forced to rebrand myself outside of the political arena using the lessons I learned from the experience. Specifically, I held on to tactics that helped me make and nurture personal relationships—following up, keeping my name (and face) out there, and using technology to remind people (hopefully without being a pest) about what I and my company were doing.

So today, when I appear as a media or political expert on the TODAY show, or other major media outlets such as CNN, MSNBC, FOX, or CBS (all of which promote my most current book, Web site, and Star-Ledger newspaper column called "Your Communication Coach"), my marketing team sends out video clips of the appearance to over six thousand clients, program sponsors, prospects, and other interested people whose names are in our e-mail database.

That same concise, one-page, mass e-mail also includes my most recent newspaper column, feature articles, excerpts from my books, and useful communication and business tips that can also be found on my Web site at stand-deliver.com. We also include video clips and promotional materials about the regular broadcasting work of our production company, which is closely tied to various PBS and commercial cable stations in the New York area. Certainly, all of this is designed to provide useful and helpful information, but it's also intended to promote me and my brand. This electronic branding effort is one of the many ways I try to balance "self-promotion" with the unselfish distribution of useful information. Further, this effort helps with securing and retaining much-needed sponsors of our television programming. Those sponsors are heavily promoted (and yes, branded) along with our TV programs in a variety of ways, including: newspaper and magazine ads, Internet ads, and via full-screen billboards on the air.

That line that separates the arrogant and boastful from the hard-working and accomplished is a thin one. My life experiences have shown me how to find that line and, more often than not, stand solidly on the right side.

As a bonus, this book stands out among others because it is not just the story of one person and his experience with self-promotion. You are going to learn about branding from a diverse collection of people and organizations who have lots to teach you. In all types of business situations, you will see that branding is a never-ending dynamic and strategic combination of advertising, PR, direct marketing, networking, public appearances, and quality customer service. You'll see that branding is about picking up the phone and just touching base; it's about sending e-mails, personal notes, or text messages just to say hello, ask about "the family," or share an interesting article or news item. Successful branding is about making a constant connection with people in your professional orbit. (Be careful, though: Many professionals use social networking sites like Facebook, Twitter, and MySpace to let the world know what they ate for dinner last night or that their kid got a B on a math test. This is not branding—this is simply "TMI," or too much information.)

You'll also see that branding is the ability to respond to ever-changing and often unpredictable market forces (see the chapter on *Newsweek*), as so many people have been forced to do during this recession—some successfully, some not so successfully. And of course, through these examples of branding strategies and the targeted lessons that follow each one, you'll see why it's important to allow yourself to be vulnerable. You have to be willing to confidently put yourself out there and take the rejection that may follow. (Oprah and Howard Stern were told by many so-called talent experts that they did not have what it took to "make it.") That's why successful branding requires a thick skin and a willingness to get knocked down and keep coming back. Are you ready to do this?

I hope so because, frankly, there is no alternative if you want to succeed in what is often a cruel and unforgiving world of business. Effectively promoting your own work and your reputation is not an option—it is a fact of business life. Like it or not, you must enthusiastically work on a regular basis to do certain things in order to consistently develop, define, and promote your brand. Remember, you are being branded by others all the time, so you may as well take charge of the image you project. This is the book that will show you how.

Focus on What You Can Control

There are many things in the world of business that we can't control or even change—the economy is at the top of that list. Therefore, doesn't it make sense to focus your energy and time on what you *can* control? Your brand is under your control if you take charge and learn how to mold, shape, and more clearly communicate who you are and what separates you from your competitors—and in that way you can survive and hopefully thrive even in a bad economy.

Don't wait until you get a pink slip or your business folds before you develop a practical and realistic plan to brand yourself along with your work to key audiences and stakeholders. This is true for every profession—from engineers to accountants and every job in between. It is not enough that you are technically proficient at your work—current and potential customers/clients need to know it.

This awareness happens when you proactively promote your own reputation. We'll see in examples throughout this book how important it can be to write articles in professional trade journals and to create a Web site promoting not just your services, but also your philosophy about your industry and about providing service to your clients. We'll see the power of providing a few testimonials from clients and customers who you've helped. This isn't bragging; this is letting people know that you've made a difference in the lives of others and that you are somebody who delivers, somebody who is really good at what you do, and somebody who can be counted on to deliver a quality product or service.

When Being Good Is Not Good Enough

Having a proactive attitude is the common thread tying together each of the successful branding strategies in this book. These examples will show you why you have to overcome the misconception that someone else should and will sing your praises. Of course, it's wonderful when that happens; word of mouth is an effective part of a branding effort. In today's very difficult economic times, however, this approach to building one's reputation is just not enough. Too many professionals hide behind the very safe but frankly passive and often unproductive approach to career development by humbling saying: "I'm just not comfortable promoting myself. . . . It just doesn't feel right." Humility is a noble trait, but you can't let a misunderstanding of what it means to be humble get in the way of building a successful and strong brand. Just ask Cake Boss Buddy Valastro.

I'm not talking about promoting yourself by boasting and bragging or being cocky and arrogant. However, I am talking about the fact that in these difficult economic times, you can't solely count on others to do your bragging for you. This advice is especially relevant at a time when so many people are losing their jobs in the blink of an eye, and along with that loss, a big chunk of their motivation, self-respect, and dignity. It's great when someone speaks highly of you, and I encourage you to do it for others. I'm a big believer in karma and the power of helping others, even, at times, your competition. Yet, not many in this fearful, competitive environment are going to take the time to talk up your strong points. They are too worried about themselves.

There are lots of examples in this book that will convince you to speak up for yourself. The business of business can be cruel to those who assume that doing a good job is enough to guarantee a successful future.

This Book Is for You If . . .

Given how important a personal brand is in today's business world, you need to stop and consider if branding is vital to your future success. I say it is . . .

- if you feel that you have something of value to offer
- if you are in a market-driven or competitive environment in which your name, reputation, and persona matters to your ability to succeed
- if you deal with customers whom you want to come back and buy your products and services again and again
- if you are confident that you can help others, but not enough potential customers know who you are and what you have to offer
- if you feel unappreciated in your current job
- if you have recently lost your job
- if you are seeking your first job out of college
- if you are trying to get back into the workforce after years of being "out of it"

If you are experiencing any one of these professional situations, have a seat, turn the page, and read on. This book truly can change your life . . . as well as your BRAND!

Tiger Woods

No One Walks on Water

When I decided to write this book in 2008, I considered writing about Tiger Woods as one of the greatest American brands ever. In fact, it was a tossup between Tiger and Oprah as to who, in my mind, was the strongest individual brand on the American scene today.

Needless to say, all that changed on November 27, 2009. Unless you live in a cave, you know the details—virtually every gory, embarrassing, graphic, and lurid detail—associated with the Tiger Woods infidelity scandal. It seems that within a nanosecond, Tiger Woods went from literally "walking on water" in an ad for the EA Sports Tiger Woods PGA Tour 2009 video game to being an international joke. Women were coming out of the woodwork saying that they had slept with Tiger Woods. Embarrassingly stupid and sophomoric text messages that Tiger sent to some of these women were released to the tabloids and posted on Web sites all over the world. Some women said that Tiger Woods had fathered their children. The golf crowds and then, in turn, the golf gods started to turn on Tiger. In the summer of 2010, it was reported that Tiger Woods lost approximately $100 million in endorsements, including being dumped by AT&T, Gillette, Accenture, Gatorade, and Tag Heuer.[1]

Further, Woods's golf game is off—way off. One wonders if his game will ever fully recover. And remember, it is Tiger's ability to win golf tournaments, especially majors, that is the cornerstone of his brand.

I don't know exactly how this story will end, but the Tiger Woods brand will never be the same—not even close. We will never have to hold a fundraiser for him, and he won't be poor, but Tiger Woods blew it big time. For a person of lesser wealth (like you and me), Tiger's mistakes would most likely be devastatingly destructive and career ending. It's worth a look at the series of mistakes that could lead to this sad end.

Infidelity Isn't the Issue

I'm not just talking about who Tiger screwed around with outside of his marriage, because frankly I couldn't care less. It's not my business. That is, in fact, between him and his wife. But at a certain point, Tiger Woods brought a lot of this on himself by allowing those who managed his brand to put him out there in the public eye as a godlike figure—perfect in virtually every way. Superhuman. Out of this world. Too good to be true. He made himself a target. And then, when it all hit the fan, Tiger proved that he was not only mortal but that he was a terrible communicator under pressure. He folded. He hid. He evaded, and avoided, and looked like a coward. By refusing to speak to police authorities about the car accident, he encouraged the media and the blogosphere to speculate and, as usually happens, this speculation and rumor mill went wild.

Tiger didn't have to give all the details. His marriage, of course, is private, but the incident was very public. There was a 911 call; he was reportedly lying unconscious on the street for five minutes; a neighbor in Florida called the police; and the tabloids were on fire. After a few days of keeping silent and not speaking to the media, Tiger posted a statement on his Web site in which he blamed himself for the accident and said his wife helped him at the scene. Said Tiger: "This situation is my fault, and it's obviously embarrassing to my family and me. . . . Although I understand there is curiosity, the many false, unfounded, and malicious rumors that are currently circulating about my family and me are irresponsible."[2]

These initial online comments didn't cut it. One thing is clear in a crisis: When communicating, you have to do it in person—especially when you are the brand. Sure, online posts are easier and much more distant, but that is the problem with them as well. When you are such a high-profile personality, people need to see you, hear you, and have a gut sense of you and your words.

Then, when Tiger did try to apologize in person, he whiffed big time. After nearly three months of no real communication, Tiger held a much publicized and much anticipated "press conference." Here, Woods communicated a lot of the right things. He said his behavior was "irresponsible and selfish." He said, "I know I have bitterly disappointed all of you. . . . What I did is not acceptable. And, I am the only person to blame."[3]

Humble words, indeed, but when it comes to protecting your brand in a crisis, although *what* you say matters a lot, *when* you say it often matters a lot more. Tiger Woods waited nearly three months to utter a single word in public. That was a dumb communication move—he waited way too long. By waiting this long, much of what Woods said wound up falling on deaf ears. People wanted to hear his apology in the first couple of weeks after the Thanksgiving incident—anytime after that just wasn't going to get it done.

By waiting three months, Woods raised the bar in terms of what people would expect from him. This was where he made his second serious communication mistake. In this first public appearance, he took no questions. He read a statement to a tightly controlled, hand-selected room of friends, family, and supporters.

By refusing to answer any questions, Tiger Woods communicated that he had something to hide. He didn't want to make himself any more vulnerable than he already was. On the human level, I understand that. But, from a practical brand management perspective, public figures owe it to their audience to take challenging questions and be held accountable—especially, given the tremendous public interest in this ongoing and highly embarrassing story that dramatically changed the image his brand was built upon.

Tiger did get points for not having his wife, Elin, stand next to him in some feeble attempt to show that his spouse still supports him (à la former New Jersey Governor Jim McGreevy and New York Governor Eliot Spitzer). Woods stood there alone because, like many of us who screw up big time, we alone must take responsibility for our actions. When the book is written on what is becoming a classic crisis communication case study, this will be one of the few things Tiger Woods did right.

However, I still don't think he got the big picture at first. His branding crisis was not fully about the infidelity. It was about the initial online denial, the silence, the stalling, and the lame first press conference with only invited family and friends. All big mistakes.

Finally, Tiger Woods held a legitimate and constructive press conference before teeing off at the Masters in 2010. This was a very relaxed and conversational Woods who seemed very sincere in his delivery. He had a healthy balance of candor (without spilling his guts) and confidence (without being cocky or arrogant). He was concise and controlled. No answer was more than a twenty-second sound bite, but he did not appear overly scripted and stiff. My sense of this press conference is that either it was a product of the most incredible coaching job around, or he's finally getting to a place that allows him to have confidence and comfort under pressure so that he can communicate effectively in these settings. Maybe he needed to go through all of that (in addition to lots of therapy) to get to this point. He didn't point fingers. He didn't blame the media. He didn't blame anyone but himself. Tiger Woods may finally be learning this lesson the hard way. Time will tell.

"Walking on Water"

Let's go back to the walking-on-water branding issue. So much of Tiger Woods's brand was based on the fact that he wasn't only an extraordinary golfer, but that he was an exceptional human being, and that clearly wasn't true. The golf part, yes. The human being part? Why imply such a thing when you know the more complicated truth?

In many ways, Tiger Woods set himself up for the fall when he told an interviewer that his family would always come before golf or any company that would pay him to endorse a product. And then again when Tiger actually approved of a video game and subsequent ad in which he walked out onto a pond with a golf club and, in his bare feet, hit a golf ball sitting on top of the water. (The original walk on water was simply a glitch in the Tiger Woods PGA Tour 08 video game. When the mistake was exposed, the brilliant minds at EA Sports decided to add the phrase "It's not a glitch. He's just that good" at the end of the video and replicate the scene in an ad for EA Sports Tiger Woods PGA Tour 2009.[4]) So there it is. Tiger Woods "walking on water." How could he be so stupid, so arrogant, so clueless to not understand that when you elevate yourself to such a lofty position, you're going to eventually sink? No one, including the most famous golfer in the world, walks on water.

What's amazing is that Tiger pleaded for privacy when the scandal broke. He said that the public and the media owed him the opportunity to work things out with his wife. That is true for most people, but not for Tiger—not once he allowed himself to be branded as not only the best-paid athlete in the world but also a guy with a squeaky clean image to go along with it. You can't expect privacy when you intentionally build that kind of pristine brand and then get caught screwing around with any woman in a skirt or a g-string.

I'm not a prude by any means when it comes to sex, but when you are the brand, you've got to know who you are at the core. Yes, Tiger Woods gave a lot of money to charity, but he wasn't Mother Teresa. He wasn't honest with himself or you and me about his weaknesses and imperfections—flaws that we all have. Of course, advertising yourself as an unfaithful husband is never a good brand builder, but when an honest self-evaluation brings up this kind of major personal flaw, it's best to avoid projecting that "perfect" image. He and his handlers tried to put him above the rest of us. Why else would they have him walking on water in an ad and video game? Who does that? Even Michael Jordan didn't do that.

Further, while I certainly don't play golf nearly as well as Tiger Woods, like Tiger, I have cursed and acted like an idiot on the golf course when I missed a shot. Yet, he has done it on network television countless times, cursing, throwing his club, barking at the gallery. I never heard him apologize for it once. I've seen him walk past little kids waiting for autographs and, in the past, he has refused to give interviews to the media if the spirit didn't move him. Does that make him a bad person? Absolutely not. But it just makes it clear how imperfect he really was well before the scandal.

Some brands implode because the public packaging is so clearly out of sync with who the person really is. If Tiger's commercial endorsements, video games, and everything about his branding had solely been about his extraordinary golf game, the scandal still would have hurt big time—but it wouldn't have been so devastating. The old expression that says, "If it seems too good to be true, it probably is," seems appropriate here. Tiger was simply too good to be true. Not as a golfer, but as a human being. He should have told his marketing people that he wasn't going to endorse the walk-on-water video game and ad because that image is inappropriate and foolhardy. He shouldn't have done interviews going on about his family being his first priority when he was juggling well over a dozen different women outside his marriage. As smart as Tiger is, he seemed not to be able to grasp that fact.

Tiger Woods may win very big on the PGA Tour again. I love watching him play golf and still root for him (yet not as enthusiastically as I once did) because I feel like I'm watching the Babe Ruth of a game I play and love. But no matter how many golf tournaments Tiger wins, he will never get his reputation back. His brand will never be the same.

Branding Lessons

While few of us will ever achieve the level of success attained by Tiger Woods in his chosen field, the lessons of his brand demise are invaluable for all of us:

- Stick with what is true. Don't try to pretend that you and your product/service are much more than they really are.

- Since we are all human, it's best to avoid projecting that image of "perfection."

- When things go wrong and you make a mistake, you've got to own it. You've got to step up and take the hit as soon as possible. The longer you hide from the media, the worse the offense seems and the longer it takes for your brand to begin the rehabilitation effort. (Clearly, this lesson is a recurring theme in this book as well as in my last book, *What Were They Thinking?*)

- In the end, it's not only true that you are the brand, but also you are, in fact, the person responsible for your brand. You can't blame brand failure on an ad agency (or those advising you) because you are the one, in the end, who reaps both the benefits when things are good and the blame when things are bad.

- Winning isn't everything. When it comes to crisis communication, your objective is to gain the benefit of the doubt. It's not about "winning." It's about whether you can get to the point where people say: "Enough. Give this guy a break." Often when we are faced with a crisis, we see it as a win/lose scenario. That's a mistake. Instead, view it as getting back to even again and gaining trust. It's a slow and difficult process. In the crisis communication game, trying to hit a "home run" is dangerous at best. The key is to move in the right direction.

- The biggest lesson in this whole Tiger Woods branding fiasco is that there is a risk in building a brand that appears omnipotent: Remember, no one "walks on water."

Buddy "The Cake Boss" Valastro

Baking Cakes and Living Dreams

Everyone loves Buddy "The Cake Boss" Valastro. My kids, my wife, and all my nieces and nephews became a lot more interested in my television work when they heard I had interviewed Buddy. "What's Buddy really like?" they all wanted to know. "Is he that much fun in person?" "You think you could take us to meet Buddy?"

Everyone wants to meet Buddy Valastro. In fact, every day at Carlo's Bakery in Hoboken, New Jersey, where Buddy and his family run a fourth-generation bakery, hundreds of fans wait in lines that wind out the door and down the street to get closer to the Cake Boss brand and Buddy's magic. His personality is big, and he also has a talent for making the kind of signature cakes that have made him and his family very comfortable financially.

It's true that the success of Carlo's Bakery is known around the country because of the TLC *Cake Boss* TV reality series. But it's too simplistic to assume that Buddy's brand is all about the TV show alone. The larger question is: What are the factors that put Buddy in a position to get the TLC series that has helped turn him into such a highly successful and potential brand empire?

The answer to that question will show that Buddy Valastro's story is not about making cakes. It is about making dreams come true and being obsessed about doing what you do with passion and dedication.

Be True to Yourself

Buddy's brand is really hot, but he's no superman. Buddy doesn't change into a costume and play a role as a super baker when the cameras start rolling. He's never tried to be someone other than who and what he is. That's one of the many reasons for the success of Buddy Valastro's brand.

When I sat down with Buddy for our *One-on-One* television series, it became clear to me why Buddy's brand is so successful. He was the same guy on my show as he is on his own: upbeat, positive, passionate, engaging, and most of all, down to earth. Buddy, who at thirty-three is a very experienced baker, took charge of the family business at the tender age of seventeen when his father died. Regardless of his celebrity status, he said that, at heart, "I'm still a baker, and I respect the profession. I want people to realize that they hurt the small business person when they go to a big box store like Costco and buy a cake the size of a tire or a pie baked a month ago. People don't realize that choosing mass-produced foods and the decline in quality and the closing of small shops are all related." Despite his fame, Buddy is still a small-town baker.

The *Cake Boss* series also features Buddy's extended Italian American family, who play a huge role at Carlo's bakery and help solidify and humanize Buddy's brand as a real family guy who happens to be a reality TV star. In the end, Buddy's pretty clear about who he is and where he comes from. "I am proud to be from Hoboken, and I would never want to live anywhere else. I am proud to be from New Jersey. I am proud of my heritage. The way you see us on the show is exactly how we are at home. We can be loud. Sometimes we yell and scream at each other. But we'd rather be yelling and screaming in the morning so we can still sit down and have dinner together after work. That's better than keeping things bottled up, and then we'd have nothing to say to each other later." Family is at the core of Buddy Valastro and the Cake Boss brand.

Vision

It was Buddy's father who passed on to him the vision of what a bakery can and should be. "I was born into this business and practically have icing in my blood," he says. He recently told NJ.com that he took his father's "old-world techniques and styles and added my own flair—the fondant, the sugar flowers, the modeling chocolate, the butter cream swirls." And this is what caught the eye of the television producers. Buddy says that the producers were looking to create a show about cakes and bakeries. "They cast a lot of different cakes and people, but then they came to me," he remembers.[1]

TLC thought they knew the kind of baker they wanted and what they wanted that baker to do, but Buddy had his own vision of what was right for him—and it worked. Even without a diploma from a culinary school, Buddy had unbeatable talent. He also had an innate understanding of what an audience would relate to. And he wasn't about to trade in this dynamic combination for the TV producers' vision of what he should be. His decision to be true to himself and stick with what he knew he could do led to the TV series contract and opportunities to bake lavish theme cakes for notable celebrities, including one for Britney Spears's birthday and one for New Jersey Governor Chris Christie's inauguration.

Determination and Persistence

Being born into the business and having a vision of what was possible was a strong foundation on which to build his brand. But these factors were not nearly enough to give the Cake Boss brand national recognition. So Buddy pushed out of his comfort zone in Hoboken and became a participant on a number of Food Network challenges. He lost several of these challenges until finally winning a $10,000 prize on a "Battle of the Brides" wedding cake challenge. That's when TLC first approached him.

A man of less determination might have felt defeated and quit trying after the Food Network said, in a variety of instances, that he really wasn't the best, not to mention the boss. Giving up is not an option. Quitting is not in the vocabulary of someone who truly wants to succeed in business and in building a brand. My sense is that Buddy Valastro could have been rejected by a dozen other TV networks and somehow, some way, the "Cake Boss" or some version of it would have been created and ultimately succeeded. A never-quit attitude is something that's found in most successful branding profiles.

Demanding and Hardworking

Buddy is incredibly talented and loves his work. That's why he is willing to work ridiculous hours on the most intricate details of his elaborate cakes. And that's why he's incredibly successful. That's also why he expects the same from others around him and why he is frustrated when he doesn't see in them that same level of commitment.

Sometimes Buddy's attitude toward his workers comes across as abrasive and unnecessarily confrontational. But in all candor, I totally relate to Buddy. I feel the same way about my work, and I know that sometimes it rubs the people closest to me the wrong way. But too often people who say they want success don't realize the amount of work it takes to claim it. The realistic view of the process of getting from desire to accomplishment is the real beauty of Buddy's show. He shows us the degree of hard work required to build a successful brand, whether you're a baker, banker, businessperson, actor, author, or accountant.

Looking at Buddy Valastro's success, some may think, "Sure it's easy to have a nationally famous brand when your face and product are all over the national media." (He is currently spinning off several new TV series and is doing a series of public appearances at major venues that are attracting thousands of enthusiastic fans.) But I have no doubt that if Buddy had never been on TV or if he were to lose the series, he would still have a highly successful and financially sound brand. He'd still be doing what he does best with vision, passion, determination, and hard work. There are thousands of bakers across this country who don't have reality TV series, but have much the same need to build their brand and their reputation in the marketplace. Simply put, they need to be the "Cake Boss" in their own market with their own customers and prospects. For many of them and others who can't even bake a cupcake, Buddy Valastro is a huge inspiration.

Branding Lessons

There is no clear-cut, iron-clad, logical way to build a brand. However, the Buddy Valastro brand is the result of best practices that any entrepreneur can learn from:

- Be yourself. You can't build a brand on an image or a façade that doesn't really exist in your soul.

- The old-school, old-style, family way of looking at things has value even in today's market. At the core of an entrepreneurial business there has to be a sense of doing whatever it takes to succeed and never ever expecting anyone else to make it happen for you.

- Vision is key to your brand. Know where you're going or you'll never get there.

- Building a successful brand requires that you never quit no matter how many times you get knocked down. Don't whine or complain, asking why things don't happen for you. One thing that is absolutely indisputable and non-negotiable is that you have to want a recognized brand so badly that you are willing to take every rejection and every hard knock as an opportunity to say, "Whatever doesn't kill me makes me stronger."

- Accept the challenge to make your brand better, to get it right, to never accept "good enough." It's never good enough. It's never perfect. But that's no reason not to try to get there.

JH Cohn

Branding for Accountants? Why Not!

JH Cohn is a full-service accounting firm. It's not in the "Big 4," but it is one of the fastest growing and most successful firms of its kind in the country. It was founded in 1919, but like any established firm, JH Cohn cannot rely on tradition alone to make its brand stand out; it has had to evolve to meet changing times and new demands.

One of those changes that forward-thinking CEO Tom Marino decided was vital to the continued success of the firm was a concerted move to raise the company profile so it could stand out in a crowded field. JH Cohn had had an office in New York City since 1954, but, as Marino told me: "No one, CEOs, business people, etc., had any recollection of JH Cohn. That's when we decided we needed to get some brand recognition where people at least know the very basic fact that we are an accounting and consulting firm."

After conducting a series of focus groups several years ago, Marino and his team at JH Cohn decided to embark on a comprehensive, multimedia marketing, advertising, and branding campaign. But because the idea of an accounting firm being so aggressive in branding itself is uncommon in the industry, the group knew this was going to be a tough sell even within the firm. In an interview with me, chief marketing officer at JH Cohn, Chuck Ludmer, said: "Initially there was concern, especially in our world where we're dealing with a group of professionals, who are conservative in nature and are not necessarily aware or comfortable with aggressive positioning and advertising. But slowly, seeing the effects of the marketplace, the partners rallied around to really support the new marketing campaign."

22

Brand Association

The firm's advertising agency suggested that JH Cohn choose something (an animal or mascot) for people to associate with the firm. Brand association is not new, but it is rarely executed effectively and never used by accounting firms. Marino didn't reject the idea immediately, but he knew he didn't want something like the AFLAC duck campaign. That kind of association just wasn't the right style for his company.

Then, when Marino was walking through Newark Liberty Airport, he saw an Accenture ad with Tiger Woods and decided to go with a testimonial ad that would help clients associate the firm with someone who embodied its values. Being the first firm of its size to use a spokesperson to promote the ideals of the company put Marino and his team under a lot of pressure to come up with just the right person—and they did. "We came up with Joe Torre, who we believe represented the things we wanted people to associate with JH Cohn: Trust. Strong managerial style. Success."

At the time, Torre was managing the New York Yankees. He was all about New York. All about baseball. All about being a great team leader. When the JH Cohn folks met with Torre, there was an immediate connection. He and Marino were kindred spirits. They managed and led in much the same way. And the JH Cohn CEO was convinced that this was the right move to build a branding and advertising campaign for the firm. The company went across the board with the Torre campaign—radio spots and full-size print ads for Web sites, newspapers, magazines, and subway stations.

The Reward

One of the JH Cohn ads featuring a full facial shot of Torre said, "Amazing how experience prepares you for things no one's ever seen . . . the experience to face the unprecedented." The ad went on to say, "Since 1919, JH Cohn has guided clients through 5 wars, 16 recessions, and 17 recoveries." Also, "Clients know they can rely on JH Cohn's experienced tax, audit, and accounting professionals to help them meet uncertain times." And, "It's why I won't face a new management challenge without JH Cohn."

This ad was featured in the middle of the 2008/2009 recession. The message delivered by Joe Torre was powerful and consistent with what the firm wanted to communicate to its clients and prospects. It was a very clear and effective brand message, and Torre was the perfect credible messenger to deliver it effectively.

Soon, people began to connect JH Cohn with Joe Torre, and brand awareness of JH Cohn in the New York market grew dramatically. In fact, Marino said, "Every year we check to see if Torre is increasing our brand recognition or if it has leveled off. We went from 0 percent recognition in New York up to 22 percent and then up to 37 percent and now we are up to 60 percent through the fourth year. Going from 0 to 60 percent is huge."

The Risk

Although the association between JH Cohn and Joe Torre turned out to be a positive one, when an established company or firm associates itself with a high-visibility celebrity, it ventures into risky-business territory. For example, consider the Tiger Woods campaign that prompted Marino to pursue testimonials in the beginning. Woods's own reputation and brand imploded in late 2009 after the sex scandal heard 'round the world. That's why when JH Cohn considered an association with Joe Torre, Marino and his team thought through the pros and cons of such an approach. When I asked Marino about the risks, he said; "We thought a lot about it. Some people threw out Derek Jeter as a possibility, and although he represents a lot of good traits, we wanted someone that was well beyond reproach. We got to know Joe Torre through his Safe at Home Foundation [a foundation created by Torre to protect and shelter victims of domestic violence and their children. Torre's mother was consistently abused by his father.]. When we talked with Joe and Ally, his wife, it even more solidified our choice. There is a risk in testimonial advertising, as Tiger has proven. We wanted someone that was not a liability."

Clearly Torre's reputation has never been sullied, but he did move from the New York Yankees to the Los Angeles Dodgers after he parted company with the Bronx Bombers in 2007. That was a critical moment for JH Cohn because the primary reason it had built the branding campaign around Torre was to enhance its reputation in the New York market, and now, he was gone. And frankly, he didn't leave the Yankees on the friendliest of terms, which could turn some fans against him.

According to Marino, "My first thought when Torre left the Yankees, even before we opened an LA office and before Torre took the LA job, was that Joe DiMaggio sold a lot of coffee well after he retired. We thought Torre was an icon here and we could continue to sell his name. But when we found out he was going to LA and we were looking for an office out there anyhow, we assessed that he was such an icon in New York that he would still be valuable."

JH Cohn's Los Angeles office and larger West Coast operation has grown considerably in the last several years. Interestingly, JH Cohn has been able to market Joe Torre as effectively on the West Coast as it continues to do on the East Coast. The messages are the same. One of the most recent campaigns features a black-and-white picture of Tom Marino and Joe Torre with the captions "Let's talk," "We turn expertise into results," and "Leader to leader."

Opening Doors with Brand Association

So, hooking up with Joe Torre was a very good idea for JH Cohn. But there is a question many still ask: Does an aggressive and multifaceted branding campaign work for any individual or corporation regardless of the professional arena?

Said Marino, "I'm not sure why everybody doesn't try to brand him- or herself. If you cold call or send out mailers and there is no association, you will not get a response. What we have found is that when we send out mailers or do rubber chicken dinners, there is an association with Torre and JH Cohn, and we have achieved that brand. Potential clients may not know how good we are yet, but there is that name association that says, 'You are that accounting firm with Joe Torre.' And that's what gets our foot in the door. It doesn't get us one piece of business unto itself, but it gets us in the door."

Of course, building a great brand takes a lot more than just connecting with a popular public figure or celebrity. It is also about consistently delivering quality work and customer service to your clients. But let's face it. Getting that foot in the door (which is often based on gaining precious and difficult-to-get "face time" with key decision makers) is something that continues to stymie countless entrepreneurs and organizations looking to grow their market share. JH Cohn is an excellent case study on using association branding to open those doors to success and then making the most of it.

Branding Lessons

Whether you are an established firm with a long tradition of service or are an upstart small business owner, association branding is worth considering if you follow these guidelines learned from JH Cohen:

- A long tradition of quality service is valuable to the success of any company; however, even companies with longevity behind them need to evolve with the times and find new and creative ways to promote their services or products.

- If your particular job/product/service is not known for high-profile branding campaigns, don't let that stop you from entering the market with gusto. Being the first can give you a big advantage.

- It takes much thought and study to successfully use association branding. You must first identify the traits and characteristics that represent your brand and then search for the person, icon, image (even a duck) that can effectively build that association in the minds of your customers.

- Remember that there are always risks with brand association. Finding a person/image that is beyond reproach and likely to stay that way is your goal. Easier said than done. Plus, no matter who or what you select to tie your brand to, there are no guarantees.

- Brand association can open many doors, but in the end it's the quality of your work/product that will make or break your brand.

Toyota

Putting the Brakes on Its Brand

Your brand is about your reputation in the marketplace. It is about how others see you, about the degree to which you are respected, and about the belief of customers and key stakeholders that you, as well as your product, services, and integrity are beyond reproach. Interestingly, in the same way that there are many ways to build your brand, there are as many ways to weaken or even destroy it. Consider the case of Toyota.

Automaker Toyota built a brand based on its reputation as the epitome of excellence, safety, economy, and customer service. The Toyota brand had it all. But then, in 2010, the company faced one of the most serious crises in business history, which threatened to destroy the foundation of that brand.

Certain Toyota automobiles were found to pose safety hazards due to faulty and therefore dangerous accelerator pedals. This problem alone put quite a chink in the armor of the Toyota brand. But the accidents, deaths, and massive worldwide recalls tied to those safety problems are not the only things that consumers will remember when they next wonder, "Should I buy a Toyota?" In addition, they will remember the way the company chiefs handled the problem, because those are the front-page headlines that will stick in consumers' mind.

The automaker's mistakes in this crisis serve as textbook lessons for all of us about how even a strong brand can go down quickly.

The Public Face and Voice of a Company

In early 2010, Toyota president Akio Toyoda spoke for the first time about this issue, which began in September 2009 when Toyota announced a recall of more than four million vehicles to replace gas pedals that could get stuck in floor mats and cause sudden acceleration. His presentation did nothing to help Toyota's image; in fact, it made the company look worse. While Toyoda spoke for nearly an hour, he was neither clear nor concise regarding Toyota's concerns about the problems and what exactly would be done to fix them. Even worse was the fact that it took this long for Toyoda, the company's president and chief executive, to speak publicly.

Much of the early, high-level communication in connection with this crisis was delegated to others. Specifically, James Lentz, a top Toyota executive in America, went on the TODAY show to represent the company. Even if Lentz had done an excellent job communicating in this pressure-filled media situation, it still wouldn't have been enough to bolster Toyota's reputation and brand. When a crisis of this magnitude hits, only the CEO has the authority and the position to speak. The fact that Akio Toyoda is a descendent of Kiichiro Toyoda, the company's founder, makes it especially important for him to have been the face and voice of the company in this situation. By initially putting Lentz out front as Toyota's lead communicator, the corporation was sending the message that the crisis, and in turn the task of protecting the company's brand, wasn't important enough to be directly handled by its top person.

Back in the 1980s, American automaker Chrysler had already shown Americans how it should be done. When Chrysler had a significant public relations problem after being accused of selling used cars under the guise of being new, CEO Lee Iacocca was the only person speaking on behalf of the automaker. He dealt with the problem directly. He said Chrysler blew it big time and was going to get it right. This approach served to build a significant degree of goodwill among consumers, which allowed Chrysler's brand to recover sooner.

One has to wonder why Toyoda didn't understand that when the brand (not to mention sales) was bleeding profusely in the United States, this required the company president himself to come here immediately and speak on behalf of his company. Particularly in this case—Akio Toyoda is the brand. In fact, his name is on every one of those cars. The fact that the "d" was changed to a "t" for marketing purposes doesn't change the fact that only Mr. Toyoda, in spite of his difficulty speaking English, was the one who had to step up and protect the brand created by his grandfather.

Finally, in February 2010, Mr. Toyoda was pressured into testifying before Congress to answer some very tough questions about what the company knew about the faulty accelerator pedals and when it knew it. Even though Mr. Toyoda apologized for putting safety second to sales, that testimony left many unanswered questions—and the brand remained tarnished.

Can It Get Any Worse?

The word "Toyota" soon became a national joke thanks to talk show hosts like Stephen Colbert, who quipped, "Toyota's slogan is 'Moving Forward'—they don't say anything in there about stopping." And David Letterman, who noted, "Critics of the automobile industry are saying that Toyota executives knew about the problems with the brakes years and years ago. And they're wondering, rightly so, why did they drag their feet? Well, trying to stop the car. That's what they were doing."[1] Once public ridicule puts a bull's-eye on a brand, can it get any worse? In Toyota's case: yes.

It got worse when new information painted Toyota as intentionally deceptive. Media reports, including a story entitled "Toyota Official in E-Mail Ahead of Recall: 'We Need to Come Clean,'" shared internal company e-mails obtained by the Associated Press (AP). According to the media, on January 16, 2010, five days before Toyota would recall 2.3 million vehicles to address sticking pedals in six vehicle models, Irv Miller, then group vice president for environment and public affairs at Toyota, wrote: "We need to come clean . . . we are not protecting our customers by keeping this quiet . . . the time to hide on this one is over. . . . We better just hope that they can get NHTSA [National Highway Traffic Safety Administration] to work with us in coming [up] with a workable solution that does not put us out of business. . . . I hate to break this to you but WE HAVE a tendency for MECHANICAL failure in accelerator pedals of a certain manufacturer on certain models."[2] Ouch.

Further, an April 12, 2010, an AP story entitled "Toyota Routinely Engaged in Questionable, Evasive, and Deceptive Legal Tactics: Reports" only made the situation worse. The public then learned that "Toyota has routinely engaged in questionable, evasive, and deceptive legal tactics when sued, frequently claiming it does not have information it is required to turn over and sometimes even ignoring court orders to produce key documents."[3]

That same article brought to the public's attention a number of lawsuits filed against Toyota over the years that would likely have gone against Toyota if the company had been honest and forthcoming with requested documents and facts. In one case, it appears that Toyota withheld documents about internal roof strength tests after a young girl was killed in a 4Runner rollover crash. In another case, involving a Toyota Land Cruiser, a Texas woman died when the vehicle accelerated backward and pinned her against the garage wall.[4] On this one, Toyota had an obligation to report a similar case that it had settled the year before—but it did not.

Toyota's response to these and other similar cases was that Toyota was simply pursuing all their options within the law; the company was simply playing by the rules. According to an official statement on the Toyota Web site: "Toyota takes its legal obligations seriously and strives to maintain the highest professional and ethical standards in its legal practices. We are confident that we have acted appropriately with respect to product liability litigation and our discovery practices, including in the cases referenced in the AP article."[5]

But here is the problem. Toyota's response in the court of law may minimize its legal liability, but in the process helps further destroy the Toyota brand. This kind of legal maneuvering sends the message to the average consumer that Toyota is more interested in protecting its hide and its wallet than in protecting innocent drivers.

Toyota may have gained some short-term legal advantage, but it surely has lost public support and that will hurt the bottom line far more than any individual lawsuit. In the end, Toyota was required to pay a $16.4 million fine, the largest government penalty ever against an automaker and the maximum allowed by law, for concealing information related to its sticking pedal recall. The fine does not release Toyota from civil or criminal actions, of which there are sure to be many, seeking billions of dollars.[6]

Headlines that call a brand evasive and deceptive and court cases that determine that a manufacturer illegally concealed information are hatchet blows to a company's reputation. Obviously, none of that is good for Toyota's brand.

Band-Aids Don't Help Your Brand

In response to Mr. Toyoda's ineffective congressional testimony and the onslaught of negative media press, Toyota embarked on an aggressive and very expensive advertising campaign, both in print and on television. Toyota ran a series of thirty-second commercials as well as full-page ads in such publications as the *New York Times* and the *Wall Street Journal* and others under the heading, "Our Pledge to Toyota Drivers."[7] The ad contained the following buzz phrases:

> The pillars of the "Toyota Way" are "respect for people" and "continuous improvement." These remain core values— and we'll adhere closely to them as we make vehicle safety our top priority.
> Toyota will set a new standard for speed of response on safety issues.
> . . . we'll be the leader in introducing advanced safety technologies. . . .

As I write this in mid-2010, it is too soon to know what will happen in the final chapter of Toyota's branding story. The company might possibly make up some of the massive market share and regain its reputation. Or it may never regain its prestigious position in the automobile industry or in consumers' minds. Either way, those interested in the effects of public scandal on a brand will learn many valuable lessons from this company, which made numerous critical mistakes in both product production and in its response to customers and media.

Branding Lessons

Some brand-related lessons that we can take from this Toyota debacle include the following:

- Never sweep internal problems under the rug hoping they won't become public. The smartest thing you can do for your brand is to address problems immediately and disclose as much as possible in an effort to communicate that you are in charge and taking care of the situation—as opposed to being pushed into honesty by external forces.

- The CEO must step up when a brand crisis occurs. The CEO is the most visible and powerful symbol of a company's brand. Never delegate crisis communication when your brand is on the line.

- Obviously, sales success is essential, but putting quantity ahead of quality will kill any brand reputation. In the long run, cutting corners to save dollars just doesn't work.

- When an initial incident or embarrassing situation occurs, look inward and never, and I mean *never*, blame consumers, as Toyota attempted to do by implying that Toyota drivers were somehow responsible for what was clearly a mechanical problem.

Michael Port

Living by the "Golden Rule"

Michael Port is a classic example of someone who was doing just fine in one profession, but decided that wasn't enough. For many years, Port was a successful TV and film actor. But in Port's case, it wasn't BIG enough for him, since he felt he had more to offer people and more to demand of himself. Then, in 2006 he published his first book, called *Book Yourself Solid*. This book became the foundation of his "THINK BIG" philosophy that evolved into motivational seminars and coaching and speaking engagements that have helped countless professionals and others transform their lives. Today Michael Port is a *New York Times* bestselling author of *Book Yourself Solid*, *Beyond Booked Solid*, *The Contrarian Effect*, and his most recent, *The Think Big Manifesto*.

No doubt Port is good at what he does and has a sound philosophy with specific tools to help his clients and readers "think big." Like a lot of people profiled in this book, he came up with a catchy and descriptive slogan (for me it's "Make the Connection" or "You Are the Brand")—*The guy to call when you're tired of thinking small*"—and used it in his books and self-help approach.

Frankly, however, books and programs based solely on such catchy slogans are a dime a dozen. There is so much more than that to Michael Port's brand. His brand is a product of the way he lives his professional life every day.

Self-Confidence

I came across Port's book at my local bookstore as I was browsing the business and self-help sections, checking out the competition as I occasionally do. As I was standing in the aisle reading the table of contents in *Book Yourself Solid*, I was struck by a section called

"Develop a Personal Brand." Naturally, I wanted to know more, not just about the topic but about the author as well.

I asked my producers at public television to book him for an interview on my series One-on-One. When I actually met Port at the TV studio, I quickly found that I was even more impressed by Michael himself than I was with his books. He was genuine and easygoing, while still projecting a sense of confidence. While both of us do many of the same things professionally, I didn't feel the slightest sense of competition or a need to engage in one-upmanship with him. This sense of ease was due to the fact that Port wasn't thinking about how he matched up against me. He just wasn't like other people I've interviewed who get caught up with comparing their success to the success of others. That's real confidence. He also wasn't like some other fellow motivational speakers I've interviewed who you know are wondering, "Why should he have this show? I'm better than Adubato!" Michael Port is confident in who he is and what he is doing. During the interview, we immediately connected and compared notes on the air about the keys to motivating and moving people. We talked about business coaching techniques and some of the challenges we face in motivating ourselves to practice what we preach. Port is clearly a successful brand himself in a very crowded and competitive field because he and his "think big" philosophy of business and life are one and the same. He believes it, lives it, and exudes it. Says Port, "All of us have the potential to think big much, if not most, of the time. And when we think bigger about who we are and what we offer the world, it results in others thinking bigger and that benefits everyone."

Port doesn't have to compare himself to anyone. He thinks big about what he's doing and his "think big" brand catches the interest of everyone around him.

You Are Your Brand

In our discussion on branding, I raised the complex and sometimes confusing issue of self-promotion, more specifically the practice of putting not just your name, but your persona and face "out there."

In Michael Port's case, we are talking about the decision to put his face on three of his four books—a decision I, too, have made and sometimes worry about. Can self-promotion be overdone? I asked Michael if it was an intentional move to place his photo so prominently on the covers of his books.

"Absolutely," said Port. "Over the years, I've received positive feedback about my look, my sound, charisma—and yes, my face—so showing that energy on my book covers is one way I can use my appearance to my advantage. If you're in a personality-based business, obviously, your personality is probably the most important component to your success. So, identify exactly what your audience finds most attractive about you and your personality and leverage it, exploit it." Indeed, you are the brand

Relevancy

Another vital aspect of Port's successful brand is his obsession with making his work "relevant." The concept of relevancy is huge for him and for me as well. It has helped me in my coaching, writing, and overall philosophy in leading seminars and workshops (as well as an on-the-air interviewer and commentator), not to mention my overall communication with others. I believe that no brand can succeed unless it is truly relevant to current and potential stakeholders.

According to Port: "Branding has to be a conscientious combination of the practical business application of who you serve and what you help those people do or get. People want to know right away: Is it relevant to me? If the answer is yes, then they will consider the second question: What does the person behind this business stand for? There are a lot of people who do what you do, but what you stand for is going to resonate emotionally with those you want to reach."

That's exactly what it means to sell a brand. In fact, Port says, "If I were to replace the word *marketing* with any other word, it would be *relevancy*. The best marketing is the most relevant. Paying for attention is not particularly effective, since there are so many products and services trying to get your attention. In today's market, we need to earn your attention and in order to do that, we need to be relevant."

Branding for All

Some might argue that people like Michael Port, or even Steve Adubato, have to succeed in branding themselves because of the nature of their work. Of course. Authors, motivational speakers, and people "out there" in the public eye have to be successful brands for obvious reasons. But what about a middle manager? A teacher? A lawyer? An accountant? Or any professional who doesn't see him- or herself in such a public light? Do these professionals have to succeed at branding themselves? Again, Michael Port is very clear on the branding of you: "If you want to be remarkable, or at least stand out, then you must brand yourself. We get anxious when we start talking about branding ourselves and standing out because our educational model is designed to prepare us to be a cog in a machine. And most businesses support this model. They are built so that they can produce a product by the least skilled people, at the lowest possible cost. This way the workers can be replaced if they underperform or are insubordinate. But here's the rub . . . insubordinate people often develop the most compelling personal brands. Which is better: to do exactly as you're told just because someone higher up the ladder told you to, or to do it a better way, the right way? I'll take the insubordinate person any day if she's producing something better because of her willingness to buck the system, to create a trend, to be a leader. Clearly, you see I would never have made it in the military. But the professional world rewards ingenuity, innovation, inventiveness, and individuality. Yes, it requires courage. Yes, it requires a willingness to be comfortable with discomfort. And, yes, it requires being fantastic at what you do."

Effectively branding yourself is not an option. To succeed you have no choice, particularly in difficult economic times when key decision makers and stakeholders must be clear on what makes you and your work stand out from the crowd. This is as true for middle managers and bank managers as it is for motivational speakers and authors.

Branding Lessons

Michael Port gives all of us important lessons on the power of practical, personal characteristics that build a brand:

- *Accessible.* Even though Port is a *New York Times* bestselling author and is obviously busy running his business and building his brand, he understands the importance of being accessible and responsive. When I first e-mailed him to introduce myself, he responded within hours. My sense is that he does the same with other colleagues as well as with professionals who may reach out to him with advice and direction. That kind of hands-on, direct communication makes all the difference when building a brand. It says to people that you care enough to be responsive and to follow up, not to mention follow through. Don't let those e-mails and phone messages pile up.

- *Generous.* Many professionals believe in a zero-sum philosophy that follows the logic: In order for me to succeed, you can't—particularly if you are working in the same industry or arena. Michael Port doesn't see the world that way. Clearly, his business philosophy is that the pie can always get larger and one of the smartest ways of succeeding is by helping other people get a bigger piece of the pie. Maybe it's a karma thing. In fact, when I reached out to Michael to ask about a particularly sensitive and challenging business situation, he immediately offered smart and strategic advice. Not a lot of people do that for people they compete with for business. But Port believes that extending your hand is a big part of thinking big and, more importantly, acting big. By being so helpful, Port has made not just a friend and a colleague in me, but also someone who clearly will sing his praises to others. That kind of word of mouth is a huge part of building your brand whether you are a motivational speaker, author, or accountant. Being small and petty is going to keep your brand small and petty—so extend a hand to others. As they say, "Pay it forward."

- *Genuine.* A brand has to be a lot more than a great slogan or catch phrase. Port lives the "think big" philosophy every day. He practices what he preaches, or at least tries to, which is all any of us can do. That kind of genuineness is appealing. It's likeable and, let's not kid ourselves, in order for a brand to be successful, it has to be well liked, whether it is a product, a service, a person, or any combination of all three. Port is a likeable guy who very much lives by the golden rule of treating others the way he would want to be treated. That approach to business and life will never go out of style.

BlackBerry

The Brand You "Can't Live Without"

I gave a speech a few years ago at a conference in Las Vegas in which I talked about some of the ways that people could make their meetings more engaging, dynamic, and inclusive. Right after my presentation, Jim Balsillie, the chair of Research in Motion (RIM), which manufactures the BlackBerry smartphone, got up and said that productive and interactive meetings were bad for the BlackBerry—implying that engaging in quality person-to-person communication gets in the way of his brand, which relies on electronic, impersonal, remote communication.

It's true that, until a few years ago, I saw the BlackBerry smartphone as an intrusive distraction that got in the way of people connecting on a more human and personal level, but now I own one and couldn't live without it. So naturally, I wanted to explore what it is about this brand that makes it a "must-have" for more than 36 million people through 475 carriers and distribution channels in over 160 countries around the world.

The Product Itself

When I finally gave in and bought a BlackBerry, I found that there was a reason for the popularity of this wireless application development platform (the not-so-smooth generic term for this form of technology). The BlackBerry is a great product. It allows me to be incredibly responsive with my clients, key stakeholders, and friends. And it's more than just a phone that lets me enjoy automatic texting and voice dialing with ease. The BlackBerry lets me connect to my e-mail, my calendar, contact list, notes, memos, and such. I can also (but rarely do) download games, news and weather reports, music, social networking sites, personal productivity applications, and so much more. It's all synchronized over the air—meaning that I don't have to do a desktop synch to update this information. This is a product that never rests—and that's important. In the technology field, a brand is only as good as it is current. Tech products lose brand value quickly if they fall behind, get slow, stagnate, get complicated, or lose the ability or desire to keep up with ever-changing technology.

However, the fact is that the BlackBerry smartphone's top competitors, particularly the iPhone from Apple and Windows Mobile from Microsoft, are also working hard to grab market share. So the BlackBerry needs more than just exciting apps to keep its name synonymous with "smartphone." That's where the branding comes in, and that starts at the moment of conception.

Passion of Invention

The BlackBerry smartphone exploded onto the market in the late 1990s with a simple and compelling message: At any time and any place, busy, mobile people, whether in their professional or personal lives, should have the ability to send and receive electronic communications. The BlackBerry provided the means to have this kind of wireless contact, and it revolutionized corporate life.

Fortunately for the BlackBerry brand, the folks at RIM introduced a quality product built on the hard work of people who passionately live, breathe, and believe in the product. As you'll see in many cases in this book, passion on the part of those behind the brand is absolutely essential to success.

What's in a Name?

Of course, there's more to the success of the BlackBerry brand than the passion of the people who created it. There's also that catchy name. It's just so simple, so easy to remember, so random. The name came about because one of the RIM executives who was developing the technology said that the buttons on this new smartphone "looked like tiny seeds in a strawberry." "Strawberry" didn't seem quite right for a name, so someone suggested, "Why not call it 'blackberry' "? And it stuck. This name was a good choice because even though not all BlackBerries are black, the name is universally known. It's fun, it's hard to forget, and it rhymes with "crackberry," which aptly describes how addictive it is. What's better than that?

Target Audience

With a solid name for the brand, the company executives then set out to target a well-defined customer—one who had the money and the authority to purchase BlackBerry smartphones in quantity. Jim Balsillie of RIM said, "We made sure the CIO was happy. The CIO has a veto and they don't hesitate to use it . . ."[1]

Further, RIM executives targeted the Wall Street crowd early on in the development of BlackBerry. They figured correctly that this was a group who could quickly increase sales of the phone through word of mouth. According to RIM vice president of corporate marketing Mark Guibert: "Wall Street professionals are heavily communications focused, heavily customer focused; what we found was many of those people could instantly justify the investment into this, even though it was of an unproven technology."[2] The plan worked. Word of mouth is a powerful way to build a brand.

It's one thing to have a great slogan or name, or even terrific commercials, which the BlackBerry does, but the buzz around BlackBerry created by people using the phone was the initial driving force behind its popularity. Once the phone hit the business world, it became a must-have accessory. People were constantly saying to me, "You don't have a BlackBerry? You have to get one! It will help you tremendously." I held out, thinking I'd rather focus on face-to-face communication and that I could easily check my e-mail when I got back into the office or got home at night. But the buzz around the BlackBerry just got too loud to ignore, and I gave in and bought one.

It's a funny thing about word of mouth—when you hear something enough times from enough people whom you respect and trust, you believe it. That's why great brands are built on buzz—a very positive buzz.

Feeding the Habit

Today the BlackBerry smartphone is ubiquitous. And yes, it is addictive. In fact, it's easy to become a "crackberry." Like everyone I know, there are times that I'm using my BlackBerry when I know I shouldn't be. Sometimes, it keeps me from connecting on a personal level with those who matter to me. And it does get in the way of family time. (I've even seen people pull out the BlackBerry while on a date!)

However, the bottom line is that the BlackBerry is an excellent example of a tremendously successful branding effort. There's no denying that in a little over a decade this tiny little technological tool has changed the way many people live their lives, and there's no reason to think that we won't keep feeding the habit.

Branding Lessons

This little product has big lessons to teach all of us about the necessity of building brand while selling products or services. The lessons here are simple:

- Having a quality product or service that keeps up with the changing times is the key to keeping a positive buzz going.

- The intense belief and passion on the part of those who create a brand has a tremendous impact on the success of that brand.

- A terrific name matters a lot. In fact, the name of your brand can make or break your ability to reach your customers.

- Targeting key consumers right from the beginning is critical not only to selling a product or service, but also to gaining the benefit of word-of-mouth advertising.

Barack Obama
A Brand in Transition

Who the heck was Barack Obama? How dare he think he could be President of the United States just a couple of years out of the Illinois state legislature? He was still inexperienced, not worldly enough, and had never served in an executive capacity. He didn't wait his turn. These were the kinds of questions and the negative perceptions that the Obama brand quickly addressed and conquered. This fascinating and complex branding story out of the 2008 presidential campaign is built on the fact that during the campaign, the Obama media marketing and branding folks knew that the biggest asset they had was the candidate himself and, oddly enough, the fact that he was new to the game.

I'm writing this chapter during Obama's second year as president, and right now the Barack Obama brand is still evolving. It clearly has problems in the wake of the BP oil disaster, an Afghanistan quagmire, and a sputtering economic crisis. The 2010 mid-term election clearly was a blow to the Obama brand. In the president's own words, he took a "shellacking," with so many Democrats, who were supportive of him and his policies, losing their Congressional seats. What President Obama does in response to such a public and humiliating loss will largely dictate his political fortunes and his long-term brand reputation and legacy. My focus in this chapter isn't on the end story, however. The focus is largely on the Obama brand that reshaped our national political landscape forever. In many ways, the Obama brand could be considered the most successful branding campaign in American history, with many lessons to teach anyone trying to make a name in a competitive market filled with veteran brands.

Political Candidate as Celebrity Brand

Obama is an innately charismatic guy, and his brand handlers wisely played to that strength right from the beginning of the 2008 race. He was the brand—the man himself would carry this campaign. But focusing on the man himself would not be easy initially, given that we're talking about a guy with a really funny last name and a middle name that sounds a lot like a notorious dictator. Barack Hussein Obama? You're kidding, right? Many Americans weren't sure where Obama came from or what he was all about. Was he black? White? A combination of both? He was from Hawaii but learned politics in Chicago. He came out of a controversial and maligned political machine in Illinois but called himself a "reformer." Who was this person who wanted to be the leader of the free world? The branding of this young politician would require calculated steps to create an image of unshakable presidential stature. But how?

The Obama campaign handlers were well aware that successful brands are always a product of word-of-mouth advertising—nothing new there. But this campaign was the first to use the Internet and the power of social networking sites to create a groundswell of personal endorsement. In the cyberspace world of Facebook, MySpace, Twitter, and every other Internet-based communication tool out there, word of mouth moved a lot faster than anyone could have imagined.

Once the word was out, Obama's rallies were choreographed in a way that had never been seen in politics. Most of the thousands of people who showed up were new to the political arena. They were not on any political party's mailing list; they had never done this before. So where did they come from? They came from savvy use of modern technology. I am sure that the growth of the Obama brand on the Internet right in the beginning of that presidential election campaign is in large part responsible for the ultimate election of the first black President of the United States. His campaign managers were the first to realize that in this age of modern technology, the race goes to the cyberspace savvy.

Add luck and influential friends to a charismatic personality with Internet presence, and the brand was gaining big momentum.

Fellow Chicagoan Oprah Winfrey loved Obama, and she wasn't afraid to show it. That kind of talk-show exposure by the world's most well-loved and influential woman quickly turned Obama into a media darling with rock star status. (See the chapter on Oprah, which examines the impact of this endorsement on her brand.) Soon, Obama was more of a celebrity than a politician, and it became apparent that the more Obama could be branded as the Brad Pitt/Denzel Washington of American politics, the more powerful his brand could be. This kind of brand was just what Obama needed to separate himself from the competition.

New Brand Beats Old Brand

In the beginning, Barack Obama was the underdog. He could not compete with Hillary Clinton in the primary race nor with John McCain in the general election on issues typical in presidential races. He didn't have longstanding political connections. He didn't have a track record of political experience. He didn't have an in-depth and personal understanding of domestic and global issues. The only thing he had going for him was the fact that he didn't have all of those things—putting this spin on a less-than-preferable situation was a major factor in his victory.

Senator and former First Lady Hillary Clinton was supposed to be the Democratic candidate that year. It was her time. Everyone said so. However, whether she had better qualities to actually be president than Obama really wasn't the issue when it came to the branding contest of their 2008 campaigns. The Hillary Clinton brand just couldn't get the job done.

Frankly, Barack Obama was more attractive on TV than Hillary was. He also seemed to be more likeable and more engaging. He seemed to be able to laugh at himself, while Hillary seemed tight, strident, and frankly, a bit too rough. Hillary Clinton wasn't a bad candidate, but Barack Obama used his youthfulness, charisma, and newness to make Hillary's brand look old and stale.

After capturing the Democratic nomination, Obama faced off against Republican candidate John McCain. Unfortunately for McCain, he couldn't escape the shadow of George W. Bush that still lingered in the Republican party. People were wary of the Bush brand, which often was characterized by adjectives like aloof, out of touch, disengaged, and frankly, not especially inspiring. This fact positioned Obama right from the start as an appealing option that was more vibrant, young, energetic, and dynamic when compared to the John McCain brand, which, in spite of his war-time heroism, was seen as too old, tired, and a bit cranky.

The Obama brand managers were smart to use the experience of Obama's opponents against them. They were also smart to build the brand around this concept and capture people's imagination with one simple word: CHANGE. Of course, one might wonder: Change to what? Change from what? How would change solve our problems? All those questions would have to be dealt with if Obama actually got elected president, but during the campaign, Obama's soaring, inspiring rhetoric about change in general seemed to get the job done. The word was perfect: How could Hillary talk about "change"? How could seventy-three-year-old Republican John McCain talk about "change" in the same way forty-seven-year-old Democrat Barack Obama could? Neither opponent could counter this angle, and Obama's brand won out without a serious fight.

You Can't Rewrite History

As typically happens when bringing a new "product" to the market, there were rough spots where Obama fumbled big time. He almost destroyed his brand and reputation with his bumbling of the Reverend Wright controversy; fortunately, the Obama brand was already well established and strong enough to withstand the slip.

Reverend Wright was Obama's spiritual leader and pastor in Chicago for more than twenty years. When it was reported that Wright had said the most racist, horrific, un-American, and, many perceived, anti-Jewish comments, Obama said he had never heard Reverend Wright say any of these things and was unfamiliar with this part of his thinking. His response wasn't credible, and it hurt his reputation and brand.

When creating a successful brand, you need to be seen as a stand-up guy (or woman), someone who admits mistakes quickly as opposed to being forced into a confession. During that time, Obama seemed disingenuous, not particularly honest, evasive, in fact "like a politician." The change he had been referring to in part was that he would be more honest than most politicians. The change was that he would tell it to us straight as opposed to giving "a political answer."

The damage was not permanent, but the incident shows how delicate even a carefully crafted brand can be. Great slogans and fiery and inspiring rhetoric, together with well-choreographed public events can't hold up a brand for long if the "product" itself becomes tarnished. The Obama brand survived in part because Obama eventually acknowledged the egregious and offensive nature of Reverend Wright's comments and ultimately distanced himself from his spiritual advisor. This decision fulfilled the hope of those who wanted to see the next president as someone who would not view the world largely through Wright's racial prism but rather, as Dr. Martin Luther King said, via "the content of our character."

With that misstep behind him, the Barack Obama 2008 campaign brand succeeded in an unprecedented fashion.

Obama . . . Presidential Brand

At the moment of victory, the next step in the Obama branding process began. The presidential image that needs to be crafted and nurtured is complex and multifaceted. Surely, building a campaign brand, as challenging as it may be, is a lot more manageable than building a presidential brand where the decisions you make and the mistakes that occur on your watch are largely beyond your control, and where no matter what you do, you are bound to offend large portions of the population.

Being president and creating a successful presidential brand requires more than slogans, great speeches, and having a nice smile and a photo in *People* magazine.

I recently interviewed Jonathan Alter, columnist and senior editor for *Newsweek* as well as an NBC News analyst who is the author of the book *The Promise: President Obama. Year One*. Alter, a long-time friend and colleague, had extensive, unprecedented access to the Obama White House. He spoke to top advisors, insiders, enemies of the president, and others to paint a powerful picture of the president's first year in office, including the impact on his lofty brand as a candidate. During that interview, Alter noted: "He's a very disciplined, decisive executive. The great surprise about Barack Obama was that we expected him to be a silver-tongued orator who would ace communications because of what he did during the campaigns, and he would struggle with executive leadership because he had no experience as a manager. It turned out that it was the opposite. He struggled in communications, he struggled to frame a message, he struggled to convince people that he was aggressive enough. In private . . . he is a very effective and decisive CEO. But in public he was not.

"So you've got this kind of 'two Obamas.' So what happens to him is he strips emotion out of it in private. He makes much better decisions by being rational and logical, not overreacting."

One of the biggest and most ironic criticisms of the Obama presidential brand is that even though as a candidate he inspired and motivated millions, as president, he's just not getting it done in the same way. He is not making a deep, personal connection that is a must in any effort to achieve brand equity. Says Jonathan Alter: "He might not use his gut enough because in public, he doesn't get the emotion back in. You can't connect with the American people without more of that emotion. He didn't connect enough to the emotional core of that issue [health care]. And he failed in that. In that sense, what happened with BP was of a piece of that. He's not reacting quickly enough. Slow reflexes; it happened on Christmas Day with that underwear bomber. People were scared, he didn't react fast enough, he didn't connect to them emotionally. He was intellectualizing it too much. . . . He actually believes that the American public can be talked to as adults because they voted for him, a guy named Barack Hussein Obama."

It seems the key to maintaining a brand is to know and understand your audience. In this area, President Obama has struggled mightily to find precise words to reach us without feeling as if he is lecturing, but ultimately tunes us out and turns us off, which is never good for your brand. Says Alter: "He's overconfident in us. He doesn't understand you've got to frame your issue with sound bites. When he talks, he's very eloquent, but it's not memorable. It is too detailed, it doesn't connect where he needs to, and that is where he's fallen short. But he can fix it, and it would be a huge mistake to underestimate him."

The Power of a Rumor to Dog a Brand

To fix the brand problems that he now faces, Obama must once again find a way to use the media to his advantage. It is ironic that it was Obama's skillful use of the Internet and other media that gave him his edge over the other candidates, but that it is now this same power of technology that is dogging his identity—his brand. Due to persistent rumors that fly through air and cyberspace unleashed and uncontrolled, there is tremendous confusion and misinformation surrounding Barak Obama's religion and citizenship—two factors that are vital to the presidential image.

The Pew Research Center took a poll before the major controversy around building a mosque at Ground Zero, which showed that one in five Americans thought Obama was Muslim—and not the Christian that he actually is. The mosque controversy only jacked up that number. Cleary, the fact that Obama's father was Muslim and that his middle name is "Hussein" helps connect his brand to Islam. Further, the fact that so many Americans believe that Obama is not an American citizen—despite the fact that he was born in Hawaii and his birth certificate has been posted online—has hurt his brand as a "patriotic president."

When it comes to branding and image, facts are often overwhelmed by media voices, including many on talk radio like Rush Limbaugh and those in the 24/7 cable news cycle (can you say FOX News?) as well as on the Internet, which is unregulated and often out of control when it comes to any semblance of accuracy. Simply put, Obama's brand has not been helped by the perception that he is not "so much American" as the rest of us.

The Obama presidential brand is far from dead, but it has been tarnished on many levels. It seems that building a brand around newness and promoting CHANGE as a panacea and promising sweeping results raises expectations unrealistically. Then when things inevitably go wrong or fall short, reputation and brand suffer immeasurably. Much more time is needed to see if the Barack Obama brand can stand strong against these challenges.

Branding Lessons

Consider the following lessons we can learn from Obama the candidate and Obama the presidential brand:

- Turn perceived weaknesses like "inexperience" into positives by framing them as "new" and "fresh." Get out there. Let potential customers/clients see you, talk to you, touch you, know you—both in person, but more importantly on the Internet. You must build your brand in cyberspace to compete in today's market.

- Don't be afraid to call on influential friends to blow your horn.

- Face obstacles and controversy directly—they will not disappear if you ignore them. Once you are in the public eye, candor is the only way to go. No matter how awful or embarrassing the event, we all admire those who have the courage to stand up, take responsibility, and own their past actions.

- Be careful of overpromising and raising expectations when building your brand. This will come back to bite you.

Coke

It's the Real Thing

I'm embarrassed to admit it, but it's true: I can't live without my Diet Coke. I know it isn't good for me, and I know I drink too much of it, but I love it. On some level, I guess I'm addicted. This attachment to a carbonated drink has nothing to do with its value as a product, and everything to do with its power as a sustainable brand built on fond memories (of regular Coke until I decided to forgo the calories) and on the ability to live in the collective memory generation after generation.

Branding on Memory

I buy Diet Coke because it's part of who I am. Like millions of others, as a little kid I remember saving empty glass Coke bottles and stacking them right next to my baseball card collection. I used them for all sorts of science experiments, including pouring Coke on the bumper of our family car—it wasn't pretty, but I can still remember how that bottle felt in my hand as I poured out that corrosive liquid.

Later, Coke became a part of my social life. I used to hang with my friends at a grocery store in Newark, New Jersey, called Mangano's. We would sit on the wooden crates that held bottles of Coke as we drank our Cokes and ate our sandwiches ("subs" as we called them). We never drank Pepsi; a few guys drank Dr. Pepper, but most drank Coke. And we weren't alone. Millions of others became addicted on some level to the whole Coke experience: the taste, the caffeine kick, the shape, the feel of the old glass bottles, and of course later, to the red and silver logo. Coke is part of the narrative of my life—this is what an established brand has going for it—its connection to memories.

If you, your product, or your company has been around awhile, there is a lot you can learn from the branding genius and the very memorable mistakes of Coca-Cola.

The Genius

In 1971, Coca-Cola launched an exceptionally successful advertising campaign built on the slogan: "I'd like to buy the world a Coke." Filmed on an Italian hilltop with 500 young people smiling and singing, the unifying message of the ads gave Coke a place in the collective memory of the baby-boomer generation.

In his book *The Care and Feeding of Ideas*, Bill Backer recalls the day when his flight to London was grounded due to fog, and he noticed disgruntled passengers calming down and joining each other in friendly conversation as they sipped their Cokes. That was the moment when, as Coke's creative director, he got the idea to pitch Coke as a bit of "commonality between all peoples, a universally liked formula that would help to keep them company for a few minutes." And so was born the famous jingle that went like this: "I'd like to teach the world to sing / in perfect harmony; / I'd like to buy the world a Coke / and keep it company."[1]

This collective memory among such a large chunk of the population positioned Coke as a reliable, dependable, and consistent common core of connection. This theme worked amazingly well for Coke—until somebody decided to try something "new."

The Branding Mistake

In the 1980s, Coca-Cola began to lose market share to Pepsi (think the "Pepsi Generation"), so the company decided to modernize the brand—in 1985, "New Coke" was introduced. Taste tests showed that most people liked the taste of New Coke, but consumers reacted to the branding change in a very negative way. They didn't understand why such a longstanding and successful brand would need to become "new." What was the matter with old Coke? The marketing geniuses behind the New Coke campaign immediately saw sales drop, and they knew that customer loyalty was in jeopardy. Time for a quick reverse.

Just a few months after New Coke hit the shelves, "Coke Classic" made its debut. "Classic" as in "stands the test of time." "Classic" as in "meeting traditionally high standards." "Classic" as in "the good stuff you used to like before we messed with it." At the time, Coke executives said, "The simple fact is that all the time and money and skill poured into consumer research on the new Coca-Cola could not measure or reveal the deep and abiding emotional attachment to the original Coca-Cola held by so many people."[2] Sometimes, branding is all about emotion.

New Coke (later renamed COKE II) was a huge branding embarrassment. The change of direction was unnecessary, and it clearly demonstrated that when it comes to the world of branding, change for change sake is very risky business. (To give Coke lovers another option with no calories, Diet Coke was developed in 1982.)

The Final Realization

Changing the taste of Coke in the hope of creating a buzz that would keep Pepsi a distant number 2 missed the point. It wasn't just the taste that Coke customers were or were not buying. Coke was more about the logo, the look, and later the red and silver colors. It was the history, the memories. It was the commercials. All of it.

Like many successful brands, the Coca-Cola brand is embedded in the minds and hearts of many Americans. There's something about Coke that is as American as Mom's apple pie and, in the case of branding, McDonald's. It doesn't have to be good for you, but it's still American, and we love it because it brings us back to our childhood and those experiences that are burned into our collective minds. This is not something you mess with.

Branding Lessons

Of course, over time brands have to evolve and adapt to consumer demands and interests. However, if you have an established, popular, and trusted brand with loyal customers, the lessons to be learned from the Coke brand are pretty simple:

- If it ain't broke, don't try to fix it.

- A brand isn't just one thing that customers latch onto. It's a complex mix of product and emotions; changing one aspect can blow the whole equation.

- "New" is not always better. When rebranding, you should never forget how visceral and nostalgic consumer connections can be.

- When rebranding, individuals, companies, and entrepreneurs need to pursue every marketing, advertising, and research tool available. But depending too heavily on such information and data can blind one to something that is quite simple: The memories associated with an original brand can be more powerful than any new ideas.

- When you see you've made a mistake by changing direction, quickly acknowledge your mistake to reestablish customer loyalty.

- Sometimes leaving well enough alone, even if your market share isn't what you want it to be at that moment, is a sound long-term business strategy.

Thirteen/WNET.org

Beyond *Sesame Street* and Bill Moyers

"The THIRTEEN brand has always been associated with integrity and intelligence as it stands apart from a lot of the pressures that impact the commercial world." These are the words of WNET.org president and CEO Neal Shapiro.

Thirteen is the PBS flagship TV station with the most public television viewers among the nation's over three hundred public broadcasters. It is also a major piece of its parent company, WNET.org, based in New York. I've been affiliated with WNET.org and Thirteen for over twenty years as an on-air host, executive producer, anchor, and creative director of numerous news and public affairs programs. While I've worked in commercial media broadcasting for many years, there has always been something special about being a part of the PBS brand, and, more specifically, Thirteen. Neal Shapiro is right. Integrity and intelligence are the right words to describe this brand. However, in the branding process, even seemingly positive words can project the wrong image. What one person sees as intelligent, another might see as high-brow or inaccessible to the average person. That's the balance between intelligent and elite that Shapiro and the rest of my colleagues at Thirteen have to strike.

How do you create intelligent, thoughtful programming that doesn't look and feel like everything else on the crowded television dial, yet is not above the interest level of the audience? This is a challenge for Thirteen and WNET.org, which doesn't develop its programming based on projected ratings, but realizes nonetheless that the audience size is critical to raising the corporate, foundation, and government dollars needed to produce PBS shows. Finding this middle ground in which to root the station's brand is the job of

Shapiro and his team. Shapiro has an extensive background in the TV world as the former president of NBC News as well as MSNBC. He also has had close ties to the TODAY show as a top executive. Shapiro knows successful commercial programming and knows the importance of building the Thirteen brand in a way that will appeal to a wide audience, while at the same time offering unique programming. At the same time, Shapiro has the added responsibility of convincing corporations and foundations to support our programs. And again, this is where "branding" comes in: One of our major selling points is that being affiliated with PBS programming helps the image and brand of these supporting institutions.

Now consider how crowded the media landscape has become over the last decade. I'm not just talking television, but there is competition from the Internet as well. People have so many choices. So many options. So the question becomes: How do you get an audience to feel that special connection to a public television station? According to Shapiro: "Many people who started watching Thirteen from its birth are still tuning in to the channel. Thirteen has the value of having generations grow up with it. Those whose first experience with public television was *Sesame Street* are now grandparents, and they can watch Thirteen with their children and their children's children and go through the cycle again." *Sesame Street*. Can you think of a better brand in the world of children's programming? Who doesn't know Big Bird, Elmo, and Cookie Monster? My kids grew up on the show, and I bet that yours did as well.

However, it's not enough to have great children's programming that touches several generations to build a successful brand in highly competitive and global markets. Our other programming, including *Charlie Rose*, *Bill Moyers Journal* (Moyers recently retired), *Frontline*, as well as newer programs like *Need to Know* and *New Jersey Capitol Report* (which I co-anchor with Rafael Pi Roman), is critical to keeping the Thirteen brand current and thriving.

Thinking Global/Staying Local

As I stated, Thirteen and WNET.org are part of a much larger brand—PBS, the Public Broadcasting Service. The venerable Roper

Poll has shown year after year that PBS is one of the most respected institutions in America and by far the most respected media organization out there. Any station knows that the PBS brand matters a lot. Its logo communicates instant credibility. I know, because for virtually all of the public television programming that I produce and host, we use the PBS brand in our print and Internet ads. We use it with our sponsors and prospective sponsors. It matters. It is a big part of the sell. It lets folks know that we are involved in a serious, legitimate, and meaningful media endeavor.

This image is the one umbrella under which Thirteen, WNET, and all PBS programming jostle for brand recognition. This need to align with the parent company while creating an individual brand identity is a constant challenge in this world of mergers and acquisitions. Even with a solid, recognizable image, television stations have to evolve and grow while still remaining loyal to their mission. Says Shapiro: "Thirteen has changed a little bit because we've had to deal with being a member of a multi-platform universe. There has been an issue as to what we are locally and nationally. Our logo is Thirteen locally, but at times, we need to expand the philosophy of Thirteen more globally, as we do business with PBS nationally and internationally. Since PBS can be Detroit, or somewhere else, the WNET branding is also part of who we are. Now we describe ourselves as Thirteen/WNET.org. Older people think of Thirteen first, and younger people think of WNET.org first. We need to expand our brand since in the future we may not be on the actual channel 13 on the TV dial. The '13' will be less important in the future as a result. As we become more national, we need to stop focusing on the 13, and focus on the WNET.org."

Brands and names evolve as organizations attempt to streamline their operations and become more efficient. One of the biggest challenges those of us on the Thirteen team must face is what exactly to call ourselves. It seems to me that it makes smart sense for Thirteen to combine Thirteen/WNET.org. Neal Shapiro is right when he argues that WNET.org ultimately will stand out and survive.

Says Shapiro: "PBS is one of the most respected institutions in the country, and fortunately, people associate PBS with us at

WNET.org. But we also produce local programming that isn't produced by PBS but is consistent with the PBS brand. We think there is a great overlap with the qualities that people like about PBS—the integrity of a highly respected brand."

Location, Location

In an effort to solidify Thirteen's brand locally, Shapiro and the leadership at WNET.org decided that it was important to create a new studio in the heart of New York City. More specifically, at Lincoln Center. In the midst of very difficult economic times, a decision was made to open a glass-enclosed, street-level studio that will be the location for numerous locally produced programs with a distinctive look and feel. The Lincoln Center Studio is now accessible to the busy and vibrant streets of midtown Manhattan. I was there at the studio's grand opening, and, in fact, hosted one of the first live programs at Lincoln Center—a live call-in with New Jersey Governor Chris Christie.

Where you do what you do sometimes really matters to the image of your organization, and in the case of Thirteen, changing its location was a key branding decision to keep the station in the public consciousness. Says Shapiro: "One of the issues that has to be considered when building a brand is how to make people aware of who you are, where you are and what you do. At Thirteen and WNET.org, we want to be in and of the community. We want to be in a place where people will see us and associate with us. In the same way that the TODAY show built a studio with glass walls, we want to have a place where people would actually want to come and visit."

The glass walls add to the Thirteen/WNET.org brand. Shapiro says that they are a metaphor for what the station stands for—transparency. "Public media has a responsibility to connect with customers," he says, "in a way that lets them see who we are and at the same time lets us better know exactly who they are and what they want. Connecting is vitally important, especially for us, because we depend on our customers to watch our show and also to financially support our programming."

At WNET/Thirteen, doing much of its programming out of this strategically located glass-enclosed studio in midtown Manhattan will have a great deal to do with the future of the station's brand.

Branding Lessons

Just because WNET/Thirteen is a public broadcasting service doesn't mean we can't learn from it important lessons about the practicalities of business branding:

- Your company/product/service is branded for a target audience. Finding the right descriptors to identify and compliment that audience requires careful thought because aiming too high can create an elitist image. Your goal is to make your brand desirable to as many target audience people as possible.

- While a long history and tradition of excellence (such as that found in *Sesame Street* and *Bill Moyers Journal*) is vital to building brand loyalty, it's not enough. Organizations must continue to produce and develop new and relevant products/services that are consistent with brand tradition, but are also consistent with the current market conditions and environment.

- The issue of transparency is critical to developing and sustaining your brand. People want to see what you do and how you do it. Be sure to be accessible to your customers.

- While promoting your brand in the local marketplace, it is essential to effectively and strategically connect that brand to the larger parent organization, which can offer residual benefits in terms of public reputation and image.

TD Bank

Beyond Colors, Letters, and Logos

Very often, creating and bolstering your brand comes down to making and keeping a promise. In the case of TD Bank, Fred Graziano, head of retail banking at TD Bank, told me that success is built on "how we execute against our brand promise, which is: America's Most Convenient Bank." Interestingly, to keep this promise, TD Bank managers didn't stop at the decision to exceed customer expectations by opening and closing their doors ten minutes earlier and later than posted hours and then sitting back feeling confident in a promise kept. They knew that the success of being a convenient bank would ultimately be tied to accessible and convenient customer service, and that's where the branding work begins and ends at TD Bank.

It's Not the Colors, Logo, or Slogans

Like many corporations today, TD Bank is a product of mergers, consolidations, and the blending of brands. TD stands for Toronto-Dominion, which acquired Banknorth to become TD Banknorth, which then ultimately merged with Commerce Bank, which was recognized in the New York, Philadelphia, Washington, and Florida regions with a big, red, capital "C."

TD's colors are green, and so clearly a change had to be made in Commerce Bank's logo, not just from a "C" to a "TD," but also from red to green. But according to Graziano, a successful brand is about so much more than colors, logos, and slogans that the change didn't matter to customers. According to Graziano: "The model, the culture, and our people are how we executed against that brand promise. I tell our people that *we* define the brand. You can change the name; it doesn't matter. We could have kept the Commerce name without affecting the slogan, but if we took away seven-day banking, the penny arcade, the live 24/7 call center, our customer-centric model, then we would not be able to execute against our brand promise. For us, internally, that made the difference."

Employees Are the Brand

So there it is. Ultimately, regardless of whether it is a bank, an insurance company, a flower shop, a baseball team, or a musical band, it is the people involved on the team who have the greatest impact on how a product or service is perceived in the marketplace. The fact is, when you walk into a TD "store" (it is not called a branch, but rather a store), immediately you are greeted with a very friendly hello. Employees are encouraged to smile, be helpful and proactive in the way they engage you. If you look lost, they will ask questions to help figure out what exactly you need and then direct you where you need to go.

When Graziano talks about the convenience of seven-day banking, or the penny arcade, or the live 24/7 call-in center, he's really talking about the convenience of quality customer service. As this book has hopefully demonstrated, no brand can succeed without exceptional customer service. My good friend and colleague Jack Mitchell, the CEO of the Connecticut clothing store Mitchell Richards, has written a great book called *Hug Your Customers,* in which he explores the importance of letting customers and key stakeholders know how much you care. Jack argues that you can't figuratively "hug" them enough by going above and beyond their expectations. The fact is, the more effectively you hug your customers, the more you solidify your brand not just in the mind but also in the heart. Hugging creates brand loyalty, which fuels word of mouth, which makes your marketing and advertising campaign that much more effective because your brand message is reinforced by objective third parties . . . customers.

So, in many ways, even in a challenging situation where a bank or any organization changes its logo, colors, and name, it can't solely rely on the effective integration of those changes to create a new brand; it must look to the culture of its workplace—the people who must be motivated to always be at their best, no matter what the organization is called. Of course, names matter a lot in the branding process, but it's not the entire game.

TD Bank knows this and has decided to build its brand on superior customer service. Says Graziano, "We created 'WOW! the Customer.' Most people look at it externally and see it as a fun thing. We asked our employees to wear green on Fridays and at events where we can recognize them for offering exceptional customer service. But at its core, WOW! reinforces a set of expectations as to the level of service from a retail perspective, and how we engage everyone both internally and externally. We reinforce this culture all the time by recognizing and celebrating exceptional customer service. When someone does something over the top with respect to customer service, we post it on our intranet site called TeamWOW! We post great customer service stories every day to get the whole organization engaged."

Says Graziano, "WOW! is that one extra degree [a reference to the book, 212: The Extra Degree by Mac Anderson and Sam Parker]. It's going the extra step and exceeding the customer's expectation. We constantly reinforce 'WOW! the Customer' in everything we do. No employee joins our organization without first graduating from a class called 'Traditions,' which shares the history of the bank and instills the culture in new employees. We tell them this is our culture, and you have to opt in or opt out. You must be 100 percent committed. I can't imagine executing our brand promise without this philosophy."

Regis and Kelly Are a Big Plus

It doesn't hurt TD Bank's brand that the two faces and personalities around which it has built its advertising are Regis Philbin and Kelly Ripa of the Regis and Kelly show. Regis and Kelly used to be with Commerce, and they stayed with TD. The commercials that Regis and Kelly appear in are fun and engaging, and they focus very heavily on welcoming viewers to "America's most convenient bank." The ads focus on the convenience of being open seven days a week, hassle-free banking, and legendary service.

While many banks could say the same thing, TD has done an exceptional job of tying two very likeable and approachable public personalities to an advertising and branding campaign that is consistent with who they are as morning hosts of one of America's most popular television programs. The fact that Regis and Kelly are seen as open, approachable, and easy-to-talk-to is not by accident. Those are the exact attributes that TD's employees must have in order to consistently achieve the "brand promise" that Fred Graziano talks about.

Branding Lessons

Effective branding comes down to team building, which is easier said than done. Consider the following tips to help you build your brand internally if you are in a position to manage employees:

- Don't be so obsessed with stopping people from doing things wrong that you are blind to the moments when they do things right. Be on the lookout for people doing a good job. It's a question of perspective and attitude. We often see what we choose to see.

- Make sure that when you recognize an employee doing a good job, you communicate it immediately after the job has been performed. If you wait too long, you lose the moment and the potential to motivate.

- The most desirable way to recognize an employee is face-to-face, but you can also use e-mail or a fax. Or, write a note on personal stationary. This communicates the message that you appreciate the effort not just professionally but also personally.

- While private recognition is great, sometimes acknowledging an employee in front of his or her peers can pay really big dividends. Just make sure you spread the praise around.

- Keep employees in the information loop. Make sure you let your people know about critical organizational accomplishments, challenges, or opportunities. Being informed gives employees a feeling of ownership over the team's destiny. Many managers let their people know when it is too late. This causes people to feel more like victims than participants. Simply put, being involved and informed is energizing.

- Other motivators include celebrating employee birthdays, anniversaries, and work-related milestones. In addition, social and recreational activities, including employee softball and bowling leagues, create a sense of togetherness and team spirit.

The Catholic Church

A Brand in Constant Crisis

The Catholic Church's brand is in big trouble. It's no secret that serious image and reputation problems for the Church revolve around its consistent mishandling of a decades-old pedophilia scandal involving the molestation of young boys. It is now known that an alarming number of current and former priests involved in these scandals were often times transferred from one parish to another—without any acknowledgment or apology until it was way too late.

The lesson of this chapter is about a powerful institution making the same egregious leadership and procedural mistakes again and again, and in the process bringing upon itself serious branding and public relations problems. The more complex and serious the set of problems, the more vital it is to have a smart and credible strategy of response. The Catholic Church pedophilia scandal has much to teach all of us about the failure to lead and the adverse and lasting impact of this failure on an organization's brand.

Leadership in Denial

In any discussion of the Catholic Church, several critical branding issues that revolve around leadership need to be put on the table. For decades, the Catholic Church's leadership strategy had been to say nothing to the media or to its parishioners about accusations of pedophile priests. Hundreds of cases have been dealt with privately in an attempt to settle out of court and obtain "gag orders" with pedophilia victims and their families. Now that word has gotten out about these highly suspect, morally questionable legal arrangements, the brand of the Catholic Church has been badly tarnished. Its actions have been clearly inconsistent with its religious and moral teachings and philosophy, which are rooted in the simple question, "What would Jesus do?" Out-of-court settlements and gag orders? I think not.

If the Church hierarchy had not opted for the strictly legal strategy of reaching out-of-court settlements, but instead had taken the public relations hit early on (and, yes, the embarrassment that went with it) and then communicated the decisive action it intended to take to address this situation, the outcome might have been quite different—and the Church's brand equity would not have been so severely eroded.

As I cited numerous times in my last book, *What Were They Thinking? Crisis Communication: The Good, the Bad, and the Totally Clueless*, the response to a crisis must come from the top of any organization. In this case, the Pope is the leader of the Catholic Church, and so he is responsible for the way these pedophilia cases have been handled. When the Pope chose silence and deception, he hurt not only his brand, but the Church was hurt as well. Simply put, the Pope's brand and reputation cannot be separated from that of the Catholic Church.

This case, in many ways, is the embodiment of my philosophy and a classic example of why you are the brand, and the brand is you.

Playing the Blame Game

Another part of the Church's leadership strategy often involved challenging or attacking those who criticized the Church on this issue, blaming the media or saying that the situation had been exaggerated. Personally, I was the target of one of these Church attacks in the early- and mid-1990s for a series of columns I had written about the pedophilia problem. In fact, not only did the Church use its primary media vehicle, a widely read newspaper called the *Advocate*, to attack editorially the way I questioned the Church's handling of these pedophilia cases, but in 2008, it became very clear to me how far certain Church officials would go to attack those who question them.

That year, I was to be given a humanitarian award by the Archdiocese of Trenton, New Jersey, for my work and affiliation with

Catholic Charities. As a lifelong Catholic, I was excited and proud to be offered this award. However, a few weeks before the event, I was called by the chair of Catholic Charities, who told me that because of some of the things I had written about the Church's handling of the pedophilia scandal and the pressure he was getting from some of my critics, the archbishop had decided to rescind the award. In response, this chairperson, a longtime friend and business associate, resigned her post. Others on the board of Catholic Charities protested, but the archbishop stood firm on his decree that I was not welcome to receive such an award because I had the audacity to question or challenge the Church's handling of the decades-long scandal that was destroying its brand bit by bit.

So instead of standing tall alongside a public figure who supports the Catholic Church's mission in many ways and yet acknowledges its weaknesses, the Church leadership chose to again make itself look small and hypocritical. This is not good for its image, a.k.a. its brand.

Attacking the Messenger

Curiously, no matter how many times the ill-conceived approach of trying to silence the media response to a "private" matter has failed, Church leaders chose once again to use the same strategy in dealing with the accusations against Pope Benedict XVI that surfaced in late 2009.

This iteration of the pedophilia scandal alleged that when Pope Benedict was the archbishop of Munich (as Cardinal Joseph Ratzinger), he approved the transfer of a German priest and sex offender in order to provide therapy for the priest. This priest later returned to the ministry and molested more children. Further, it is now known that in the 1990s, a Vatican office headed by Ratzinger failed to defrock an American priest accused of molesting 200 deaf boys in Wisconsin.

In the spring of 2010, in churches across the country, Palm Sunday and Easter homilies centered on attacking the media and the Pope's accusers. At Saint Peter's in Rome, the Pope himself offered a prayer "for the young and for those charged with educating them and protecting them." He also said he would not be intimidated by "the petty gossip of dominant opinion."[1] At another time, the Pope addressed the media attacks by saying, "Jesus did not react when insulted."[2] Comparing yourself to Jesus (even for the Pope) is never a smart strategy. Playing the victim rarely if ever makes your brand look good. (See the Tiger Woods chapter for more on the downside of playing God.)

At this same time, Cardinal William Levada, an American who heads the Church's Congregation for the Doctrine of the Faith, wrote a piece on the official Vatican Web site about the New York Times' reporting of the sex scandal involving Pope Benedict. He wrote: "I ask the New York Times to reconsider its attack mode on Pope Benedict XVI and give the world a more balanced view of its leader it can and should count on."[3] Additionally, noted Italian exorcist Father Gabriele Amorth commented that the defamatory reporting on Pope Benedict XVI, especially by the New York Times, was "prompted by the devil."[4]

However, David Clohessy, national director of SNAP (Survivors Network of Those Abused by Priests), was not swayed by this attempt to switch the focus of blame. He noted, "It is, at best, disingenuous and at worst, deceitful and unhealthy to try to shift focus away from child sex crimes and cover ups into the alleged motives of journalists."[5]

I'm not saying that if the leadership of the Catholic Church had not tried to quiet the media and not tried to deflect blame onto others that its branding and reputation problem would have gone away. But I am saying that it would have had a much better chance of getting some people to offer the benefit of the doubt if it had immediately apologized, communicated that there was no excuse for what happened, taken responsibility, and then made sure that the victims and their families were treated with empathy and compassion.

Like millions of others, I am a practicing, but often confused and conflicted, Catholic who has great respect for some of the Church's moral teachings and much of the Church's efforts to help the poor and suffering across the globe. But it is impossible to ignore the fact that the Church's brand is in serious trouble—due to the pedophilia scandal, and because of its flawed response in terms of leadership and communication that has been consistently repeated. It didn't have to be this way.

Branding Lessons

The lessons to be learned from the Catholic Church's branding problems revolve around leadership and communication:

- Business leaders of private companies who try to cover up problems because they falsely think the problems are "*private* matters involving a *private* institution" don't understand that branding will always be about your *public* image, with the need to attract and retain customers. Whether it's the Catholic Church, a corporation, or a private university or school, these principles are the same: It's the public brand image that allows us to raise money/capital and build strong relations with key stakeholders, which in turn allow us to grow and succeed.

- Because a brand is innately public, over time, you can expect some public relations problems. Negative information or rumors may show up on the news, in the paper, or on the Web. When that happens, do not try to defend your brand by blaming the messenger. This approach rarely works and often makes you look defensive.

- Communicate well or die, particularly in a crisis. Do not try to hide. Do not lie. Do not cover up. Do not stall. Do not deflect. Admit the problem. Apologize if needed. Communicate a solution. Your brand will take a hit, but the damage will be far less than it would be if you use the Catholic Church in the pedophilia scandal model as your guide.

Toast

Knowing Where Your Bread Is Buttered

I met Amy Russo several years ago when I stopped in a new restaurant in town called Toast. I was intrigued by the name "Toast," which is always a branding plus. However, as soon as I met Russo, I knew that while her restaurant had a catchy name, it was Russo herself who had the passion, enthusiasm, and all-around big personality that was driving the new Toast brand.

"A Jack of All Trades"

As I entered the restaurant for the first time, Russo was not only greeting people as they came in and sat down, she was also going back and forth from kitchen to tables, totally engaged and involved. She was also constantly checking in with the kitchen staff. While the restaurant has been open for only a few years, it is popular and growing. It has loyal customers, nice word-of-mouth, and Russo is pursuing opening up a second Toast restaurant about fifteen miles away from her initial location in Montclair, New Jersey.

Russo is a typically exuberant and energized entrepreneur who created the concept of Toast and ran with it. Here's what Russo says: "When I came out of college, I did marketing. Then I was home for five years starting our family and decided to get into the restaurant business because I liked to feed people and talk with people. One day when I was at a restaurant that opened at 8 A.M. and closed at 4, it dawned on me that I could do the same thing. I always loved breakfast and brunch, and Montclair, New Jersey, which was my stomping ground, had a big gap in this area. It was a matter of lifestyle and careers crossing paths."

But what about the name *Toast*? Did Russo hire a high-priced marketing or PR firm to conduct focus groups and come up with it? Think again. Russo says: "Toast came from my work in my former life. When I was living overseas, I craved comfort food. I just wanted to come home and have toast with butter and cinnamon. The name of my restaurant was either going to recall that memory or be a name like Home Fries. I settled on Toast because it was simple, easy, and you could take it two ways: toast like breakfast toast, or, if I ever wanted a liquor license, a toast to good health would work, too." I told you she was good!

"Hey, Who's with Me on This?"

Russo didn't tell her family about her business plans until nearly six weeks after she decided to open up Toast and had put the wheels in motion. When she did inform her family members, the reaction was less than positive. "I didn't tell my family—my mother, brothers and sisters—right away," she remembers, "because I didn't need the criticism. When I did tell them, they wanted to know what would happen when it didn't work. In fact, 80 percent of the people in my life asked, 'What happens when it doesn't work?' But there were 20 percent who rooted me on."

Consider this: Russo had the drive, the energy, the commitment, and undoubtedly the personality to own her own restaurant. She had researched it and was ready to go. But that didn't mean others would stand behind her. Remember, no matter what some people say around you, if you truly believe in a particular idea or initiative, you have to go for it. Of course, you want to succeed, but even if you don't, imagine how you are going to feel if you don't try it? You will wonder about it for the rest of your life. *Could I have done it? Would it have worked out? Why didn't I try it?* And finally, *Why did I listen to everyone around me instead of to my own heart?* Russo went for it, and it paid off big. If she hadn't believed in herself and taken the leap, I wouldn't be writing this chapter about Toast.

Living the Brand

When starting a new business, it's important to have a clear image of the brand—the concept that people will hook into that separates this business from all others. Russo notes: "I grew up in a town with a coffee shop that everyone went to for breakfast and lunch. I wanted it to be like that shop, but I wanted to make my place a bit bigger. It would be a place where all customers would be treated equally, whether I see them seven days a week or whether I'm seeing them for the first time. I also knew I needed to hire employees who would want to be here. Building a brand is building a reputation."

As is true in many cases in this book, successful entrepreneurs live the brand every day. Russo knows this while admitting: "It is not like I'm a Jonas Brother, and the show can't go on without me. But I am almost always around and that means that what you see is what you get. If someone wants to see the owner, and I've just come in from running on the treadmill at the gym, well . . . I'll be in my gym clothes. But it works because the whole atmosphere is really laid back, and we have really great food."

This kind of "laid back" style works for Russo because she is confident in herself and comfortable in her own skin, or, more specifically, in her gym clothes without a lot of makeup. This approach is not only refreshing, but it's also comforting to know that you don't have to be anyone else or present an image that is inconsistent with what you feel and who you really are in order to succeed.

"Guerilla Marketing"

Being a small-business person, Russo didn't have a huge marketing or advertising budget. So she knew that if she was going to brand Toast effectively, she was going to have to be creative and think out of the box. She would have to behave in ways described by Marc Levison in his landmark book *Guerilla Marketing*. More specifically, she had to inexpensively take advantage of the burgeoning social media environment. Says Russo, "In the beginning, things like Facebook didn't seem that useful. Now, I get a lot of information out to my customers through Facebook. In fact, I use social media and the Internet much more than print marketing.

"Of course, TV is also great. On National Pancake Day I got a spot on WPIX Channel 11, a local TV station based in New York.

People still make the jaunt in from Brooklyn and Staten Island because they saw me on TV."

Yes, TV is a nice PR coup, but no one can consistently rely on that kind of coverage to strengthen a brand. Getting a feature story on TV is a crap shoot. Translation: Every day, news organizations get pitched countless ideas and guests for stories. And even if your idea hits the jackpot and the producers commit to cover you or your event, any number of things or "news of the day" can knock you out of the box.

This means that you have to be smarter about creating your own media content. You have to use existing technology and information platforms to reach current and potential customers. That's what Amy Russo has done with Toast. She has a great e-mail list and uses it regularly to let those who know and like her and her restaurant know what is going on, what events she has coming up at the restaurant, what causes she is supporting and how customers can get in on them, too. She is creating a community who cares about her and her restaurant. That's smart branding.

Your People Are an Extension of You

Although Russo is the face of her brand, she is smart enough to know that it's not her face most customers see. No matter how good Russo may be at marketing and promotion or how committed she is to Toast, in the end, her success is largely determined by her employees.

"A learning curve for me," admits Russo, "was knowing who is a great server and who isn't. I want employees who are here for the right reasons. I have had people who were great servers, but they didn't care about the products on the plate—now, I can see right through them. At the same time, I have interesting people here who have taken my brand to a new level. Whether you are making $10 an hour or $40 an hour, we are here to put great food on the table and to give people a good experience." That's what people remember when they leave and talk to their friends and spread the word about a business.

Keeping an eye on all employees will become even more challenging as Russo attempts to expand Toast to a second location. "I will have to make sure," she says, "that this place doesn't suffer while the other place gets going. I feel like my manager, my chef, and my employees keep the culture going here, so I will spend more time at the new place. Then I will take the feedback to determine if my absence hurts my business. It's hard to run a mom-and-pop shop in two locations, especially knowing that I'm an independent who is independent. I want to keep everything the way it is as far as quality and culture are concerned."

I'm betting that Russo will keep up the quality and culture of Toast because she knows what it takes to build and keep brand reputation—she knows there is no time to rest on one's success. She will think and at times obsess (a requirement for many of us who work at our business virtually every day). Says Russo: "It's been great. We are holding our own in the three years we've been open, and I'd say I have a fairly successful business. Every once in a while, I'll sit at a different table to get a new perspective, hoping to see something I can improve on. If I sat there and thought 'Yea me,' I am afraid I will get complacent. I keep looking at new products and ways to do things better."

That's what truly great entrepreneurs do. They are always looking to connect the dots, to coach their staff, to bring in new blood, and to develop new and exciting ideas. They don't rest on their laurels. If you haven't yet heard of Toast, there is a good chance you will in the years to come because Amy Russo herself is as much of the brand as is the restaurant, and that is a part of her success as an entrepreneur.

Branding Lessons

Amy Russo's small, start-up business has a lot to teach anyone in any business about how to create, build, and keep a brand:

- Even if some people (including some family members and friends) tell you that something you want to do won't work, if you truly believe in it, you owe it to yourself to try it and give it your best shot.

- Relax . . . just be yourself. Trying to create an image or persona that does not reflect who you really are will weaken your brand and send mixed signals to your audience. Be honest and genuine.

- Remember, even when you are the owner of your own company, you are often times the VP for marketing, branding, and PR. Be creative, think out of the box, be proactive, and use social media to its fullest advantage. You better, because no one else is likely to swoop in and do it for you.

- As committed as you may be as the top dog, your people need to be committed as well. You may be the brand, but you can't perform every job. Hire well and when it doesn't work out, don't be afraid to "fire fast," as Jim Collins, author of *Good to Great*, likes to say!

The New York Yankees

A Lot More Than a Baseball Brand

I'll never forget the first time I walked into Yankee Stadium. I was seven years old in the summer of 1966, and the New York Yankees were playing the Cleveland Indians. My dad and I walked up the entrance ramp as the crowd roared in the bottom of the first inning, and I knew there was nothing like it on the face of the earth.

Of course, I didn't know or care anything about branding, but this was my introduction to one of the greatest brands of all time, and I'll never forget it. Today, I'm more certain than ever that the New York Yankees have a lot to teach us about the complex, multi-levels of branding—even if we don't have the deepest of pockets to pay for the best talent to fill in whatever hole we have on our team.

It's All about Tradition

The Yankee brand is about understanding that tradition sells. People want to be a part of an organization/brand that connects them to the good ol' days when things were simpler. Tradition also gives us a shared history, a common bond, a sense of comfort. Hip-hop stars, celebrities, politicians, colleagues, and the guy down the street, all know the Yankees. Across generations, whether you talk to people who saw Ruth, Gehrig, or DiMaggio (whose quote "I want to thank the Good Lord for making me a Yankee" is one of my all-time favorites), we're talking about the Yankees and wearing that Yankee cap with the interlocking "NY."

I'm a big baseball fan, and I live in New Jersey. But I can tell you that if tomorrow, there was suddenly a great New Jersey professional baseball team, I wouldn't be a fan. That team just couldn't compete with the New York Yankees for any New Jersey fan because the New Jersey team would have no tradition, no history, no connection to Mickey Mantle or Babe Ruth. Yeah, for that, I'd ride right through New Jersey, past its baseball stadium, and head out to the Bronx to support the team I was raised on. Good brands built on tradition command loyalty.

Leadership

Tradition alone won't keep a brand afloat. So what else do the Yankees have? They have something that all of us must strive for—a reputation for having leaders with strong personalities.

George Steinbrenner, whether you loved him or hated him, was a leader with a strong personality. His obsession with winning and having Yankee players conduct themselves in a respectful and professional manner is something to admire. On how many other teams is facial hair banned? Did you see the difference between Johnny Damon with the Red Sox versus Johnny Damon with the Yankees? On the Red Sox he played with a full beard and a mane of hair halfway down his back. When he came to the Yankees, all that changed. With Steinbrenner at the helm, Yankee players had to look the part—no exceptions. Only a strong leader can make this happen.

The Yankees are also known for managers who are giants among mere mortals. These legendary leaders include the great Casey Stengel, who was one of the all-time characters of the game. There is also Billy Martin, who was hired and fired more times than any of us can count, but who always knew how to fire up his team. And then there is Joe Torre, who interestingly created his own successful brand as a thoughtful, sensitive motivator who knew his players and exactly what buttons to push at the right times, which earned the Yankees four world championships. In a large organization, management is part of the brand. Today, Joe Girardi is the Yankee manager who wears the pinstripes with pride.

Rank and File: The Brand within the Brand

The Yankee brand is also a product of the players themselves—what the rest of us call the employees. For the Yankees, these are the men who transcend baseball and become social and cultural icons. We know them. We love them. And we associate them with the brand. From Mickey Mantle (the favorite of me and millions of other kids in the 1950s), to Babe Ruth, to Joe DiMaggio, to Yogi Berra, all the way to Derek Jeter, great brands often are tied to great names within the organization. And those individuals carry the mark of the brand in whatever they do.

The fact that Derek Jeter always looks sharp and carries himself with class and dignity as the Yankee captain does, in fact, impact the Yankee brand in a positive way. (However, both the Yankees brand as well as Jeter's lofty Yankee reputation was not helped by the very public and at times acrimonious contract negotiation involving the Yankees icon in late 2010.) That's why when we read in the *New York Post* and the *Daily News* about a supremely talented player like A-Rod sunning himself with his shirt off in Central Park, or caught up in some embarrassing off-field controversy or distraction (including the use of steroids), we can't help thinking, "That's not what Yankee players are supposed to do." They are also not supposed to cheat on their wives in such a public and crass fashion— it hurts the Yankee name, so we don't like him for it. Yankee players are far from perfect, but when they make mistakes or do something wrong, we expect them to step up and take responsibility.

Even good brands with strong personalities behind the product can run into trouble sometimes. Even the Yankees can't ignore the problems with steroids and performance-enhancing drugs that plagued Roger Clemens, Andy Petttite, Jason Giambi, and yes, A-Rod. Did that scandal tarnish the Yankee brand? Of course it did. But notwithstanding this controversy, and many other problems that have affected the Yankee brand throughout the years, the brand endures. That's because these few individual players are only one piece of the branding puzzle. When one piece of the brand gets tarnished, the other pieces—the tradition, the leadership, the good and honest players, the twenty-seven championships—hold it together.

Be an Elitist

Many Yankee fans are baseball snobs. And that's not a bad thing. We believe in our hearts that our team is better than any other team.

And we believe that those who root for our team are better than other sports fans. We make fun of any other team or fan that tries to pretend to be as good (and that goes double for Mets fans—we're talking about a second-rate brand over there in Queens). Yep, we're snobs and we like it that way.

And that is the funny thing about brands. When a brand earns unwavering loyalty, the result can sometimes border on obsession. I, for example, have a room filled with framed Yankee photos and other memorabilia. I keep adding to the collection as I find "classic" Yankee black-and-white framed photos. I know it's nuts to dedicate this much money and space to a ball game, but I also know I'm not the only middle-aged guy with all this Yankee stuff. These pieces of the team connect us to great memories and milestone moments in our lives. They help us connect on a deep and personal level—and that's what a good brand must do.

Moving the Brand Forward

Finally, the Yankee brand anchors itself in the aura of Yankee Stadium itself. The new stadium that opened in 2009 is bigger; the seats are more comfortable; and obviously the tickets more expensive. But because the brand is built on tradition, when you go to the new stadium, it's very obvious that management has made exceptional efforts to transfer from the old stadium all the things that make the Yankees the Yankees: Those oversized framed pictures of Yankee greats are everywhere. Ruth, Gehrig, DiMaggio, Mantle, Berra, and the other greats are hovering everywhere you look. Yankee management isn't stupid. It knows that in order to succeed it can't throw out the old and go with the new. The new stadium also boasts a store dedicated to selling "old school" Yankee memorabilia. You go with the new, but you try to make it look like the old. That's why the Yankee Stadium façade still looks the same when you look out in right field. Of course, it is newer material that will hopefully last a long time, but it looks like the old stuff. And even many of the advertising sponsors are posted on billboards in exactly the same places they were in the old Yankee Stadium. That's not by accident. It may not be the house that Ruth built, but for the foreseeable future, it is the house that the traditional Yankee brand will flourish in.

Branding Lessons

None of us has the deep pockets that have helped the Yankees brand themselves as the greatest sports team of all time. (Yes, I know that some may say this is an exaggeration; I, however, believe it in my heart.) Still, there are very basic branding lessons that this team gives to all of us, free of charge:

- Identify and build on the elements of a business, product, or service that have staying power. Whether your brand is old or new, building tradition will create loyalty.

- The leaders of a business are a part of the brand. There's no way to hide them. So make sure that your leaders have strong personalities that represent the qualities of the brand.

- Every member of a company's team also has the opportunity to be a brand within a brand. No matter how small or large your role is in a larger organization, distinguish yourself with a reputation of excellence.

- It's okay in the branding business to be a snob. If you want others to think your brand is the best, then you must live, think, and breathe that attitude yourself.

- Don't dump the old just because it's old. Move your brand forward and adjust to changing times, but bring the things of value from the past along with you.

The Kennedys

The Rise and Fall of America's "Royal Family"

The Kennedy name is synonymous with American culture and politics. In fact, for decades, the Kennedys were considered America's "royal family" by many. However, today the Kennedy brand is a struggling one that has clearly seen better days. Its rise, fall, and attempted resurrection make for interesting analysis.

In the Beginning

It was Joe Kennedy Sr. who first understood the importance of building a Kennedy "brand." Beginning in the 1940s, Joe Sr. introduced a campaign strategy still used today, built on marketing, media, money, and personality.[1] He originally intended to implement this strategy through his eldest son, Joe, whom he felt had great potential for national office. Vincent Bzdek, author of *The Kennedy Legacy: Jack, Bobby, and Ted and a Family Dream Fulfilled*, says that Joe Jr., a naval aviator in World War II, felt the need to compete with his brother Jack for "hero" status in his dad's eyes and so he "started volunteering for riskier and riskier missions even after he was supposed to come home." Then in 1944, his explosives-laden plane detonated in flight, and he was killed.[2] Many felt that he would ultimately have become president if it were not for his untimely death.

Joe Sr. then turned his attention to son Jack, helping to create an heroic military image and, yes, a brand that was crystallized in the story of the PT-109 incident. "The trigger was a night in August 1943, when a Japanese warship sliced in half a Navy Patrol Torpedo boat commanded by Jack. Ten of the 12 men on board the PT-109 survived the ordeal, in part because of Jack's decisions. Jack returned to a hero's welcome."[3]

Fast forward to 1960 when Jack is being groomed to take the highest office in the nation. During this campaign, the Kennedy brand was created and broadcast to the nation in a way that had never been done before, thanks to the magic of television. The most memorable stamp of modern branding on the Kennedy campaign is found in the senator's smooth and highly telegenic presentation during a series of televised debates with Richard Nixon. For many years to come, Kennedy's performance would be the prototype for how a candidate, or for that matter any male public figure, should come across on television: calm, smiling, attractive, and comfortable with himself. In 1961, the Kennedy brand added "president" to its dazzling public image. The Kennedys also promoted the family's political brand by holding hundreds of coffee clutches in the 1960 presidential campaign, in which Jack charmed and dazzled countless women voters while he was accompanied by his mother Rose and his very photogenic wife Jackie. Those touch football games at the Kennedy compound that always seemed to be recorded in black-and-white photos also promoted the Kennedy brand as young, athletic, and vibrant.

The Kennedy Curse

The Kennedy brand is rooted in the so-called Camelot story of President John F. Kennedy and his wife Jackie in the early 1960s, but unfortunately it is defined by the events of November 22, 1963—the day JFK was killed in Dallas, Texas. I was in grammar school at the time, and as it did for millions of other school-aged children, the assassination effected my childhood and my sense of who the Kennedys were and what they represented to our country. The powerful and poignant black-and-white images of widow Jackie and children Caroline and John Jr. would be etched in the minds and hearts of a generation of Americans. Five years later, when Robert F. Kennedy was killed in Los Angeles, again by an assassin's bullet, as he was campaigning for president, the Kennedy brand became firmly connected to modern-day martyrdom.

It's hard to imagine a more high-profile American political family who has experienced so much public suffering. In fact, it's impossible to separate the Kennedy name from tragedy. First, tragedy struck Joe Jr. in World War II. It also fell on their sister Rosemary, who had severe mental illness and was put in an institution, where she spent the rest of her life. Then in 1969, Ted Kennedy faced the tragic events in Chappaquiddick that led to the death of Mary Jo Kopechne. In many ways, that incident ensured that Ted would never be elected president. The Kennedy curse, as some might call it, continued into the 1970s when Ted's son, Teddy Jr., lost his leg to cancer. Through the following years, the family seemed plagued by drug overdoses, car accidents, and serious alcoholism and addiction problems. This tragic legacy continued until John Kennedy Jr. and his wife Carolyn were killed in a horrific small-plane accident on July 16, 1999.

In many ways, the Kennedy brand may have died in that plane crash. Young John had it all. Looks, charisma, likeability, and a sense that he was the legitimate heir apparent to major national office. If he had not died so tragically at such a young age, things might have been different for the Kennedy brand. He may have been the brightest family star, but, it often seems that the surviving Kennedy family members are their own worst enemies and therefore largely responsible for the demise of the family name.

Circling the Wagons . . . Protecting the Brand

The Kennedy brand is often now seen as privileged and out of touch with the lives of everyday American citizens who must abide by the law and pay the consequences when they break it. It was bad enough that twenty-eight-year-old Mary Jo Kopechne died in that car with Ted Kennedy in 1969, but in many ways, what was so much worse for the reputation of the Kennedy family was the apparent effort to cover up what happened, and the fact that Teddy was not only driving the car, but clearly had been drinking heavily before the accident.

This history of irresponsibility and freedom from the consequences of that irresponsibility would become a pattern that the Kennedy family would replicate time and time again. When one of them broke the law, the family would seem to circle the wagons and close ranks. They would lawyer up and be less than candid. It often seemed like they were incapable of taking responsibility, and instead chose to hide behind privilege and high-level relationships with those in law enforcement, the media, and government.

In fact, in July of 2010, a *New York Post* headline entitled "Driving While Kennedy" seemed to capture the essence of how the public came to see the descendants of the original Kennedys who had done so much to build the initial brand. The *Post* article stated, "A member of the Kennedy clan drove blotto, hitting a curb near a school jammed with kids near her Westchester home. Fortunately, no one was hurt. In keeping with family tradition, Mary Richardson Kennedy, 50, whose hubby, Robert F. Kennedy Jr., has filed for divorce, last week avoided jail or any meaningful punishment by pleading guilty to a reduced charge of driving with ability impaired. She'll lose her license for 90 days, pay a $500 fine and attend two (!) anti-drunken-driving classes. If she stays out of trouble for a year, her record is magically cleansed. Nothing about being forced to hire a driver, which should be required by law for those named Kennedy."[4]

Certainly, many of the Kennedy children, even those who have had serious personal problems including Robert F. Kennedy Jr., Rory Kennedy, and Teddy Kennedy Jr., have made significant contributions to society both in the for-profit and not-for-profit sectors. However, it is the "dark side" of the family legacy that remains at the forefront in the American press and has served to seriously tarnish the Kennedy brand. It has been noted that "the dark side of the family story also endures: two assassinations and thirteen children who grew up without fathers; accidents that claimed and damaged lives, and men behaving badly toward women, one generation after another. Kennedys have been idolized and demonized for decades, romanticized as the second coming of Camelot and splashed across tabloids as exemplars of self-indulgence." "Sooner or later," says Laurence Leamer, author of three books on the Kennedy family, "we'll get a balanced vision of what they were."[5] Boston University historian Thomas Whalen says anyone in a family, especially a large one, can relate to the adventures and misadventures of the Kennedys. "They are America's family," he says, "both good and bad."[6]

You Know . . . You're No JFK

Despite the dark side of the Kennedy clan, for years it was perceived that the Kennedy name and brand alone was tantamount to political success. Patrick Kennedy had served in Congress for Massachusetts for many years (despite a series of embarrassing public situations due to his drug and alcohol problems resulting in highly publicized stints in rehab). His cousin Joe served in Congress for Massachusetts, and Uncle Teddy became a highly effective legislator who would come to be called the "lion" of the U.S. Senate, and was lionized upon his death on August 25, 2009. (Ted's endorsement of Barack Obama in the 2008 presidential campaign helped Obama and demonstrated that, while the Kennedy name was seriously wounded, it was not dead.)

John Kennedy's daughter, Caroline, also stepped into the Kennedy political circle when she flirted with the U.S. Senate seat in New York in 2008, hoping the Kennedy name and legacy would carry her into office. As I was reporting and providing political commentary on her quixotic candidacy, it became clear that the Kennedy name alone was not going to get the job done (the luster had long worn off the family name) and that the Kennedy children were going to have to stand on their own and be judged as harshly as other public brands when it came to the ability to connect, motivate, and move people. Caroline just couldn't get it done.

Carolyn Kennedy is admittedly a very shy person who had avoided the public spotlight and didn't have much experience giving speeches or communicating in public. Watching her initial steps into the political ring, it became clear that her lack of communication training and awareness was a problem. Consider this excerpt from a Kennedy interview: "You know, I think, you know, sort of, of, oh, sharing some of this experience. And, um, as I've said, he was a friend. [Referring to another public figure] was a friend, a family member, and, um, so, and oh, obviously, he's you know, he has also had an impressive career in public service."[7]

Being shy is one thing. But bumbling through a nationally televised interview that would immediately go viral on YouTube is another. This practice of breaking up complete thoughts and statements with fillers like "um" or "like" or "you know" is deadly. It communicates a lack of confidence and clarity. One of the most important qualities of a leader is confidence. Not arrogance or cockiness, but confidence. We need to believe that a leader or any person in a significant position believes what she is saying and has the ability to communicate it in a clear, concise, and coherent fashion.

Carolyn Kennedy's Senate bid died before it ever got off the ground. In as much as honest, direct communication abilities bolstered the reputation of her dad, John F. Kennedy, lack of these same skills caused the public embarrassment of his daughter. Leaning on the reputation of the Kennedy name without possessing the traits that made the brand great to begin with sets even the most entrenched brands up for a tumble.

In the End

So while the Kennedy brand and name survives, it has become a complicated equation. It no longer stands for American royalty or political star power—today it stands most notably for a family firmly entrenched in American culture and history that was at its peak in the 1960s with Jack and Bobby and ultimately died with the untimely tragic death of JFK Jr.

My sense is that there is a chance, albeit an outside one, that a younger member of the Kennedy clan will emerge and become a successful brand name once again on the American landscape. But as of now, that's a long shot. Fair or not, the brand has seen its best days, which were nearly two generations ago. It will be hard to resurrect the glitter and shine of those bygone days.

Branding Lessons

Your name doesn't have to be Kennedy to learn from these branding lessons:

- You can't live off the past forever. No matter how successful a family or organization brand may have been, future success relies on constant nurturing of the qualities that made that brand special in the beginning.

- The American public loses its patience over time with erratic and irresponsible behavior. Additionally, any hint of "privilege" that places a brand above the average citizen is destructive to long-term success.

- No matter what your last name is, you still must perform under pressure and perform competently in the marketplace.

- Your ability to communicate is often the first and most important criterion of evaluation that can make or break you, no matter what your reputation or family name.

- Some brands just run their course, whether it is a family, a company, a sports team, or an entertainer.

Hospital Brands

Hospital Branding in Challenging and Uncertain Times

Much of my coaching and consulting work revolves around marketing, communications, and, yes, branding in the world of healthcare. Many of my clients are hospitals or hospital systems trying to figure out how to manage and meet their bottom line in a constantly changing environment, including national healthcare reform, government reimbursement reductions, new and ever-changing regulations, and intense competition, not just for patients but also for qualified physicians. All the while, these hospitals are trying to keep their brands strong in the marketplace and their employees engaged, enthused, and involved, while also cutting costs and sometimes laying people off.

This is the backdrop for this chapter, which features three hospitals/hospital systems that I have worked with for many years—each has unique stories to tell but all are trying to accomplish the same thing. What you are about to read barely scratches the surface of the entire branding game plan for each of these institutions, but even this basic overview provides valuable lessons to anyone trying to build, sustain, and promote a brand in a large, diverse, and complex organization.

Saint Barnabas Health Care System: 4 Boxes . . . One Philosophy

All four of my children were born at Saint Barnabas Medical Center, which is part of the Saint Barnabas Health Care System (SBHCS), the largest health care system in New Jersey and one of the largest in the nation. SBHCS includes six acute care hospitals, a psychiatric hospital, outpatient centers, two children's hospitals, geriatric centers, a state-wide behavioral health network, and comprehensive home care and hospice programs, at fifty sites throughout New Jersey. System facilities treat over two million patients each year.

Within this complex structure, excellence thrives. The specialties of Heart and Heart Surgery at Newark Beth Israel and Neurology and Neurosurgery at Saint Barnabas Medical Center were named in their specific areas among the 50 Best Hospitals in the United States (and in fact, are tops in New Jersey) by *U.S. News and World Report*. *Modern Healthcare* named SBHCS among the 100 Best Places to Work in Healthcare in the United States and SBHCS is recognized for being among the top 10 in the nation in volume for heart transplants, renal and pancreas transplants, and burn care.

I know the hospital and the system well. I've dealt with top executives, doctors, nurses, and orderlies, as well as with the people who greet you at the entrance, and I have led seminars and workshops with hundreds, if not thousands, of employees throughout the Saint Barnabas Health Care System. While no system or hospital is perfect, and mistakes occur no matter how many precautions are taken, there is a philosophy at SBHCS that focuses on excellence in terms of patient satisfaction and customer service. This philosophy starts at the top with CEO Ron Del Mauro.

The branding focus of SBHCS is exemplified in what is called the "four boxes" in the SBHCS logo. Each box stands for a particular pillar of the Saint Barnabas approach, which includes: Quality; Patient, Employee and Physician Satisfaction; Cost Efficiency; Execution and Sustainability.

When I asked Del Mauro about the significance of the four boxes in the branding of the Saint Barnabas Health Care System, here's some of what he had to say: "People are always looking for something unique as far as a logo is concerned. At Saint Barnabas, we believe that it's not the logo that makes the philosophy; it is the philosophy that makes the logo. We came up with these four boxes because we liked the way they looked, and they stood out. When all is said and done, however, it's what we did to make those images special that created the impact of the logo. First, we created something that we felt was visually appealing and marketable, and then we asked ourselves how we could make people identify the image with the SBHCS philosophy, which is that patients' and family members' expectations will be met every time they come to any of our fifty sites in New Jersey. It is the execution of our philosophy that makes the logo so special."

I then asked Michellene Davis, senior vice president for Policy Development and Government Affairs for SBHCS, how difficult it is getting every element of this complex organization to be supportive of one brand and marketing approach, centered around the four boxes. She responded: "It's like watching siblings. Everyone wants to say 'me, me, me,' but the truth is that the power is in the family unit as a whole. In a family situation where you have a healthy, sibling competitive edge, the one great methodology there for parents is the fact that the strength and virtue of the family comes from all the individuals that make up the family. In the same way, this dynamic is what constitutes who we at SBHCS really are. The power is in the family."

So there it is. Any hospital or hospital system can have four boxes or four stars or four triangles in its logo. It can be visually appealing and look good in a print ad or on a billboard, but that doesn't make the brand by itself. It's living up to what those boxes stand for that matters most. This is particularly challenging with an organization that employs 18,500 people, which is the case at SBHCS. As this book has demonstrated, one of the biggest challenges to a successful branding effort is to get employees to "buy in" to what you are doing, because ultimately *they* are the messengers who matter most. We will see the truth of that in action in the Campbell Soup chapter.

According to Del Mauro: "The most difficult task that we've faced since we became a system in 1996 has been putting together such a diverse organization in such a short period of time. The success of this effort depended on the integration of the culture— on everyone assuming a similar philosophy. Everyone in the System bought into the philosophy of creating a special experience from the time you step on our property to the time you receive a bill. We believe every employee is important in conveying our philosophy and our mission—whether that's our security guards, housekeepers, nurses, or surgeons, each plays a vital role in creating a healthcare experience that we believe makes SBHCS unique. The ultimate goal is that when people see the four boxes in our logo, they know that the clinical and personal care they will receive at SBHCS distinguishes us from all others. The credit for our success goes to the 18,500 employees in the System (SBHCS is the second largest private employer in New Jersey) because each of them is responsible for carrying out that philosophy."

But even if the integration of a singular, unifying philosophy is done well, in an organization that has so many moving parts and is so geographically spread out in different buildings and communities, problems are bound to occur. Mistakes will happen. When I asked Del Mauro about this, I focused on the role of the CEO and leader of an organization in protecting brand equity when an incident occurs. (I asked Ron this question at the height of the BP oil spill fiasco in the Gulf.) Here's what he had to say: "I truly believe it is my responsibility to know about and be involved with any and all negative instances that take place in our system. We are far from perfect, and mistakes happen, but it is critically important to me that we are involved in every issue and respond to that mistake, analyze it, and take corrective action to keep it from happening again. It is important to me to know if a patient has a problem with service—even if that problem occurs at 3:00 A.M. on a Sunday morning at some remote location; if it is brought to my attention, I have to respond, and I would expect anyone in a leadership position to do the same. To me, all the issues are important as far as protecting the brand. . . . That is why we extensively analyze patient surveys. If a letter of complaint from a patient comes in, it is addressed, and we try to correct the problem. It is my responsibility 24 hours a day, 7 days a week, 52 weeks of the year. It is an obsession with creating that experience that must distinguish us from all others." Again . . . It's about being "obsessed."

Michellene Davis, who before joining the SBHCS held several top healthcare and other policy positions, including state treasurer in New Jersey, said this of Ron Del Mauro: "Branding SBHCS as a healthcare organization of the highest quality is an easy thing to do once you encounter the System's corporate leadership. Quite honestly, the compassionate corporate leadership that Ron Del Mauro brings to his role as CEO of the organization sets the tone and tenor of the delivery of service at every level. In my short tenure with this organization, I am most impressed with the institutional character of the organization and have readily observed that it has trickled down from the leader of the organization."

Throughout *You Are the Brand*, you've been introduced to some pretty "obsessed" leaders and CEOs. We're talking about people who think about their organization's brand and reputation all the time. Excellence is their standard and anything less is just not acceptable. Ron Del Mauro of SBHCS is one of those people. Del Mauro pursues excellence in every facet of his life, including on the golf course, where we have played some very competitive and intense matches with his longtime associate Barry Ostrowsky, who serves as president and chief operating officer for the System. But Del Mauro's pursuit of excellence is most intense when it comes to the Saint Barnabas Health Care System, as he explains: "We have to seek perfection. We treat two million patients, and of course we can't be perfect, but we need to seek perfection in all two million cases."

RWJ: Going from Twenty-one Logos to Three Letters

Consider, also, the case of Robert Wood Johnson University Hospital (RWJUH) and the Robert Wood Johnson Health System. Unlike Saint Barnabas Health Care System, RWJUH is a private hospital tied to one of the state's great public medical schools: University of Medicine and Dentistry of New Jersey—Robert Wood Johnson Medical School. RWJUH CEO Steve Jones and his vice president of communications and community relations, Michael Knecht, have played key roles in taking on the challenge of coordinating, simplifying, and streamlining a plethora of logos, names, and philosophies that were spread throughout this very large health care system. They knew from the start that the lack of a unifying brand was getting in the way of Robert Wood Johnson University Hospital being recognized for its excellence, particularly in terms of research and clinical outcomes.

When I asked Jones about the Robert Wood Johnson brand, he said that when he took over in December 2006, branding was one of his top priorities. (Jones has held a variety of leadership positions at RWJUH for twenty-eight years.) He knew that as CEO he needed to lead this effort, and to do that, some drastic changes were needed. He told me: "We wanted a visual identity that would be a symbol that instantly brought Robert Wood Johnson to mind. A decade ago, there were twenty different logos associated with the hospital. We woke up one day and found out we had twenty-one. The trauma center had its own logo, as did the children's hospital, the heart hospital, the cancer program. We had brand confusion and didn't have clarity. It became our goal to have one visual identity that symbolized Robert Wood Johnson University Hospital. We do have different names for different service lines, but we want people to know that they will have the same high-quality experience when they interact with the RWJUH brand no matter which part of our hospital they are using. To tie all of our different brands together we chose the unifying theme of just three letters: RWJ."

Clearly, Steve Jones was on the right track. But knowing what's right, smart, and strategic from a branding point of view is very different from executing that strategy successfully, particularly when people have become so used to doing things "their own way." This fact is a challenge, but it's not a reason to give up. According to Michael Knecht, it is CEO Steve Jones who has played the most important role in this massive brand transformation at this sprawling and complex institution: "The CEO role clarifies the vision. The CEO is the chief strategist, cheerleader, fundraiser, and he or she is the brand champion—being cognizant of what it means to have a strong brand, knowing its strengths and weaknesses. I may be the chief communications officer, but Steve sets the tone. When he is in a board meeting, at a community event, on the sidelines of a Rutgers University football game, or working with the media, everything he does shapes or reinforces the brand. He understands that any misstep can do damage to the brand. He gets it; he supports the efforts we do to make sure the brand is integrated across all of our entities. If I am the 'brand cop' behind all the logo fights, he is the 'brand attorney general' and will make the final determinations. His role is critical for advancing the brand externally and internally."

So what do those letters RWJ really mean to the tens of thousands who come in contact with this healthcare organization, which has been recognized as one of "America's Best Hospitals" in 2010 by U.S. News and World Report? According to Jones: "The RWJ brand stands for excellence, high-quality technology, new techniques, and compassionate care. If there is that recognition and meaning behind a brand, then that is the place I want to go, the place where I know they will take care of me. That umbrella can cover many different things. Therefore, if we put our cancer program, executive health program, cardiac program, or any other service we offer under that umbrella, we bask in the glow of that brand." The RWJ academic medical center brand encourages the public to see the synergy between RWJ University Hospital and the great UMDNJ-Robert Wood Johnson Medical School.

A major theme in this book focuses on brand partnerships, and RWJ offers a good example of how that concept can work successfully. Steve Jones is a big Rutgers University football fan. I've been to games with him, and I've seen how he really believes in this team and has great respect for his good friend Coach Greg Schiano (who was the chief architect of the Block R logo at Rutgers, which is featured later in this book). As I sat in Jones's office recently and looked at the shelves filled with books on health care and leadership, I also saw countless Rutgers University football souvenirs, all of them emblazoned with the huge Block R—a football signed by Schiano and many of his players, cups, hats, pennants. All of them clearly showed how enthusiastic CEO Jones is about RU football. However, my sense is also that seeing that Block R influenced him on some level to simplify his own organization's brand into the letters RWJ, and that's a good thing.

But for Jones, it isn't just about going to football games. It is about a smart, strategic, and carefully aligned brand partnership with Rutgers, which was in part facilitated through TJ Nelligan of Nelligan Sports Marketing (see TJ Nelligan chapter).

Says Jones: "You are judged by the company you keep. Clearly we are looking for partners, whether clinical partners like RWJ

Medical School, or community outreach such as Rutgers University and Princeton. [This is a reference to RWJ's effort to connect its Robert Wood Johnson University Hospital Hamilton facility with Princeton University and the larger Princeton community. The RWJ Health System was recently designated as the Official Hospital System of Princeton University Athletics.] We serve the community, so people at the Rutgers football stadium, 50,000 people at the opening game, and 8,000 screaming at the Rutgers Athletic Center, will see the hospital's sponsorship banners, electronic scoreboard graphics, and the hospital ads in the game programs. Every football game, women's basketball game, and men's basketball game give the opportunity to reinforce the RWJ brand and partnership with Rutgers University. We also have a clinical relationship with the Rutgers University College of Nursing and the College of Pharmacy. The Rutgers University Ernest Mario School of Pharmacy has had personnel stationed on the RWJUH campus for more than thirty years. Our relationship with Rutgers is strong and logical. It is a natural fit, and it reinforces the high-quality brand."

When analyzing successful brands, it often becomes apparent that there are similarities worth noting and perhaps even emulating. In the case of Saint Barnabas Health Care System and Robert Wood Johnson University Hospital, it's interesting to note that both have smart and effective naming, cross-branding, and philanthropic relationships with the New Jersey Devils ice hockey team and Rutgers University football program, respectively. Clearly, forming partnerships with entities that share a common population is a wise move.

Hackensack University Medical Center: Scoring a "Touchdown"

Hackensack University Medical Center (HUMC) received two rankings in U.S. News and World Report's "America's Best Hospitals." It's considered one of the top hospitals in the country, particularly when it comes to geriatrics and heart surgery. The medical center is the only New Jersey acute-care hospital to be ranked in two specialties. The rankings underscore the medical center's philosophy that patients have always been and will always be its top priority.

Yet, with so many areas of clinical expertise, much of its "branding" effort revolves around promoting and highlighting specific service lines. Most specifically, kids, cardiac, and cancer. In an effort to expand upon an already-impressive marketing and promotional campaign, HUMC, located in northern New Jersey (in the heart of the country's number-one media market, New York City), teamed up with the New York football Giants to create something called "The Touchdown Fund: Score for Kids, Cardiac, and Cancer." In fact, you can't go to the new Meadowlands Stadium, which houses the Giants and the Jets, without seeing HUMC's brand all over.

HUMC president and CEO Bob Garrett felt the greatest connection to the football Giants. After a series of meetings in which both organizations pursued the partnership and brainstormed ways of getting together, the Touchdown Fund became a reality. When I asked Garrett why the Giants and why this particular initiative, here's what he said: "It made sense. Two companies have an incredibly positive image in their respective fields, the NY football Giants in the field of sports and HUMC in the healthcare and hospital world. It made sense for those two to get together in terms of brand recognition and striving for excellence. Then there is geographic synergy. We are both in the northern part of New Jersey and are servicing the same types of people—our patients are often the core of the Giants' fan base." Another reason why the football Giants are a logical branding partner with HUMC is the fact that the team has moved into a brand-new stadium with a variety of promotional bells and whistles that simply didn't exist in the old Meadowlands. According to Garrett: "The new stadium affords us opportunities to get more exposure. As people come in, they see two power boards where our messaging will be running for three hours prior to game time. This year, our message will run on tower boards outside the stadium all day long. HUMC will also be on the 2,200 high-definition TVs that are placed throughout the stadium. The enhanced technology in the stadium provides us great exposure."

Hackensack University Medical Center could have gone with a very simple "naming" opportunity in which the name of the organization would be placed on a Giants-related building. However, Garrett was looking for a living, breathing branding initiative that had legs and could create a buzz and excitement, and frankly, give more value for the limited and precious advertising dollars that his system was willing to put up. Says Garrett: "That's where we came up with the Touchdown Fund, which would create a sense of philanthropy in these tough economic times. You have to be careful you are not going back to the same people and companies over and over again, as there is diminishing return at some point. The Touchdown Fund expanded our opportunities for new fundraising with A-list partners, sponsors, and season ticket holders—those are folks that we did not have access to in terms of philanthropy before this partnership. It was attractive to both sides. When you take a $25,000 membership in the Touchdown Fund, that membership gives you VIP privileges at Giants games and all Giants events both on and off the field. You have VIP status to go on the field during pregame practice. You have an opportunity to see the training camp and have first access to a limited number of away games. In addition, the dollars that you give go directly to HUMC Foundation, designated for the children's hospital, the cancer center, or the heart and vascular center. It is truly a win-win."

In addition, according to Anne Marie Campbell, vice president of public relations for HUMC: "What is important about the way the Touchdown Fund was structured is that Bob wanted to be sure that the partnership philosophically met the mission of the hospital—that it wasn't just a partnership with the hospital, but that the moneys came back and provided services to the community and patient care in the areas of kids, cardiac, and cancer; those are our three major service lines here at the hospital."

This philosophical match between these partners avoids the problems facing many other branding campaigns. Too many partnerships are not really well thought out. They are not strategic. They are not tied directly to the organizations' missions and values. Too often, they are desperate attempts to put the name and logo on as many things as possible, hoping and praying that some of it will stick in the minds of the public. Well that just doesn't work. It's sloppy, wasteful, and, in these very difficult economic times, a luxury that few can afford. Further, when the partnership is mismatched, even if people remember your name or what your logo looks like, they can't connect it to anything meaningful or deeper—something that will stick in their minds as well as their hearts. There is no synergy. That's why promoting kids, cardiac, and cancer care is so important to the Touchdown Fund.

It isn't just the creative alliteration of kids, cardiac, and cancer that sticks in the memory when one hears about the Touchdown Fund. It's what those clinical services stand for and who is helped by those dollars raised. According to Garrett: "The feedback has been great. We have about a half a million dollars pledged so far through the Touchdown Foundation. It's off to a very good start, but we've just scratched the surface. The Giants are helping us in terms of calls, promoting, etc. They have four corner sponsors: Verizon, Pepsi, Budweiser, and MetLife. With the help of the Giants, we started talking to the corporate execs at these companies to see if they would be interested in the Touchdown Fund. As a result, Verizon Wireless CEO Lowell McAdam not only agreed to be a Touchdown Fund member, but he agreed to be the honoree at our 2010 gala. A branding partnership is all about opening doors. It is good for the Giants because it lets the community know they are invested in them, and it is good for HUMC because it helps us carry out our mission to offer excellent medical care to our patients."

Partnerships like the one between HUMC and the New York Giants that are well thought out and strategic have the potential to build an organization's brand—not just in terms of recognition with the general public, but also with respect to relationship building with key opinion leaders and influential CEOs of other industries. That is clearly the case with the partnership between HUMC and Verizon Wireless. Who will Mr. McAdam tell about his positive experience with HUMC as the honoree of the hospital's annual gala (which is being held on the field where the Giants play at the new Meadowlands Stadium)? Who will be with him that night? Who will hear about the success of HUMC? Who will then be a potential investor/contributor to the Touchdown Fund? Some people simplistically call this "fundraising," but it's not. This is all part of a comprehensive, multifaceted branding program that, yes, does raise money, but also builds brand equity among people who matter.

Branding Lessons

- Whether your business has two million or two hundred customers, the value of a meaningful logo, strong leadership, and smart and strategic partnering cannot be understated.

- It's not the logo that makes the philosophy of a company; it is the philosophy that makes the logo.

- The strength of a brand depends on all the individuals within an organization. Just like a family, greatness comes from the members within. Employees are the brand messengers or ambassadors who matter most.

- The CEO must be the chief strategist, peer leader, fundraiser, and he or she is the most influential brand champion.

- It is a sign of a healthy brand when those at the top are quick to get involved in every negative incident or problem, analyze it, and take corrective action to keep it from happening again.

- Successful brands are often led by leaders who are obsessed with excellence and who refuse to accept anything less.

- Even when an organization has many divisions / branches / satellites, it is essential to have one unifying brand.

- Your brand is often judged by the company you keep. Look to strategically partner with organizations that share your vision and philosophy.

- Especially in tough economic times, it is wise to create a sense of philanthropy among your employees and customers by partnering with in-need organizations.

- Don't associate your name and logo with just any partner. Partnerships that are intended to build a brand must be well thought out and strategic—not just in terms of recognition with the general public, but also with respect to relationship-building with key opinion leaders and influential CEOs of other industries.

Starbucks

"Your Usual, Steve?"

I'm not exactly sure why I started going to Starbucks to drink my coffee, read my newspaper, and eventually brainstorm and write in the cozy back corner. When I first stepped into the store, I'm sure I had no idea that the place would eventually become my home away from home. I also don't know when I decided that I was willing to pay $4 for a cappuccino, or when exactly I switched to a Venti-one-and-a-half-shots-half-caff-skim-extra-hot cappuccino. But, now I do these things four or five times a week. I especially look forward to Sundays, when I spread out several newspapers at "my" table to do some reading and brainstorming. It has become a ritual. It has become a part of my life. And although I can't say exactly why, I know I would never even think of spending as much time or money at Dunkin' Donuts, or IHOP, or any other "coffee shop."

The Starbucks "experience" for me isn't really about the coffee, and it isn't solely about it being a good place to hang out or about being another place to do work, and it obviously is not like home. But it is a hybrid of all three on some level, and that's the power of the Starbucks brand.

An Accidental Brand

The folks behind Starbucks say they never set out to build a brand. In fact, for years, Starbucks did not engage in big-time advertising campaigns. (That's changed recently.) Its reputation was built on word of mouth and excellent customer service—and the brand naturally followed. That brand is now so powerful that candid photos of celebrities from Barack Obama to George Clooney generally show them walking around with a cup of coffee featuring that unmistakable green, white, and black Starbucks logo. An accident? I don't think so.

100

According to Howard Schultz, the original chairman and CEO of Starbucks, in his book, *Pour Your Heart into It: How Starbucks Built a Company One Cup at a Time*: "Our goal was to build a great company, one that stood for something, one that valued authenticity of its product and passion of its people. . . . Then one day I started getting calls 'Can you tell us how you built a national brand in only five years?' It was unusual, people told me, for a brand to burst into the national consciousness as quickly as Starbucks had."[1]

For sure, Starbucks was doing something right. But then the company began to lose market share (especially in the late 1980s), and it looked like the quick rise in popularity was about to take a speedy fall. Looking back, it's clear that the way the owners handled the problem is one of the biggest reasons Starbucks is as strong as it is today. Starbucks's owners remembered that their original goal was to cater to the passion of the people, and so they began an aggressive campaign to survey their customers, asking for their opinions about why Starbucks was losing customers. Schultz says in his book that, from the customer responses, he concluded that "the key threat to the Starbucks brand was a growing belief amongst customers that the company was becoming corporate, predictable, inaccessible, and irrelevant." According to Schultz, the Starbucks brand was seen by many as a "faceless corporation."

Like most great companies with sustaining brands, Schultz and his colleagues responded aggressively to the negative feedback they received. Changes were made, particularly in an effort to attract twentysomethings, who told Starbucks market researchers that they "want a place that is funky and unique, not necessarily well-lighted and efficient." They found that "what matters to them is a place to hang out at night, not a quick to-go latte on the way to work."

Making a Connection with Customers

Although Starbucks clearly caters to its customers' needs, it did not put the customer first when building its brand. Schultz makes this very clear, saying: "We built the Starbucks brand first with our people, not with consumers . . . because we believed the best way to meet and exceed expectations of customers was to hire and train great people. We invested in employees who were zealous of good coffee." Schultz goes on to talk about the secret of the Starbucks brand being "the personal attachment our partners (employees) feel and the connection they make with their customers."

It may sound unconventional to put the needs of employees first, but the results speak for themselves. Most Starbucks employees I've met over the years seem to be genuinely happy people who like their jobs. And that positive energy makes the customers feel happy. I know it sounds corny, but in my case it is true. I really like the people who sell me my overpriced cappuccino or on occasion my "Awake" tea at Starbucks. One employee in my hometown Starbucks is a perfect example of what I mean. When I walk in, the server, Tara, greets me in a friendly, polite, and always accommodating way—no matter how early or late it is or how many cups of coffee she has already served, she's always wearing that great smile: "Your usual today, Steve?" Nearly every time, she gets it right, and we're not talking about a simple drink. Either she does it herself, or she repeats it to one of the baristas behind the espresso machine. I can count on it being hot and correctly mixed. If it's not right, she'll just do it again—with that smile.

This makes Starbucks stand out. In too many other coffee shops and retail establishments, I feel like a number. The employees don't know me—they don't want to know me. I might as well be at an impersonal ATM machine at the bank handing over my PIN number. I don't care how good the coffee is, and I don't even care if it's cheaper than Starbucks coffee, I just don't feel like sitting down and spending some leisure time at those places. Why? What's the big deal about an employee knowing my name and my favorite drink?

I think the reason Starbucks draws people in is something like what happened on the *Cheers* TV series set in Boston in the 1980s. Why did people go to this local bar? As the theme song says: "Because everyone knows your name." A favorite character, Norm, would walk into the bar and everyone would turn and yell "Norm!" He'd sit at the bar, they'd bring him his favorite beer, and in that moment Norm felt he was "at home."

I know it sounds crazy, but there is actually a "Starbucks community" that makes people feel at home. Most of the people don't know each others' names, but we all know we are paying too much for a cup of coffee, and we like the feeling of being around other people who have made the same (often irrational) decision. I feel oddly connected to the people in this particular coffee shop. Starbucks has captured this feeling and turned it into a brand.

Building on "Comfortable" and "Familiar"

Another aspect of Starbucks that promotes the "community" brand is the aesthetics of the place itself. In most Starbucks across the country, you'll find a few upholstered chairs and some comfortable high-back chairs grouped around coffee tables strewn with the day's newspapers. There will be scattered tables and high-top counters where customers can rest their coffee cups and open up their laptops.

Although each store has a unique setup, none is sterile, corporate, or uncomfortable. Whether I'm in my local Starbucks or in one in New York, or LA, or Chicago, I get the same at-home feeling. And I have to say that once I sit down in any Starbucks in any city and I hear Etta James singing "At Last" or Frank Sinatra crooning "Night and Day" in the background, it feels like home. That's what Starbucks is selling.

Branding Lessons

The bottom line is that the Starbucks brand may not be for everyone, but for people like me who have bought into it, there is a tremendous sense of loyalty and comfort associated with it—that's because the Starbucks brand is built on a "feeling" rather than the product itself. That feeling has been carefully created with attention to certain aspects of the business that you too can work into your branding campaign if you have a product or service to sell:

- Know what your customers want: ask them and respond. If you're not filling their needs, they won't come back. If you listen and actually make suggested changes, you'll have those customers for life.

- Make your employees happy. Treat them like partners. Watch their respect for your company or product transform itself into respect and kindness toward your customers.

- No point throwing money at an advertising campaign that will bring in customers if those customers don't feel special and valued when they arrive. Even before quality and pricing, customer service is tops.

- Atmosphere matters. The best product or service can fall short of its potential if the customer doesn't feel comfortable in your space.

- Make your customers enjoy the experience of giving you their money. Make them "feel" good.

Blackwater

Changing Your Name
Doesn't Fix Your Reputation

Sometimes, a brand has to rebuild itself. Sometimes a new name is necessary. Sometimes it's worthwhile to start all over again. Sometimes, however, this approach to improving the company brand is a bad idea—a very bad idea if the company has been involved in an egregious or embarrassing incident and then tries to rebrand simply by coming up with a new name. Take Blackwater Worldwide, for example.

This private security company was founded in North Carolina in 1997 by its chief executive Erik Prince, along with a group of fellow Navy Seals. Blackwater (whose name came from the murky water that runs through the swamp land of North Carolina) built its brand as an organization that could achieve things on the battlefield that no one else could. The company got government contracts that no one else could get to do work that few others wanted to do.

While few understood how Blackwater was able to achieve things that the U.S. military couldn't, not many questions were asked about its methods or practices. But all that changed in 2004 when four of its contractors were killed when insurgents in Iraq ambushed them in Fallujah. The bodies of the Blackwater contractors were burned, mutilated, and hung from a bridge for all to see in worldwide media coverage.

Those visuals outraged Americans, who began asking questions. What was Blackwater? What did it do that the military couldn't or wouldn't? How could its contractors be put in such a vulnerable position to be made into pawns by Iraqi insurgents?

With these questions still not answered to everyone's satisfaction, in September 2007, there was a shooting in Baghdad that tarnished Blackwater's brand even further. Simply put, the folks at

Blackwater engaged in a firefight that resulted in the deaths of at least a dozen Iraqi civilians. This kind of unintentional tragedy in war is often called "collateral damage," and although understood to be an unavoidable evil of war, in the case of Blackwater, the brand damage was significant. The news of this event was confounding to the American public because, again, no one questioned what private contractors, retained by the U.S. military, were doing in the middle of a war in Iraq in which they had no official part.

The 2004 incident involving the killing, mutilating, and burning of four Blackwater contractors in Fallujah was bad, but combined with the 2007 killing of Iraqi civilians, the company hit its tipping point. Congressional hearings ensued and members of Congress questioned Blackwater's training methods and investigated how exactly the company worked officially and/or unofficially with the U.S. government and military. Many in Washington called for Blackwater to be banned from any military operations in Iraq, and the State Department refused to renew Blackwater's contract to "protect diplomats" in the Middle East. Blackwater was out. The company was blacklisted. The brand was tarnished so severely that the thought of a comeback was inconceivable.

What's Xe?

So what did the company execs do when the brand hit rock bottom? They acted as if the incidents never happened. They decided simply to change the company name and start over. They called themselves Xe. That's right. Blackwater became a new company overnight with the indecipherable name that is pronounced like the letter "z."

Further, what was known as the Blackwater Lodge and Training Center was renamed U.S. Training Center, Inc. (the use of "U.S." implying, or making it seem, that the U.S. government was involved). This branding switcheroo fooled no one. According to Katy Helvenston, who sued Blackwater after her son was killed in the Fallujah incident, "They have established themselves as the bad guys. . . . They've established such a horrible reputation. Why else would they change their name?"[1]

However, according to then-Blackwater president Gary Jackson, the new names reflected the change in the company's focus: away from the business of providing private security. Said Jackson in 2007: "The volume of changes over the past half-year have taken the company to an exciting place, and we are now ready for two of the final, and most obvious changes."[2]

In a memo to employees, Jackson went on to say that the company was "not interested in actively pursuing private security contracts" and would be focusing on "training and providing logistics." Added Jackson, "This company will continue to provide personnel protective services for high-threat environments when needed by the U.S. government, but its primary mission will be operating our training facilities around the world, including the flagship campus in North Carolina."[3]

According to Backwater spokesperson Anne Tyrrell, the name change from Blackwater to Xe/U.S. Training Center, Inc. had nothing to do with the embarrassing incidents in Iraq in which Blackwater performed so poorly. "It's not a direct result of a loss of contract, but certainly that is an aspect of our work and we feel we were defined by it." The company also replaced its bear paw logo with a "sleeker black and white graphic based on letters that make up the company's new name."[4]

But here's the deal. Changing your name alone rarely improves your brand. I don't care how ingenious, imaginative, or catchy the new name is or how professionally designed an accompanying logo may be, Blackwater is Blackwater. Its history is its history. Those horrific incidents from 2004 and 2007 are burned into the psyche of key stakeholders and decision makers related to the military defense and security arenas. Those who are in a position in the U.S. government to hire the newly named Xe or U.S. Training Center, Inc. have a sense of history. They know that the same people, who are running this newly named company, are the ones whose actions virtually destroyed its brand in the past.

It was naïve and simplistic for those who ran Blackwater to think that changing the name to Xe would make it all better. It didn't. Xe has not been particularly successful in getting government contracts. If Blackwater was blacklisted and cut out by the government, why would that change because the company changed its name? The folks at Blackwater in many ways expressed a cynical and disingenuous attitude by thinking that we would somehow forget those four Blackwater contractors burned, mutilated, and hanging in the Fallujah square or the innocent Iraqi citizens killed for no apparent reason. Changing your name is not the easy way out.

Branding Lessons

Blackwater had an opportunity to regain its reputation and protect its brand, but that opportunity was quickly lost. From this mess, we all can gain a valuable list of do's and don'ts to follow if something bad happens to our brand:

- Don't fool yourself into believing that you can maintain a positive brand reputation simply by changing the name of the company.

- When things go wrong, don't try to pretend they didn't happen.

- When faced with a problem, don't insist that you're moving in a new, exciting direction and therefore need to update your name and logo.

- Don't insult the intelligence of your customers.

Do:

- Keep the company name but try to understand what went wrong.

- Make sure the company leaders acknowledge their mistakes and then take full responsibility.

- Improve practices and procedures.

- Publicly state how those changes will put the company in a better position to provide customers with a valuable service.

- Take a longer term view of rebuilding your reputation, image, and brand.

Campbell Soup

Engage Your Employees . . . Awaken Your Brand

In the early 2000s, Campbell Soup Company was called a "beleaguered old brand."[1] Its sales were down, employees were not engaged, and the company was losing some of its most talented performers. There were constant rumors that Campbell was for sale.

But then, according to a 2009 *Forbes* profile, Campbell's brand turned around dramatically. A new group of leaders and managers was brought in—some promoted from within, others recruited from outside the company—to set the tone and follow through on performance; soon, employees were more engaged and involved, and sales rose dramatically.[2] The biggest reason for this impressive brand turnaround is the fact that Campbell got a new president and CEO in 2001. Doug Conant became the eleventh leader in Campbell's 140-year history. As with many organizations, it is leadership from the top that sets the tone for how a company will communicate and engage its employees and ultimately lead what is commonly referred to as a "turnaround."

To start the turnaround, CEO Conant actively promoted employee engagement, which, in turn, had a direct impact on building and bolstering Campbell's brand both internally and externally and on improving Campbell's performance in the marketplace. Here's how it happened.

What Does Your Workplace Look Like?

Physical surroundings communicate a lot about how an organization sees its brand and itself. When Conant first arrived at Campbell's world headquarters in Camden, New Jersey, he was struck by the fact that some parking lots were surrounded by barbed wire. To many, it resembled a prison. Immediately, the new president and CEO replaced the fences, the first step on a journey to improve Campbell's Camden campus, which culminated in 2010 with the completion of the Campbell Employee Center, an 80,000-square-foot building with state-of-the-art café, fitness center, company store, training and development center, and other amenities for Campbell's employees.

What Conant realized was that the physical surroundings in which people work can send a powerful message regarding how leaders view the organization as well as how they communicate internally and externally. To engage employees, barriers must be broken down, be they barbed wires or departmental silos.

So How Are We Doing?

Conant also believed that it was important to get a baseline of employee engagement, no matter how ugly the results may be. Conant is fond of saying, "You must confront the brutal facts." Campbell and Conant engaged the Gallup Organization in 2002 and found that 62 percent of Campbell's employees said they were not actively engaged in their jobs, and 12 percent said they were "actively disengaged." Of course, no one wants to see those results. However, you can't know where you're going unless you have a sense of where you came from.

According to a *Gallup Management Journal* article, Conant argues, "I strongly believe that you can't win in the marketplace unless you win first in the workplace. If you don't have a winning culture inside, it's hard to compete in the very tough world outside. Our mission is to build the world's most extraordinary food company by nourishing people's lives everywhere, every day. You can't ask employees to achieve extraordinary results if they're not fully engaged. That's why we focus a great deal on getting the workplace right so that people are engaged and proactive—so that people are moving forward arm in arm and competing with a spring in their step. As they become more engaged, they find ways to win in the marketplace that are sustainable. You do have to shift your tactics every once in a while. You always have to bring something new to

the engagement mix to bring it to life again. It can be a big thing
or a little thing."[3]

Honesty Is Still the Best Policy

Campbell's turnaround was also boosted by Conant's efforts to promote honest, open forums, along with confidential communication vehicles, for employees to express their concerns as well as
recommendations for improving things. One of the biggest mistakes leaders make is to avoid holding such forums for fear of negative things that might be said publicly. But the fact is that people
are saying these things anyway. Why not get them out in the open
so you can do something about it? Organizations that stonewall or
try to ignore that employees are disengaged pay a heavy price.

I recently had the opportunity to speak with Doug Conant
about the value of open, honest communication. This is what he
had to say on that topic: "It goes back to the employee engagement
notion. We have something called the Campbell's Promise here. It is
a simple yet powerful concept: Campbell valuing people. And, in
turn, people valuing Campbell."

Conant established this promise on his first day as CEO in January 2001 at a company-wide meeting with employees. "Back in
2001 we needed to demonstrate to each individual employee that
we valued their agenda. Once we demonstrated that we valued
them, they in turn would value the company's agenda. Today we
still need to value every employee every step of the way. The way
you get employees to achieve extraordinary results is to lean in and
be helpful to them in unique and tangible ways, and create opportunities for them to feel valued every day. The more time we spend
taking care of our employees, the more they take care of our agenda
and what we are trying to achieve. It is incredibly powerful. Most
companies have this episodic focus on some form of employee
engagement, but for us, it's been a ten-year drum beat. It is not a
survey once every three years. We have been doing it for ten years
and people know we mean it. We have an enormous array of programs to meet people's needs whether it is recognition programs,
workplace flexibility, affinity groups, training and development,

and others. We lean into these programs in a way that people see and feel."

Each year, Campbell collects employee feedback and measures engagement using the Gallup Q12 Survey. Once this valuable employee feedback is received, the leaders in an organization have to create action plans in concert with the members of every work group to make sure the issues of the day are addressed. They have to focus on action because all the talk in the world about engaging employees won't matter if the reality doesn't match the rhetoric. In fact, if you don't respond to employee feedback, it is clearly recognized, and negative consequences, including loss of trust and encroaching cynicism, are likely to occur.

According to Conant: "Each year we do the survey and employees are essentially able to vote on how we are doing—and, importantly, how their direct manager is doing. Once we have this data, managers can sit down with their teams to see what we can be doing better and develop action plans. Having an action plan to address the feedback is critical. Then, the next year, we come back and ask whether we achieved what we said what we would." That's putting action behind your words.

Being "Obsessed"

Conant is determined to stay in touch with his workforce—he sends approximately twenty handwritten notes to employees every day on topics ranging from thank you's to words of encouragement. These notes are sent to people at every level of the organization. In fact, you can see many of them displayed at employees desks. When Conant began this ritual, word got out that the CEO himself was engaged, which, in turn, raised expectations for employees. Remember, employees don't care what you have to say until they know how much you actually care.

That message doesn't come through just in note-writing, however. It's broadcast in other ways. For instance, Conant holds lunches with a dozen or so employees from all parts of the organization every six weeks as another way to stay in touch. Lately, he's taken to walking the halls as a way to get some exercise while also talking and listening to employees. Says Conant, "I have a pair of sneakers, and whenever I have a half hour free, I put on my sneakers, and I start walking the halls. I stop and talk to people. And it gives me a sense of the pulse of the company. But the main reason I do it is because when the world's feeling a little shaky, it's important for the leader to be more physically present."[4]

Conant sees his note-writing and hall-walking as part of a larger "obsessive" commitment to his direct and active involvement in promoting Campbell's brand. Says Conant when I spoke to him: "As a leader, you have to walk the walk and be the change you wish to see in your company. I am incredibly involved in employee engagement. I do it in a personal way. I walk the building every day. I celebrate the successes. I know who every manager is out of our 525 managers; I know which managers are in the top 10 percent of employee engagement and which are in the bottom 20 percent. We celebrate the top 10 percent and work on improving the bottom 20 percent. And I know virtually every one of these managers by name."

"Further," says Conant, "you have to pick your focus areas. We focus on three things: 1) Winning in the workplace, as measured by employee engagement. Over the past five years, we have continued to increase employee engagement to world-class levels. In 2010, our engagement ratio was 17 to 1. Gallup defines 'world class' as 12 to 1. You can't manage it if you can't measure it. 2) Winning in the marketplace, as measured by total shareowner return. During the past five years, we have delivered cumulative total shareowner returns above the S&P Packaged Food Index, an index of our peer companies. And 3) winning in the community, as measured by the Boston College Center for Corporate Citizenship. This gives us a look at how we are building a better world and how the world views us. On this front, in 2010 we were recognized for the third year in a row as one of the ten most socially responsible U.S. companies. We report on all three of these measures each year in our annual report."

Imagine the impact that highly engaged and committed employees have on promoting the Campbell brand by word of mouth. These kinds of employees become ambassadors and cheerleaders for the company. In the same way a disgruntled, unhappy, and disengaged employee trashes his organization's brand, most of the folks at Campbell are singing its praises.

How Relevant Are We?

Conant and his team have managed to spark employee engagement and boost performance at Campbell. But the work is never done. You never really "get there" when it comes to branding. As Conant likes to say, "We can do better." To sustain Campbell's success, Conant knows he will have to go beyond employee engagement. Conant has to find a way to keep this established, 140-year-old brand new and exciting.

According to Conant, it's all about staying relevant. "You have to continuously celebrate what's special about your brand," he says, "but constantly reinvent it as well. The language we use in our mission statement and our advertising conveys the message that we will not rest on our laurels. We are obsessed about meeting the needs of consumers faster, better, more completely and more uniquely than anyone on the planet as it relates to our categories. Andy Grove from Intel said, 'Only the paranoid survive.' That's very true—so I will not be the leader that lets Campbell slip."

Conant respects Campbell's history and tradition but plans to keep Campbell out front with the high-tech consumer base of today. "We have a special relationship with consumers," Conant acknowledges. "Soup is viewed as a nourishing food, good for the heart and soul, and good for the family. Other food companies may have similar missions and visions, but everyone I come in contact with has a story about being nourished by Campbell's soup. So people want to like the brand; as long as we keep it contemporary and fresh, they are rooting for us. Not many brands have the type of emotional connection with consumers that we do. But we need to keep that relationship alive and relevant for every generation. In today's market, that means finding new ways to communicate through things like Facebook and Twitter and staying relevant. The consumer packaged goods industry is very Darwinian: You either grow or die in this business. It is a mindset that you must live every day. We choose growth."

Branding Lessons

If you are in a position to lead employees to obtain "M'm M'm Good" results, these lessons from Campbell Soup Company can help you lead the way:

- Highly engaged and enthusiastic employees are the best ambassadors and cheerleaders to promote your brand by word of mouth.

- Even the most established and successful brand can never rest on its laurels. It has to constantly be "obsessed" with being relevant and responding to feedback both from employees and customers as to what will improve the product/service in the marketplace.

- As this book has shown, time and time again, organizations, no matter how good they are, don't run themselves. You can't go on autopilot. That's why enthusiastic and committed CEOs are as much of the brand of their companies as anyone or anything else.

- Don't be afraid to hear negative or critical news or information about how your brand is doing. Rather, confront the facts, embrace that feedback, and use it to make constant improvements and remain relevant.

Nick Matarazzo

Staying in the Game

Nick Matarazzo spent twenty-seven years as a top sales and marketing executive at Hachette Filipacchi Media (the publisher of such popular magazines as ELLE, *Woman's Day, Car and Driver,* and *Road & Track*). His views on personal branding were solidified the day in mid-2009 when he became the victim of downsizing. Matarazzo was let go because his salary was too high and costs needed to be cut. This situation was an all-too-common occurrence for millions of mid- to upper-level executives and managers in corporate America at that time. What happens next to these loyal but "expendable" employees often depends on how they have built their brand as a member of that company.

Branding Yourself before the Ax Falls

Nick and I met back in college when he was a star basketball player and a leader both on and off the court. When he was later inducted into the Montclair State University Hall of Fame, no one was surprised. As far back as I can remember, "Nicky Mats," as he is affectionately known, has always been a winner.

That's the terribly frustrating part about downsizing. Being let go wasn't about Matarazzo's performance or his sales numbers and definitely not about his work ethic or attitude. This was a guy who passionately loved his job and gave it his all. In my capacity as a communication consultant, I coached him and many of his colleagues as they struggled with shrinking ad revenues due to strategy shifts in ad spending from traditional to nontraditional content media platforms in the increasingly digital publishing world. I came to better know and understand Nick Matarazzo the businessman. And I had further opportunities to see Matarazzo in action when he brought me in to Hachette to provide a series of leader-

116

ship and communication seminars as well as executive coaching for the publishers, editors, and managers at a variety of their magazine brands.

That's why, despite all the challenges in the publishing industry, I was floored when Matarazzo told me he was being let go by Hachette. The news didn't make sense to me. Not Nicky Mats. Not when he was at the top of his game. Not after twenty-seven years of being one of the best salesmen and team leaders around. Matarazzo was a legend in the publishing industry who had been written up in trade publications and talked about not just for his performance but for his bigger-than-life personality.

Fortunately, a layoff doesn't take away a person's brand, because the company can't hold on to the employee's reputation and work ethic. Your brand is probably the most important thing you can take with you when you walk out the door. And that fact kept Matarazzo alive and hopeful.

It's Not Easy to Stay in the Game

Even though he tried not to show it, Matarazzo was seriously hurt when he was shown the door by the company that he started working for soon after we graduated college together. He told me: "When adversity hits on the job—a new boss comes in and wants his own team, or assets are sold and a company downsizes and you lose your job despite the value you provided for years and the monetary value you created for the company, you can expect to go through the typical five stages identified by Dr. Elisabeth Kubler-Ross that people often go through following a serious loss, which are denial, anger, bargaining, depression, and acceptance." Nick explains how he dealt with each of these stages:

1. Denial: This was my first reaction and the same reaction of 99 percent of the rest of the company as well as of the clients we serviced. This can't be happening.

2. Anger: Why my career? Why me? How dare they treat me like this! For me, this stage lasted for about twenty-four hours before I could realize it wasn't about me; it was just business.

3. *Bargaining*: I was thinking that because the layoff was the result of an economic decision perhaps I should offer to take a major pay cut. Should I try to make a deal to gain back what I lost? This stage also lasted about twenty-four hours. It took me that long to remember my value.

4. *Depression*: This is the most dangerous stage of grief that can last a long time if nothing new takes the place of the old. I was fortunate to skip right past it. Within forty-eight hours of my layoff, I was getting calls from clients and competitors asking for my consulting services.

5. *Acceptance*: This isn't about bells and fireworks. It's a decision to be at peace with the way things are. To know that no amount of denial, bargaining, anger, or depression is going to change anything. It's not good or bad . . . just how it is.

Moving Forward with Your Brand Intact

Sure, Matarazzo was down, but not out. Once he was let go, Matarazzo quickly formed his own consulting company called Rainmaker Media Solutions and was later hired as a consultant by *TVGuide* magazine by the former CEO of Hachette with whom he had worked for years.

During those nine months, Matarazzo had the time to think about his professional experience, the meaning of personal branding in the marketplace, and what he wanted to do for the rest of his professional life. While he was putting all the pieces together, in the spring of 2010, Matarazzo got a call from the same CEO at Hachette who had let him go. Hachette wanted him back to run a division of Hachette Filipacchi Media called Jumpstart Automotive Group in San Francisco. Sure, it had to feel good to know that his former employer realized his true value. Still, Matarazzo didn't gloat. "I was humbled that I got a call and was told that they made a mistake and they wanted me back," he says. "It takes a special type of person to make that call. It takes a special type of company to allow that to happen. I don't think this happens at a lot of major companies because there are too many egos at the top—which is why I was honored when I got the call to be back at the helm managing and leading several brands that I had built with some very talented people."

Ultimately, Nick Matarazzo did take the job in San Francisco as CEO of Jumpstart Automotive Group.

Branding Lessons

Because Nick Matarazzo is such a close friend, not to mention a great guy, I was thrilled that he was given the opportunity at Hachette to show once again how valuable he really is by taking over a team and an operation that wasn't meeting the company's expectations. But the question for others who may not be so lucky to have their former employers ask them to come back to work is: "What are some of the key lessons that can be learned from this round of layoffs that disposed of very talented and valuable people?" Matarazzo's answer to this question focuses—not surprisingly—on branding. "You can work for a great company and have great products, but if you are mediocre, you will not achieve maximum results. However, you can be the best there is and have mediocre product and still outsell your competitors because people want to do business with you. Despite the hard economic times," he says, "there are a few things that ring true if you want to brand yourself, and that I believe have served me well throughout my career:

- *Work ethic*: I have always worked harder and smarter than most people around me. But that doesn't mean I can or should do it all myself. I learned over the years that it's important to assess the strengths and weaknesses in each employee and then assemble a team that brings out the strengths so that we all can get the most work done.

- *Superior attitude*: A can-do attitude is a must. I never wait until tomorrow to finish something I can do today. And I always research and prepare diligently before meeting with clients or superiors (in fact, I treat my superiors like clients).

- *Humility*: When I got to the top of the organization I never asked a subordinate to do anything that I would not do myself. I have led by example and tried my hardest to inspire the people around me. And I always try to keep a sense of humor.

- Confidence: If you are not confident about what you do, it comes through to your client or your boss. You must genuinely believe in your people and your job, the product or service you are selling and approach it with unwavering conviction. When you do that, your staff, your clients, your boss are then confident in you.

All of these things create you—*you are the brand.*"

Martha Stewart

Boy, . . . Was I Wrong

I was convinced that going to jail and doing real time would destroy the Martha Stewart brand. There was no way that this woman, whose brand was predicated on seeking perfection in everything—from the way to bake a cake to what to wear and how to speak—could survive a jail sentence and keep her reputation intact. Boy, was I wrong.

At first I had good reason to doubt the strength of the brand. The way Stewart had handled the fallout of the much-publicized insider trade scandal was a classic case study in how not to communicate under pressure. When the whole IMCLONE stock debacle exploded in 2002, she chose to be silent and act like it didn't happen. I still have to shake my head when I think about her disastrous appearance on CBS's *Early Show*, where she did a weekly cooking segment. She was asked about the controversy but insisted that it wasn't something she wanted to talk about and that she had to "keep chopping the salad." Her response was embarrassing and awkward—far from perfect. How could someone who had spent two decades in the public eye not understand that she needed to face this scandal head-on?

In the short term Martha Stewart's brand took a huge hit. Her company stock dropped, and many people stopped buying her products. She was approaching her mid to late sixties, and there were younger, more energetic daytime domestic divas, such as Rachel Ray, who were clearly invading Stewart's turf and brand. But go figure, by mid-2005, Martha Stewart was back! She was back every day on television, she was back selling her stuff, and she was back with a loyal audience that forgave her for all wrongdoing.

How did she manage to do that? A look at the Stewart brand offers an interesting lesson in the value of successful branding.

The Power of a Good Product

I asked my wife if she had any idea why Martha Stewart's reputation and brand had not been damaged by Stewart's run-in with the law. While no big fan of Martha Stewart, her response was clear, "Her stuff is pretty good." That's not the whole story, but it's a big part of it. Apparently there are a lot of people out there who like to build a home and entertain friends in ways that leave a lasting impression. And Martha Stewart—the guru of homemaking with homemade style—helps them do just that.

There's no doubt about it. Stewart products have a quality reputation, and so the Stewart name sells across the economic spectrum. She has successfully lent her name to an impressive collection of brands, individualized for a wide array of products such as: the Martha Stewart Collection of bedding, bath, cookware, and dinnerware at Macy's; Martha Stewart Crafts; Martha Stewart's 1–800-Flowers.com; Martha Stewart Living at The Home Depot; Martha Stewart for Grandin Road for indoor and outdoor decorations, costumes, and entertainment supplies for holidays; Martha Stewart Clean for nontoxic, fragrance-free home cleaning products; Martha Stewart Floor Designs for eco-friendly carpet tiles; Martha Stewart Stationery with Crane & Co. for customized wedding programs, place cards, menu cards, thank you cards, and table accessories; Martha Stewart Kodak Gallery for personal keepsakes with customized photo books, cards, and stickers; as well as, my personal favorite: Martha Stewart KB Home for new residential communities inspired by Martha's homes in New York, Connecticut, and Maine.

Love her or loathe her, the Martha Stewart brand is one worth studying. I guess it's true that what doesn't kill you can, in fact, make you stronger.

She Is the Brand

Even though she presents herself in what I see as a stuck-up and inaccessible fashion, Martha Stewart has very loyal fans. And her brand has always been predicated on staying visible in the media on many platforms to reach those fans. This is a woman who knows that truly successful brand identity depends on market penetration, on being "out there." (This is a major reason I do so much television work on multiple networks. It keeps me on the radar of current clients, sponsors, and prospects. Plus it promotes my books, Web site, and my overall brand.)

As founder of Martha Stewart Living Omnimedia, she has used publishing, broadcasting, and merchandizing outlets to make sure that you and I know her name and her products. She secured her own syndicated talk show, *Martha*, continues to write bestselling books, and publishes *Martha Stewart Living* magazine. In case you haven't gone looking for her in these outlets, you'll also find her as a frequent contributor to CBS's *Early Show*. Oh, and then there was her adapted version of the TV show *The Apprentice*, called *The Apprentice: Martha Stewart*, and her special appearance on the comedy-drama series *Ugly Betty*. And not to slight the Internet, you can be sure that Martha Stewart has a Web site and online catalog business that sings and dances.

So, I ask you: Now that we've all seen this woman all over the place (whether we want to or not), what's the difference between Martha Stewart the woman and Martha Stewart the brand? The answer: nothing. Martha is the brand and the brand is Martha. You can't separate them. I'm convinced that even if Martha Stewart's products were solidly practical and useful, they would not move off the shelves if Martha wasn't selling them.

Ya Gotta Believe

If the product alone really is that good, you might wonder, why would consumers confuse the product for the person? Why does the reputation of the spokesperson speak as loudly to you and me as the quality of the items we buy? Good questions, with a simple answer: The ever-present connection of a person to a brand tells us that the person believes in that brand in a big way. Even though she's approaching age seventy, Martha Stewart's energy and intensity tells us that she deeply believes in herself and the philosophy that she is selling. That's why her name is all over everything. In the beginning of her empire, I have no doubt that marketing experts spent countless hours and a lot of money coming to the decision that Stewart's logo would have her name all over it. The decision has paid off mightily.

Some might say that for someone in her late sixties Martha would be better off having someone else be the company spokesperson, who could appeal to a younger demographic. In this case such a branding strategy wouldn't work. No one could sell Martha Stewart better than Martha Stewart in spite of a stint in jail. She's not ashamed, she's not embarrassed, she hasn't slowed down, and I have to say that I was wrong about Martha Stewart. I thought she was dead in the water a few years ago.

However, her success proves that building and sustaining a brand is far from an exact science. Rather it is a combination of many factors including those that are subjective and emotionally visceral and, in Martha Stewart's case, very personal. The people who love her absolutely love her, and the people who are turned off by her are turned off in a big way. But like I said, to succeed with your brand, not everyone has to like you.

Branding Lessons

Martha Stewart couldn't care less if I don't find her appealing—the last time I checked, she was laughing all the way to the bank as I was learning these valuable lessons from her continued success:

- Know your audience. Martha Stewart knows her audience very well. She also knows what they want from her. This has caused her to be laserlike in the content she produces on air and in other media venues.

- You need chutzpah when it comes to branding. Many, including myself, would resist putting themselves out there in public so quickly upon getting out of jail. But apparently Martha Stewart and her team were planning for her public return to the marketplace even while she was incarcerated. They acted as if the "jail thing" never happened.

- Believe in yourself. The success of the Martha Stewart brand clearly shows that believing in yourself and your abilities is crucial to successful branding. Without it, you won't survive the slings and arrows (much less the rejections) of a sometimes vicious marketplace.

Bobbi Brown

Keeping It Real

Bobbi Brown is a makeup maven—Bobbie Brown Essentials is one of the most successful brands in the cosmetic industry. When asked how she did it, Brown's answer is a bit surprising. She says she didn't do it with a lot of market research or a big-time advertising budget. In fact, in his book *The Authentic Brand*, Christopher Rosica quotes Brown as saying, "I didn't know what marketing was. I had never really heard the word. . . . I did not have a marketing person for the first ten years in my business." Even after achieving success, Brown wasn't so sure she believed in intentional branding, saying, "How do you brand something? It has to be organic. I don't understand people who think you can take something and brand it into something. It's got to be just organic. It's got to happen."[1]

Bobbi Brown's "just happened" description of how she branded her cosmetic company into a multimillion-dollar empire, which was ultimately bought by Estée Lauder, is an honest one. However, the fact is that, whether intentionally or unintentionally, she has worked hard to build an incredibly successful brand that is the product of very specific and crafted factors. Any person, company, or product can learn a lot from this woman who had a dream, started from scratch, and believed in herself and her product.

Being Authentic

I've known Bobbi Brown for over a decade. I remember that one of the first things I noticed about her was her passion. To this day, she believes deeply not just in her makeup products but in a philosophy about women that is deeply embedded into everything she does. Se has told me in several PBS interviews that, although cosmetics can highlight a woman's beauty, real beauty comes from within. Brown is convinced that unless a woman feels good about

125

herself on a personal level, there is no cosmetic product that can really show her true beauty. This philosophy makes Brown's approach to the business of "beauty" quite unique in an industry where the "plain" woman is not considered beautiful until she is covered with makeup.

It is an interesting lesson in branding that Brown's success stands firm on her countercultural beliefs about women and beauty. Standing barely over five feet tall, Brown talks candidly about the sense of insecurity she has felt when standing alongside six-foot-tall fashion models. She knows that sense of vulnerability in women who are not externally gifted. She took that experience and those feelings and poured them into her work. She created makeup—first lipstick and then other products—that were simple and basic, that would not cover up but rather enhance innate beauty.

More than the products themselves, Brown's authentic philosophy became her brand. She stood up for the average woman who needed to feel better about herself and her appearance but was being shamed by the cosmetic industry into hiding behind "coverup." This unique turn away from an established norm did far more for the Bobbi Brown brand than any big advertising budget could have done.

Brown also believed that using her own name, "Bobbi Brown," was critical to her success. Let's face it. "Bobbi Brown Essentials" is a great name. In order to be a great brand it helps to have a pretty cool name.

Promotion Is Not Only about Ad Dollars

Brown believes that in order to build her reputation (we'll call it her brand), she had to be the face and the image of the company. That's why so much of her success is a product of public appearances. Says Bobbi, "I still do in-store appearances around the country about twenty times a year. . . . Women are still coming up to me and saying, 'Oh, I brought all the girls in my office in to see you,' or, 'My sister brought me in,' or 'Here's my Girl Scout troop to see you.' I know how much my business relies on word of mouth."

Brown still does not focus as much on her advertising budget as on the value of public relations. She believes that if people read or hear something about you that you're not paying for, they're much more likely to believe it. As she told Rosica, "We are a huge PR business. People will much more believe what they read in a magazine article or a quote than they will in an ad anyway. I'm lucky that I have relationships with all the editors at the magazines and they are really supportive of things and actually excited, so we get pretty good coverage and I feel really fortunate."

Bobbi's being modest when she says she's lucky to have these PR opportunities. Those relationships don't come easy. Building a successful brand has a lot to do with building strong and enduring relationships with people connected to your industry. Those relationships are the result of being true to your word, having integrity, following up and following through, and being responsive. You could have all the money in the world to put into advertising, but if you have poor relationships with key stakeholders, none of it matters.

Bobbi Brown gets that. She knows that successfully building a brand is a marathon and not a sprint. People who look for the quick buck miss the opportunity to build good will and foster relationships that have people talking about them and their brand in a positive and constructive way.

Give It Away

Brown's naturally generous spirit has helped her build those key relationships. She believes deeply in giving of herself, her money, and her time—not to mention her products. It's not only generous but it's also smart business and smart branding. Says Brown, "I've always believed in giving a lot away . . . right from the beginning, I gave because it's what I believe in."[2]

Brown's charity work is notable and, whether intentional or not, it has helped her create the positive image associated with her product. Highlights of her charitable work include her involvement with Dress for Success, in which she gives underprivileged women professional attire to wear to job interviews, Bobbi Brown makeup, and the opportunity to have their makeup done by her makeup artists for free. Brown also supports the Jane Addams High School for Academic Careers, and has participated in its PENCIL partnership program. And in her hometown of Montclair, New Jersey, Brown offers her celebrity connections and her home to host the "Stars Come Out for Kids" event that raises money for the town's Community Pre-K program. Through these programs, Brown is giving away her time and gaining key relationships.

There are also opportunities to "give it away" and build a brand outside of charitable causes. "You cannot imagine," Bobbi told me, "how many new customers we've gotten because we always give away good stuff." Bobbi's right, you have to give things away. Certainly, she doesn't make big money as the exclusive beauty editor on the TODAY show (I gladly do the show for free), but how do you calculate the positive public relations you get out of appearing on a regular basis on the country's most popular network morning program? Branding is built on buzz. Being on TV or hosting a charity event often creates buzz. It has people wanting to know more about you and, dare I say, what you're selling. I'm a big believer that those who look to make a difference and help others achieve their dreams wind up having a much better shot at achieving their own, which in turn means enhancing your brand.

Whether it's distributing free cosmetics, or in my case conducting free seminars on public speaking, hosting a charity event, or writing an article in a magazine or journal that you don't get paid for, it's all a part of building your brand and reputation. People who want to be paid for everything they do don't understand the bigger picture.

Bobbi Brown never had to depend on a lot of market research or a big-time advertising budget to build her business, because she herself became the brand, and she is one heck of a lady who knows the value of personal passion, pride, and human connection.

Branding Lessons

The branding lessons from Bobbi Brown are as simple and basic as the woman herself:

- It's a brand whether you know it or not. Any successful person who says, "I never thought about building a brand," has done all the right things through an innate understanding of the value of reputation. We're all always building our brand.

- Be genuine. You don't have to change your beliefs to sell yourself or your service or your product. The passion you truly feel for something is your best sales tool.

- Public relations is not the same thing as advertising. The more you can ingratiate yourself through personal appearances into the community where you sell your service/product, the less advertising money you have to spend to tell everyone how great you are. Word of mouth will do that for you and it's free.

- Give it away and reap the returns. Giving away your time and product is a proven way to get new customers and make key relationships. There is an upfront cost to this strategy, but the growth in sales afterward will more than balance the expense.

Oprah

The "Babe Ruth" of Modern-Day Branding

Oprah. Like Madonna, Sting, Bruce, and Sinatra, Oprah Winfrey doesn't really need more than her first name to conjure up a brand, an image, or, in her case, a powerful media force of nature that has changed the landscape of American pop culture forever.

I'm not one of Oprah's biggest fans, but I am also not a detractor. I like some things she does, but other things seem way over the top. I don't even think she is the greatest interviewer around: she often doesn't follow up and press people (especially if she happens to like them), even though important and pressing questions need to be asked. But none of this really matters when it comes to Oprah's brand. She is by far the most successful media brand of our time.

A few numbers put the power of Oprah into perspective. *The Oprah Winfrey Show*, which is syndicated and distributed to well over one hundred countries, reaches over 30 million viewers each week in the United States alone. Oprah's been on the air nonstop, every day, for nearly a quarter century. She heads an entertainment empire composed of television, film production, and publishing enterprises. Recently, she created her OWN network, standing for (of course) Oprah Winfrey Network. She also co-founded Oxygen Media in 1998, which is a twenty-four-hour cable network. Her picture is on the cover of virtually every O magazine, which comes out monthly. And as a philanthropist, she's got to be one of the most generous celebrities in the world. She's given away millions and raised millions more through her Oprah's Angels network.

As I write this, Oprah is winding down her daily talk show produced by her production company, Harpo, Inc., and distributed by King World. She has made millions, in fact billions, of dollars, not just for herself but for those connected to her brand. But given that there are so many talk show hosts out there, the question needs to be asked, What makes Oprah's brand so unique and successful?

Knowing Yourself . . . and Your Audience

Clearly Oprah's brand is strongest among women, particularly those who are looking for direction and motivation. According to a *Fortune* magazine article: "To understand what makes Oprah Inc. such a powerhouse business, you must first understand the simple message that makes Oprah the new queen of soul . . . simply put, says Oprah, 'My message is, "you are responsible for your own life." ' " According to *Fortune*, this foundation for a brand is "as consistent a selling proposition as McDonald's convenience or Wal-Mart's every day low prices."[1]

That message about being responsible for your own life is an authentic one coming from Oprah. This is a woman who has practiced what she preaches from the early days in her career, when she was told by more than one TV executive that she just didn't have the right look or really didn't have what it took to make it in the business. The station execs in charge of Oprah's first major TV job in Baltimore wanted her to change just about everything, including her hair, lips, and nose.[2] But Oprah would have none of it. She believed in herself, or what she would later call her "authentic self." She didn't change anything, but just kept plugging away until in 1983 TV executive Dennis Swanson recruited Oprah to Chicago, where Oprah was encouraged to be herself. The rest is history.

The powerful and enduring connection that Oprah's brand has with her audience is based on this "authentic self" image. People trust her and what she says—this is priceless in any business. Her open and honest relationship with her viewers and fans begins with the fact that she has been candid about so many things in her life including the fact that she was molested as a young girl and got pregnant. She has also talked openly about her struggles with her own weight—in a media venue obsessed with vanity. She famously wheeled out sixty pounds of fat in a red wagon after one of the many times she dropped a lot of weight to show what she was carrying around all those years.

But while Oprah's weight has been a roller coaster ride of epic proportions, it's never hurt her brand. In fact, I'm convinced that Oprah's physical imperfections are a big part of why so many people relate to her.

The Risks of Political Endorsements

The other thing about Oprah's brand is that she doesn't give it away easily—she never endorses products. But once in a while, she does promote people. In fact, her endorsements have helped create other brands like Dr. Phil, Rachel Ray, and Dr. Mehmet Oz. Endorsing a political candidate, however, can be risky business, as Oprah well knows.

Oprah took a big risk in 2008 when she endorsed Barack Obama for president. Clearly Oprah felt an emotional connection to Obama. She liked him, believed in him, and put it all on the line for him on the campaign trail. The problem was that he was running against Hillary Clinton in the Democratic primary. Lots of women didn't appreciate what Oprah did. In the eyes of many, this hurt her reputation among a group of disproportionately white women who felt that Oprah was picking race over gender, which could be a problem when your key demographic skews so heavily to women. Simply put, engaging in partisan electoral politics is very risky business when your brand is based on appealing to a mass audience.

According to Lester Spence, an assistant professor of political science at Johns Hopkins University, "Oprah literally talked about stepping out of her pew (in church) to endorse him . . . when she steps into the world of politics, a world she has always been above, and anoints someone [Obama] it is coming from someone that millions of people, especially women, trust and revere." According to this article, written by David Carr, "After her endorsement of Mr. Obama, however, the message boards on Oprah.com are alive with allegations of 'betrayal' and 'sellout.' Mr. Obama's base may have been engaged, but part of Ms. Winfrey's base is livid."[3] Oprah saw and felt this reaction and started pulling away from Obama. Sure, she was there at the end when he was running against John McCain in the general election, but by then it didn't matter that much.

A Quick and Effective Response

Even when things look bad, Oprah always lands on her feet because she recovers pretty quickly. When James Frey promoted his autobiography, *A Million Little Pieces*, on Oprah's show, she told everyone to go out and buy the book. She praised Frey for his brutal honesty and candor.

But when it came out that James Frey had made up huge chunks of his book, his reputation and brand cracked into, you guessed it, a million little pieces. But not Oprah's. She sensed very quickly that there was an opportunity and a responsibility to step up and challenge James Frey on the same TV set on which she had praised him only months before. On his return visit to Oprah's couch, she killed him. She demanded answers to hard questions, like why he lied, not just to his readers, but to her. She showed genuine anger and hurt. She didn't give him an inch and exposed him for the fraud that he was. Oprah masterfully dissociated herself from an endorsement gone bad. She not only survived the fiasco, but she grew from it.

In a similar way, Oprah stepped forward when a sex scandal became public at the Oprah Winfrey Leadership Academy—an elite South African school founded by Oprah herself. Fifteen girls at the school claimed that they were sexually molested by a "dorm matron." Given how proud Oprah was when the school opened and how hopeful everyone was about its impact, she was clearly upset and emotionally overwhelmed by these reports—particularly because Oprah had been the victim of rape as a child. Yet, in that press conference, despite her own emotional involvement, Oprah proved the power of superior communication skills in a crisis. Her words and actions demonstrated how a leader should handle a serious problem.

On October 6, 2007, when Oprah Winfrey was informed of the sexual abuse allegations, she took charge immediately. Not hiding behind a cadre of lawyers and PR types, Oprah got out in front of the crisis. She hired private investigators to find out what happened to the girls. She dismissed school administrators who should have been more on top of the situation. She showed sensitivity and compassion for the girls involved, and she got her hands dirty in the process. She explained the relevant details of the case, and (unlike most executives) she allowed a horde of journalists to ask her any question after her powerful opening statement. Her answers were candid and forthright; she didn't plead the Fifth nor duck the tough ones. She took them head-on. While the judicial process had to play out for the twenty-seven-year-old woman accused of sexually abusing these young girls in Oprah's school, Oprah knew that true leaders often cannot wait for the slow-moving courts to dictate their communication and leadership timetable in a crisis. Her candid communication style sends a powerful message to all those who lead and are responsible for protecting the organization's brand.

Not only did Oprah put herself on the firing line to protect her young charges, she was able to use the situation to serve as a role model. The girls in South Africa in her leadership academy are part of a society that does not encourage women to speak out for themselves. Says Oprah, "They represent—those fifteen girls—a new generation of youth in South Africa who fearlessly take back their voices to speak up about their concern about their fellow classmates. . . . This is really what we're trying to teach. This is what leadership is all about—to use your voice, no matter what the personal consequences."[4]

Business, government, and the media are littered with case studies of people who got it wrong when facing a crisis or scandal. Whether it's the Catholic Church, BP, or Toyota, top executives consistently get the communication game all wrong. Oprah gave us all a case study in crisis communication that sets the bar extremely high for all leaders.

Oprah Knows She Is the Brand

Oprah's astronomically successful brand is a product of her survival skills that push her to step up and take responsibility when things go wrong, and of the fact that she is a very shrewd businessperson. She knows she's the brand. She knows she's the product, and she is not shy in any way about using her name, her likeness, and her reputation to make it all work.

There's a lesson here for so many who are so reluctant to "put themselves out there" for fear that it looks too "self promotional." I'm not saying your name and/or face needs to be on *everything* connected to you and your work, but there is a powerful branding lesson in Oprah Winfrey's career. She's always known that even with the best producers and the most enterprising staff, her TV show would never have been as successful if she were not the host. Further, she also knew that just as many people tuned in to hear what *she* was going to say or do, as those who tuned in to hear her guests.

Of course, when one believes very strongly in one's own value and ability, that person risks becoming (or perceived as being) narcissistic or egotistical. But I choose to see Oprah's strong sense of herself as the ideal example of "supreme confidence"—the kind of confidence that can catapult a brand, designed to spotlight an overweight African American woman in a media industry dominated by middle-aged white men, to unimaginable heights.

Branding Lessons

Oprah's got it all. Looking for just a few lessons, I'd emphasize:

- When you are the brand, your physical appearance, your business ethics, and your personal life, are all fair game. So, be your authentic self—whatever that may be.

- Be wary of endorsements. Standing behind a product or person allows you to gain from their popularity, but you also stand to lose the business of those who do not support that product or person—this is especially true in politics.

- When your brand is associated with someone or something that becomes involved in a scandal, don't hide. Seize the opportunity and take responsibility to step up and challenge that person or thing to apologize to you and your customers.

- In a crisis that involves your own brand reputation, get out ahead of the crisis. Proactively, demonstrate with words and actions how a leader should handle a serious problem.

- There's a lesson here for so many who are so reluctant to "put themselves out there" for fear that it looks too "self-promotional." If self-promotion is built on substance and relevance, I say be proud and confident of yourself and your brand.

BP Oil

Total Brand Destruction

Sometimes it's not what you say that delivers your message, but rather the context in which your comments are received. Consider the case of British Petroleum—BP—the company responsible for the largest uncontrolled oil disaster in American history that devastated the Gulf of Mexico. This is a case study that clearly illustrates for all of us that ultimately it is how an organization and its leaders deal with a crisis that firmly establishes the brand and reputation in the marketplace.

You Can't Run from Your Record

When it comes to protecting a reputation or brand, the company's track record can sometimes matter as much as what it says in a moment of crisis. In BP's case, no matter what company executives said at the time of the Gulf of Mexico catastrophe, their message was received in the context of an abysmal safety and environmental track record.

For example, in 2000, by its own admission, BP dumped hazardous waste into Alaska's North Slope. Then, in 2001, BP promised it would clean up polluted air from its refineries after it reached a settlement with the Department of Justice based on requirements of the Clean Air Act. Then, in 2005, a BP refinery exploded in Texas City, killing fifteen people. At the time, BP apologized profusely and reached an agreement with the federal government to assure that such an incident would never happen again. Then, just four years later, the federal government found that BP had over 700 safety violations of that very agreement and fined the company $88 million. These are just a few examples of the countless incidents in which BP was found to have sloppy and dangerous practices involving its oil refineries—every time, the company apologized and promised to do better.

So when BP said "sorry" about the Gulf Coast oil spill, that apology was seen in its historical context. Who can blame us for being skeptical of BP's sincerity given the industry's track record?

Sometimes a company and its leaders can say all the right things. They can apologize. They can promise to fix things and do better. But if that company has a history of saying all the right things and continuing to do all the wrong things, eventually, their stakeholders won't listen to anything that company has to say when the next crisis hits. There's no more credibility and no benefit of the doubt offered. At that point, the brand and reputation have been destroyed. That was the case with BP. Its message of contrition bordered on worthless.

"Foot in Mouth" Disease

BP's CEO and chief spokesperson at the time of the Gulf oil spill was Tony Hayward. Hayward was trying to communicate a lot of the right things in this crisis, but he failed miserably. His insensitivity to the countless victims of this horrific oil spill served only to erode BP's brand to the point where it became unsalvageable.

Some of Hayward's most egregious public statements on behalf of BP in the spring and summer of 2010 include the following: "This is not our accident, but it's our responsibility."[1] (You can't have it both ways, Tony.) Later, once the BP crisis was nearly fifty days in progress, Hayward actually had the gall to say in public: "I'd like my life back."[2] Hayward was clearly ignoring the fact that so many people, as well as innocent wildlife, would never get their lives back in large part due to BP's sloppiness, insensitivity, and downright dishonesty in connection with this disaster.

From the beginning, Hayward, who was the public face and brand of BP, got it all wrong. BP was reluctant to release any of the video showing the spill in progress until forced by Congress to do so. Hayward would also make some absurd statements implying that the spill wasn't that big of a deal. Said Hayward: "The Gulf of Mexico is a very big ocean. The amount of volume of oil and dispersant we are putting into it is tiny in relation to the total water volume."[3] Simply put, Tony Hayward took whatever was left of BP's reputation and threw it in the ocean. His words, his face, and his attitude became the BP brand, offering all of us another example of exactly how you are the brand of your organization.

Ultimately, there were calls for Hayward to step aside. In June of that summer, BP began having others speak on behalf of the company in an effort to move attention away from Tony Hayward. But by then it was too late. Hayward's comments and BP's actions had devastated the company in the eyes of most Americans. If people didn't trust Tony Hayward as the leader of BP, then they couldn't trust the company itself.

So . . . Who's to Blame?

To protect your brand or reputation in the middle of a crisis, you must realize that no matter how justified you think you may be in pointing the finger at anyone else, you must avoid the temptation to do so. In the case of the BP oil spill in the Gulf of Mexico, playing the blame game further eroded BP's public brand.

There were three corporate players in this case: BP was the principal developer for this project, essentially leasing the land and equipment and overseeing and directing the drilling. Transocean was the contractor who leased the deep-water drilling rig to BP. And Halliburton Energy Services provided the cement that was supposed to keep gas from escaping up the well pipe to the surface. At the time of the spill, BP America chairman Lamar McKay, Transocean CEO Steven Newman, and Halliburton president Tim Probert gave testimony before a Senate Environment Committee hearing. Predictably, each pointed the finger at the other.

When pressed in Washington, D.C., BP boss Lamar McKay said it was Transocean's fault that things went terribly wrong when a safety seal failed. McKay's argument was that since Transocean owned the rig, it was of course to blame. Not so, said Transocean boss Newman, arguing that when it comes to drilling projects, responsibility begins and ends with the operator. In this case, that would be BP. So BP blames Transocean, Transocean blames BP, while both of them imply that somehow Halliburton is to blame because there were problems with the company's cement surrounding the rig.

When will people in business finally get the message that when it comes to crisis communication, blaming others never helps your brand? Most people are looking for leaders to step up and lead, to take responsibility, even if a leader believes that someone else is partly responsible for a bad outcome. Great leaders take responsibility for the part of the problem to which they contributed. Bottom line.

So, if BP leased the oil rigging equipment from Transocean, then BP must take responsibility (or blame) for not monitoring or overseeing that leasing in a more responsible fashion. If there was a problem with Halliburton's cement, then whoever brought in Halliburton has to take *some* responsibility (or, yes, blame) for that decision.

When it comes to communication and leadership, professionals should spend less time trying to figure out who they can point the finger at and more time looking in the mirror and asking this question: "What should I do or could have done to decrease the odds that something might go wrong?" Or, "What was I responsible for that didn't turn out right?" Nobody likes a whiner. Nobody wants to hear excuses. And nobody wants to hear you blame anyone else. It's a lesson that we as parents teach our kids every day. So one wonders when "leaders" in corporate America are going to finally learn that lesson themselves.

Talk about Bad Timing

In the midst of this crisis, BP decided to spend over $50 million on image-repairing TV spots. At the same time, the company gave out a massive $10.5 billion in quarterly payments to its shareholders. Talk about bad timing.

As for the ads? Slick ads not only don't help your brand in the midst of a crisis; in fact, they only make things worse. President Barack Obama, whose reputation and image as a leader was also impacted negatively given the Gulf crisis, said of the multimillion dollar advertising campaign: "I don't have a problem with BP fulfilling its legal obligations, but I want BP to be very clear—they've got moral and legal obligations here in the Gulf for the damage that has been done. And what I don't want to hear is, when they're spending that kind of money on their shareholders and spending that kind of money on TV advertising, that they're nickel-and-diming fishermen or small businesses here in the Gulf who are having a hard time."[4]

Simply put, the president was telling BP that every dollar spent on either itself or its public image is seen as a dollar that could have, and in fact would have, been spent on plugging the damn leak that was destroying the waters, and sands, and businesses, and livelihoods in multiple states along the Gulf Coast. Just one more dumb move on top of the others ends the branding saga of BP.

Branding Lessons

In spite of the fact that the well was ultimately capped and the leak contained in mid-July (eighty-seven days after the incident), BP's brand and reputation is shot. The question now is whether other major American companies and organizations will learn some valuable lessons from BP's experience and not repeat their horrific crisis management and communication efforts and their poorly conceived crisis rebranding and advertising campaign. A few lessons for all of us include these:

- A company's track record will always influence its credibility and brand reputation in times of crisis. For this reason, it's important that the reputation of your brand remains as unblemished as possible throughout your career.

- The way an organization's leader communicates in public, regardless of the company's actions, can either help or hurt the brand in a very big way. Yes, one insensitive, uninformed, or clueless person whose face becomes associated with the crisis can bring down the whole company.

- Blaming others never helps your brand. No matter how many people or organizations contributed to a crisis, a leader must step up and take responsibility and add a dose of accountability and integrity to the brand reputation.

- No matter what your lawyers or your marketing people tell you, there is a huge risk in spending big bucks trying to publicly rehabilitate your brand at a time when the incident or crisis remains unresolved.

TODAY

It's about Yesterday, Today, and Tomorrow

I'm a bit biased when I talk about NBC News's TODAY show. That's partly because I've been on the program many times over the past several years as a media and communication expert and have greatly enjoyed every appearance on what many consider to be the number-one network morning show on the air. The TODAY show is turned on first thing in the morning in my own house as well as in the homes of many other relatives and longtime friends and professional colleagues. You become a bit partial when you have such emotional, direct connection to such an enduring institution.

The TODAY brand is highly successful in a world where media success is so fleeting. We live in an age dominated by short-lived "reality show" gimmicks that create incredibly popular brands one day, but whose names we can't remember the next. This fact makes it especially impressive on many levels that the TODAY show brand has become such a strong part of our American culture for fifty-eight years. The show is an institution. It is an icon. And that doesn't happen by accident.

Regardless of your profession, there are many lessons to be learned from how the TODAY brand has been built and more importantly how it has sustained itself through so many decades and trends.

Something for Everyone

TODAY is a powerful television brand that millions of Americans relate to on a very deep and personal level. Viewers feel like they know Matt, Meredith, Ann Curry, and of course Al Roker. These people are so familiar to us that we feel like we know them, even though we haven't actually met them in person.

TODAY's appeal to a wildly varied demographic is illustrated in my own family. I've already told you that I'm a fan. But it's unusual that any TV show that I love grabs the loyalty of my wife and eighteen-year-old son also. My wife watches the *TODAY* show every morning and works out while watching the show on a regular basis. My son Stephen also loves the program. He has been to the *TODAY* plaza on numerous occasions at ridiculous hours of the morning to see acts such as Beyoncé, Alicia Keys, and Jay-Z. In fact, while not many members of my family pay much attention to my own TV work, they are attentive, impressed, and even accompany me to the studio on occasions when I do a *TODAY* show.

The diverse appeal of *TODAY* is not unique to my family. Every time I've done a *TODAY* show, I get e-mails, text messages, and phone calls from people across the country that I haven't talked to in years. This shows me in a very concrete way that the *TODAY* show's audience is very diverse and far-reaching, and more important, very loyal. This audience doesn't flip around to other morning programs—a factor in sustaining a brand that is incredibly rare in the 24/7 multimedia platform world that we live in today.

Why is that? The answer to this question is what we all need to know about building a brand if we hope to appeal to a wide and loyal consumer base.

Begin with Trust

I have a good relationship with *TODAY* executive producer Jim Bell, who has been at the helm of the show since April 2005. When I asked Jim how he would describe the *TODAY* brand, he responded: "First and foremost, the key word is trust. We are on television at a time of day when most people wouldn't want to talk to or spend time with friends or family. Mornings are challenging, especially for parents as they prepare breakfast, find socks, and pack lunches and homework. We take it very seriously that this is a vulnerable time for people to let us into their home.

"There is a relationship, a connective tissue, which exists in morning television that is unique. This is not to say that the same people don't have the same feeling in the evening, but if you walk around with Matt, Meredith, or Al, you can feel the difference. I had an interesting experience when I went with Matt Lauer to a speech he was giving. A guy came up to talk to him and said he felt awkward being so informal with Matt, but he felt like he knew him. And I said that he shouldn't feel awkward. You see, it's all about trust."

I feel the same way about the TODAY show host I've most often worked with—Meredith Vieira. She is consistently prepared, engaging, upbeat, and accessible. Off the air, she is quick to ask about my family, share stories, and has gone the extra yard in greeting my son Stephen when he comes to the studio. I've also seen her be just as friendly and accessible off the air with others.

Jim Bell is right. Brands can't be successful without that trust factor, whether you are a TV program, an airline carrier, a celebrated sports figure like Tiger Woods, or an automaker (think Toyota). Build trust, then work on the brand.

Consistency

The TODAY show has a unique physical set-up for a morning news show that adds to it appeal. The outdoor plaza, at 30 Rock in the heart of Manhattan, always generates tremendous excitement among its fans. Every single day, whether the weather is freezing cold or humid and hot, people from everywhere across this country mob the plaza holding up signs, trying to get on camera, trying to say hello to Al, Ann, Matt, or Meredith.

So, you might wonder, does this give TODAY a branding advantage that others can't hope to emulate? Is this unique aspect of the show the reason for its branding success and therefore has nothing to teach me? Surprisingly, the answer to both questions is no.

Says Jim Bell: "The plaza crowd is important, but the show did fine for years without it. Actually, on NBC's video site on Hulu.com, you can see the first-ever TODAY show episode in 1952. Dave Garroway was the anchor. That very first time he says, 'Well here we are . . . ' And then he goes on for two or three minutes and talks about what the show is and why they are there. It is powerful. Not to get too goofy about it, but it is impressive how the things he says in there are the same today. It is the same show. It is bringing the world into your home. It is taking the viewers to places they can't get to. The relevance of his statements so many years later stays true to the *TODAY* show."

In many ways, according to Bell, *TODAY* is very much the same as it was when Dave Galloway kicked it off almost sixty years ago. The introduction of the plaza audience in the early 1990s may have added a new element of interest to this morning show, but it did not make the brand—a consistent approach to meeting the needs of viewers is what keeps the *TODAY* show alive.

Keeping Up

Even with a solid and consistent foundation proven over decades, Jim Bell and his team know that a brand has to continually evolve, especially in an effort to identify with younger, more technologically savvy consumers.

Says Bell: "We are trying to evolve and change, but at the same time do so with the reliability and trust that we've always had. I think we feel great about the way we are positioned to do that with an extraordinarily powerful Web site. At todayshow.com, each month we have more video streams (which is a huge metric on the Web right now) than on the entirety of ABC and CBS news sites combined. I think it is because we have some compelling programs, and we make it a priority to drive people there. We have smart stories that particularly lend themselves to the Web. The Web is a level playing field. It is not about celebrities; it is about content. It is about compelling interviews, blogs, guests, recipes, and so much more. We have to try to evolve to keep up with the industry as best we can and yet keep the foundation of the house rock solid."

Even a brand with history and reputation as solid as *TODAY* can't sit still. We all have to keep up with the times and use the power of the Internet to stay alive.

Team Personality

Every successful brand must have a strong and compelling Web presence, but that's not enough. Much of *TODAY*'s brand still comes down to flesh-and-blood people—to the on-air personalities who represent and embody the show every morning. Without Matt, Meredith, Ann, Al, and the others, where would TODAY be—no matter how great its Web site?

When you really examine the success of the TODAY show, it becomes clear that building a successful brand is about having a great team both on and off the air. It is about how team members work together supporting each other, making each other look good. It is as true for the TODAY how as it is for any corporation.

According to Bell, the role of the on- and off-air team at TODAY is critically important: "Most people on the show, like Meredith and Matt, don't humor or flatter themselves to think they are the show. We are all the caretakers. The people who work here—the editors, producers, and big talent—are all caretakers. We get to hold this thing for a little while, and then we get to give it to somebody else. The hope is that when we give it to someone else, it is in as good a shape or even better than it was when we got it."

In your company, you do need to brand yourself. Your own brand does matter, but the company brand has to come first if your personal brand is to have any value. Of course, Matt, Meredith, Ann, and Al all must have strong and popular brands that make each one of them identifiable, likeable, and approachable. A huge part of the TODAY brand is the level at which audience members relate to the on-air talent. But TODAY was around a long time before they arrived, and it is likely to be still standing long after they're gone—just ask Katie Couric.

Branding Lessons

Although you may not be trying to brand a morning TV show to compete with the likes of TODAY, there are many ways your brand can be improved by keeping in mind the factors that helped build the TODAY brand into a legend in its industry:

- Many companies can expand beyond a niche consumer group to make their brands appeal to a wide and loyal consumer base. Although there's a fine line between having a diverse base and trying to be all things to all people (which can be deadly to a brand), when a company has the opportunity to grow its market carefully and wisely, it's good for the brand.

- Your customers have to trust you and your product/service. They have to believe that they can depend on getting the same quality every time they "tune in," and they have to feel that you know and understand them and their needs. If they trust in these things, they will be loyal customers.

- While holding tight to tradition and fundamental business practices, allow your product/service to evolve. The technological advancements in the world today no longer apply only to certain types of companies, and they are certainly not a passing fad. Whatever you do, or make, or sell, or service, your brand needs Internet exposure.

- The brand of the company must be strong enough to give value to the individuals within. This is an important lesson for those who think that their personal brands are more powerful than the organizational brand that they represent. The fact is, no one is expendable—not even the biggest and most popular star or "brand."

- Taking the "extra time" to remain accessible and friendly matters. Do what you do with a smile and upbeat attitude. Your brand is greatly influenced by your demeanor, not just your technical skills. Remember that.

Howard Stern

"The King of Media"

If you're working hard to earn your "15 minutes of fame," you can give up the idea of having a successful brand right now. Successful branding is about making a name for yourself that keeps you competitive in your field over the long haul. Enter Howard Stern.

When it comes to the self-professed "King of All Media" (giving yourself a great nickname is important), we are talking about one of the most enduring and successful brands in the history of entertainment media. Stern has been on the radio for over twenty-five years. He became number one in markets all across this country, big and small. He ultimately came to the number-one media market, New York, to WNBC in 1982, and it didn't take him long to become the king of New York radio. You don't have to like Howard Stern or his humor to appreciate his success and his extraordinary ability to create a brand that is anything but a flash in the pan.

Exuding Confidence

Howard Stern built his brand on his unwavering belief in his own ability to be the best. He has always had tremendous confidence in himself; in fact, in every radio market he entered, he announced publicly that he was there to be on top. He held public rallies at which he would make a spectacle of himself and put on often outrageous and sometimes crude performances. At first he attracted hundreds of fans—then tens of thousands as he gained free attention from the media, who gave him the label "shock jock." Every antic was calculated to draw attention to himself, his program, and his brand and to make people remember him. It worked.

The wild on-air antics that have swelled Stern's audience into the millions are the visible part of his arrogant confidence that have made him stand out in a crowded field of shock jocks. His interviews with porn stars, his strip beer pong contests, the world's strongest naked woman competition, and the popular Gary the Retard's Birthday Show are all examples of outlandish programs that keep his show alive when others around him bomb like old jokes. He farts in the face of convention and a whole lot of people love him for that. (At the same time, in more serious segments, Stern has demonstrated exceptional interviewing skills.)

Yes, Stern loves his crude and rowdy skits, routines, gags, and big-name guests; they are an integral part of the brand he's built over time. His listeners keep tuning in because they've come to respect and trust his "shocking" personality. To put it more simply: They know he's one crazy guy and that he never disappoints.

Stern made this style of promotion work for him, but not everyone can—I can't. I'm not building my business on being a shocking guy. I'm not trying to sell anything that's wild. I'm not going to throw insults at whole groups of people, knowing the media will put the spotlight on me tomorrow. But still, I've learned valuable lessons from Stern. For starters, I can clearly see that as I build my brand, I have to identify exactly who I am and what I'm selling, and then I must have the confidence to promote that without hesitation or doubts. I am what I am and make no apologies to anyone.

Climbing Down Off the Pedestal

After many years on the radio making millions, Stern decided to expand his brand by writing a book. In *Private Parts*, he shared the most intimate aspects of both his public radio life and his private life. That book was turned into a movie of the same name that further expanded his audience base and his brand.

It's worth our time to analyze why this book was so wildly popular and why it solidified his standing in the entertainment business. (The book debuted at the top of the *New York Times* bestseller list, and the movie grossed over $40 million in the United States alone.[1]) The success of this autobiography starts with the fact that its brutally honest quality let Howard Stern fans into his life and made them fans forever. This book brought Stern down from the "celebrity" pedestal and made him "one of us." Throughout his career, Stern has shown the ability to be self-deprecating and to make fun of every aspect of himself and his physical appearance (including a running joke about what Stern calls his incredibly small penis size). You can't criticize or make fun of him in a way that is hurtful because he does it first.

Howard Stern takes his work very seriously, but not himself. This is what has made his brand so likeable for so many. We relate to Stern, the gawky, geeky teenager who tells stories about being beaten up in his hometown of Roosevelt, Long Island, never getting the girl, and going to Jewish summer camp, and never feeling adequate enough. He talks about getting yelled at by his father Ben Stern, who was a radio engineer—Stern has even shared with his listeners a taped moment of a typical family dinner when he was a kid; we can hear his father ask him a question, and we hear Stern give a wise-ass answer. Then we hear his father yelling at him: "Shut up sit down." Ha! Sounds like home to me.

You may not actually write a tell-all book about your life in order to strengthen your brand, but you can still take a lesson from Stern on this approach to successful business practices. Placing yourself above your customer is a mistake. People feel more comfortable and confident and trusting of others they view as "like me."

Going with His Gut

Another quality that has helped Stern build an enduring brand is his willingness to follow his instincts and blaze his own trails to protect his craft, art, and professionalism.

This independent streak of Stern's was highlighted in one of the funniest moments in the movie version of *Private Parts*. Stern had finally realized his professional dream to work at WNBC radio in New York, one of the most successful radio brands in the country. Stern was not a particularly well known commodity at the time, and management at WNBC expected him to take clear direction from program manager Kevin Metheny, whom Stern jokingly nicknamed "Pig Vomit." In the scene, Metheny is trying to explain to Stern how the station expects its on-air disc jockeys to say "WNBC" with the emphasis on the "N." Repeatedly, Metheny tells Stern the call letters are "WNBC" and Stern half-heartedly tries to comply, but never gets it right—clearly, which letter gets which emphasis was just not on top of Stern's priority list.

Soon after, we see that Metheny is calling Stern into his office on a daily basis complaining about his on-air approach, which involves refusing to use the call letters as required and, in fact, making fun of his program director and the network itself. Stern believed deeply that his reputation and also his brand was predicated on being authentic and real, even if that meant being crude and embarrassing the people who were paying him millions—in this case WNBC. He would later do the same thing when he was fired at WNBC and ended up at K-Rock, which helped syndicate him across the country in countless media markets.

Staying true to his authentic self, in 2004, Stern announced that he would be moving to Sirius, a satellite radio system. At the traditional terrestrial radio of K-Rock, he had racked up hundreds of thousands of dollars in FCC fines for what the government perceived to be indecent broadcasting. Stern decided to follow his own instincts and leave popular radio behind and move to an untested, satellite radio system that few people knew about and even fewer had access to.

Many people predicted that very few Stern followers would leave terrestrial radio and follow him to satellite. Those people didn't understand how powerful a respected brand can be. When Stern left K-Rock in late 2005, the station's ratings during his former time period plummeted, and the station's brand ultimately suffered and changed its format dramatically. Today, K-Rock is gone—not even a blip on the New York radio market. But, millions of his loyal listeners bought Sirius satellite radio to get Stern and are still there for him every day from 6 to 10 A.M. Since Stern has been on Sirius, he has not only expanded his own brand, but he has helped Sirius build its brand.

Throughout his career at WNBC, K-Rock, and Sirius, Stern remained successful because he remained true to himself—and to his "shock jock" brand. He has never changed his image to fit the needs of someone else, or the popular trends, or even the dictates of his supervisors. Stern knows who he is, and his audience has learned to trust that he will change, not because someone says he should, but only when he decides it's appropriate (as he did after the tragedy of 9/11, when he became downright serious, bringing people together in the most painful of situations). That's a true brand.

Moving from one station to another with his loyal fans right behind him shows all of us what can happen if we stay true to ourselves, and it also shows us that the success of your brand is not based on where you do your business. Offer a product or service that customers can count on to be consistently the best, and they'll follow you anywhere.

Building Versatile and Enduring Relationships

Some people may try to diminish the strength of Stern's brand by stereotyping his loyal fan base, calling them unemployed, poorly educated, "trailer park" folks. But that's simply not true. Stern's demographic is diverse and crosses into every socioeconomic category—from Main Street to Wall Street. In fact, Time magazine has included Stern in its list of the one-hundred most influential people in the world,[2] and Forbes ranked Stern thirty-ninth on the "Celebrity 100" list.[3] These acknowledgments of Stern's popularity do not come out of a fringe market.

Admittedly, some people do find Stern's style and humor extremely offensive, but even this group is a diverse one. There's no single category of people who love him or hate him, and that is magic in the world of branding.

As we all work to build a brand, it's important to recognize that we're not going to wow everyone. Yes, some people will not like you or your product/service. But that doesn't mean you should assume your customer base is limited to only one narrowly defined target group, or that you should change direction or goals when some people don't respond positively to what you have to offer.

The work of Howard Stern is a how-to example of the powerful results that can be gained when one is unwaveringly authentic. Stern would never give up his audience just because he thought another one might be more lucrative or because his boss says he should, or because some people criticize him. He has spent a lifetime building an enduring and emotional attachment with a wildly diverse audience that knows what it gets when it tunes into Stern's show: Day after day, Stern will be revealing, interesting, provocative, and at times, shocking.

Branding Lessons

Love him or hate him, the Howard Stern brand is a classic case study we can all learn from:

- Embrace your wild side, only if you have a wild side. Wild antics intended to draw attention to the brand worked for Howard Stern because that's who he is—one wild antic. He was and is confident in his ability to sustain the image he portrays in his media events. However, wild attention-grabbing strategies usually fail for people who are not selling a wild and crazy product. The accountant or lawyer who strips naked in the center of town will get attention, but it won't help his or her brand. We all must have the confidence to show who we truly are and stick with that authentic image.

- Share some of yourself. Whatever image you convey as part of your brand, don't set yourself apart from your customers. Letting customers see your personal side, your human side, may be just what's needed to cement their loyalty.

- Know who you are and what you're selling. Of course, we all need to accept change into our professional lives as the world changes around us; however, your customers have to be able to trust that your brand is rock solid. Who you are and the quality of what you offer should not be constantly reinvented to satisfy each new trend that blows through your field of business.

- Remember that you are the brand—not your location. The success of a brand is not based on where you do your business. Customers will remain loyal to a brand, no matter where it is located, if it consistently offers them what they want.

- Reach for a diverse yet loyal customer base. Your brand doesn't have to be liked by everyone in order to be successful if you make sure that those who like you, like you enough to remain loyal to you and if you return that loyalty in abundance.

E*TRADE

When Your Brand Is a "Baby"

How important can a baby—who can't even talk—be to a brand? Just ask the folks at E*TRADE, the online trading company that created the YouTube sensation (as well as "water cooler" conversation) when it kicked off a series of entertaining, highly digitized TV commercials featuring babies, in particular a really cute baby "talking" about the importance of investing. With the debut ad during Super Bowl XLII in 2008, E*TRADE's brand was embedded into many people's minds. That's what a creative, entertaining, and memorable piece of communication can do for a brand. But there's also a potential downside to this branding strategy that serves as a lesson to all of us.

Baby #1: The Face of E*TRADE

In this now-famous ad, a baby is sitting with another baby at a computer screen. They are clearly in a child's room, but they are talking to each other in "adult" voices. The first E*TRADE spot that really grabbed everyone's attention was the "Broken Wings" song spot. In the commercial, the lead baby tries to persuade the other baby that he'd have better luck if he invested via E*TRADE rather than messing around with the lottery. The other baby starts singing the line "take these broken wings" and is then scolded by the lead baby. It is a very funny and memorable commercial. When you're branding, being memorable is key, and this campaign hit a home run on that point. (Think about how many commercials you forget.)

I'm not sure how much of E*TRADE's services people actually remember or purchased from this ad, but they clearly connect these babies (particularly the lead baby) with the E*TRADE brand. It wasn't just his face, but it was his expressions and the exquisitely matched "adult" voice. All in all, E*TRADE got two years of successful advertising footage from Baby #1—the ad drew to the E*TRADE Web site many people who wanted to find out more about what these babies were "selling." The little tyke even developed an online following, with 12,000 fans on Facebook and 3,000 followers on Twitter.[1] But, as is often the case with kids, the babies got older, and their looks changed. So, E*TRADE had little choice but to put out a casting call for a new baby.

Baby #2: Cute, But . . .

You might think that a baby is a baby and all babies are cute, but while the new baby that was picked for the 2010 E*TRADE spots was cute enough, he just wasn't Baby #1. Some media experts say he didn't have the right face. He didn't have "the look." He just didn't connect with viewers. That's the funny thing about brand recognition, whether you're talking about babies or financial service companies, the image needs to hit you viscerally in the gut—not just the head. That's the way a lot of branding communication works. It's subjective but no less significant.

E*TRADE certainly isn't the first company to hit it big using a cute kid as a branding strategy. Years back, Gerber created an incredibly successful brand by putting the so-called "Gerber baby" on its baby food jars and boxes. It was easier back then. The same baby could appear on millions of packages of baby food for generations without change. The baby didn't have to talk or appear "live" on the Internet. Coppertone suntan lotion, too, created a visual brand with a little girl and a dog that stayed cute and adorable in print for ages. Branding via print advertising is very different than efforts in today's digital world.

Then came the TV ad for Life cereal in 1972 that gave the first hint that the electronic age changes things. One of the biggest reasons I liked Life cereal when I was a kid was because Mikey liked it. In the TV commercial, Mikey's brothers weren't sure if they wanted to taste the cereal because allegedly it was healthy food: "I'm not gonna try it—you try it!" Then one brother says, "Let's get Mikey. He hates everything!" But of course, Mikey did like it. The kid was adorable. The way he ate the cereal was genuine and engaging. It felt real. Only catch? Mikey grew up and there were no more Mikey commercials. (Quaker Oats did try a new commercial for Life cereal with a new Mikey in 1997, but it just didn't have the punch of the first one.)

Fast forward to today: As the media become more sophisticated and moving video becomes more dominant in brand building, products have to evolve beyond print and even TV. Although E*TRADE gets points for being creative, imaginative, and gutsy in its advertising campaign, it set itself up for a major branding problem by tying so much of its identity and image to Baby #1.

"The reality is that babies do grow up," says Nicholas A. Utton, chief marketing officer of E*TRADE Financial, in a company statement.[2] So Baby #1 had to go, and there was no pretending that the new baby was an identical stand-in. So E*TRADE now finds itself hoping that it can hold on to the magic with a series of babies. That's a risky plan, but it just might pay off if the evolving concept catches on. In a clever move, E*TRADE gave Baby #1 a public send-off by having him explain on Twitter why he was leaving the campaign: "Why am I leaving? Because I'm getting old. And old people follow the sunset. Plus I just took up windsurfing."[3] If viewers begin to look forward to each baby's funny farewell as part of the whole E*TRADE image, the company might minimize the downside of losing E*TRADE Baby #1.

Branding Lessons

Some communication and marketing messages to consider with all this "baby talk" about E*TRADE:

- Don't put all your eggs in one basket when creating a multifaceted marketing/advertising plan. Sure, the talking baby got your attention, but too much of E*TRADE's campaign was based on that baby. There was no Plan B. Branding with babies can be very risky business.

- Getting the attention of your customers is hard enough with all the information and communication they see every day. But, *keeping* their attention is even harder. Remember, truly effective communication must be more than eye-catching. It's got to keep you engaged and involved throughout the entire message, whether it's a TV commercial or a sales presentation. Don't let opening bells and whistles in the beginning drop off to a dull message in the end.

- Take advantage of technology when creating a communication and advertising plan. However, be aware that you can get too cute with this approach, and then the message about what you are actually selling gets lost in an effort to be entertaining.

Gibbons

One Name Can Communicate So Much

Branding a law firm to stand out in such a crowded professional arena is no easy task. A law firm is a collection of individuals who provide clients with individual service; each lawyer has his or her own personality, style, and approach. How do they all contribute to one brand? Having a long and distinguished history adds another level of difficulty to law firm branding. Consider the case of Gibbons P.C., a 230-lawyer firm with five offices in four mid-Atlantic states and a long and distinguished history. Gibbons stands out in the legal community for having great lawyers who provide excellent client service, primarily geared toward middle-market corporations in the range of legal areas, as well as toward major companies in their middle-market matters. It is one of the most innovative and successful brands in the country—but it didn't start out that way.

In fact, the firm named after John J. Gibbons (former chief judge of the United States Court of Appeal for the Third Circuit and one of the most respected people in the legal community) was actually founded by Andrew B. Crummy in 1926. According to Gibbons Chairman and Managing Director Patrick C. Dunican Jr.: "For many years, we were known as Crummy lawyers." Think about that. "Crummy lawyers." What's in the name? A lot.

Over time, the firm became known as Crummy, Del Deo, Dolan, Griffinger & Vecchione. Then in 1990, Judge Gibbons, who had originally worked for the firm for twenty years before serving twenty years on the bench, came back, and in 1997, the firm became Gibbons, Del Deo, Dolan, Griffinger & Vecchione. All those names were important and all those lawyers were important to the firm's history and to building its reputation for excellence.

However, Patrick Dunican and his closest advisers knew that something had to change. According to Dunican, "In 2007, we took a hard look at the name. We commissioned a study, and a market research professional talked to our clients, our lawyers, and others in the legal community to make sure that changing the name to simply *Gibbons* was the right thing to do. That was perilous for us because people across the country knew the firm as Gibbons, Del Deo and every variation of that. We knew this was a change we had to make, but how would we do that while also capturing the history and legacy of the Crummy firm and the Gibbons, Del Deo, Dolan, Griffinger & Vecchione firm?"

A Delicate Balancing Act

That question was hard to answer. Along with his Chief Marketing Officer Dawn Afanador, Dunican and others involved in leading the branding effort needed to balance tradition, legacy, and history with what made the most marketing sense for today's world. These people of vision knew that not only did the name need revising in order to allow the firm to reach its brand potential, but the entire way the firm looked at marketing, public relations, community outreach, and social media needed to evolve as well.

To start, the firm's name was changed to just one word. *Gibbons*. Sure, there was some resistance, but largely through Dunican's strength of personality and persistence, along with the trust that he had developed, a multitiered, sophisticated branding effort was undertaken, not just to change the name to Gibbons, but also to expand the firm's name and reputation outside the insulated legal arena.

A charitable arm of the firm was created, called "Gibbons Cares," which now gives away over $1 million a year, some of which is raised by Gibbons employees themselves through sponsoring monthly "wear jeans to work for $5" days and other efforts.

To further reinforce the firm's new name, Gibbons endowed $1 million to the Seton Hall University School of Law to establish the Gibbons Institute of Law, Science & Technology, which is focused on educating and training the next generation of attorneys in the technology and scientific communities. The firm also donated $500,000 to a major New Jersey law center and created what is called the Gibbons Conference Room.

In addition, in 2007, Dunican made the decision to relocate the firm to a major piece of prime real estate in downtown Newark, New Jersey. To make sure everyone knew that the firm was there and there to stay, Dunican and his team, including Executive Director June Inderwies, arranged to have installed on the building a big, bold sign that read, simply, GIBBONS. According to Dunican, "The sign heralded a new way of doing business for us. We were offered the most attractive lease deal, and we knew it would save millions of dollars over the life of the lease. We decided we were going to save our clients money by offering lower billable rates than our competitors did."

Dunican continued: "We said to our lawyers, this is not your grandfather's law firm. You are not going to have the large corner offices. We are going to cut the size of your offices in half so we can fit more lawyers in less space. We are going to give you systems furniture, not leather and oak furniture. We understand the importance of being efficient and cost effective for our clients; these changes allowed us to hire more lawyers without raising our rates, and we are out there with our clients talking about that fact—that we understand their needs. In September 2008, when we were hit with the recession, we were positioned perfectly to let our clients know how much we were saving them."

Going Very Public

Dunican and Afanador also realized that building a successful legal brand requires extensive interface with the media. Gibbons began to sponsor and partner with entities such as NJBIZ, New Jersey's most prominent business publication. They published articles and placed advertisements in the publication, but also nominated the firm and its attorneys for a variety of awards sponsored by NJBIZ— 40 under 40 Business Leaders, Leading Women in Business, Corporate Citizen of the Year, and Company of the Year. In fact, Gibbons has ranked among the top ten companies on the publication's "Best

Places to Work in New Jersey" list for five consecutive years. Duni-can explained: "Gibbons achieved this recognition in part due to its 'Gibbons Experience,' a generous suite of benefits offered to all employees, and 'Gibbons Academy,' its formal employee training program. This recognition was important, because we earned a place on this list alongside our clients. It gave us another opportunity to network with leading businesses in the state."

Further, Gibbons began sponsoring strategic news and public affairs television programming that helped promote key aspects of the firm, including its government affairs operation. In the name of full disclosure, those programs include several series that I am affiliated with on numerous public television networks on the East Coast, including a live, call-in series with New Jersey Governor Chris Christie, as well as a public policy program called *New Jersey Capitol Report*, which looks at political, social, and cultural issues affecting the people of New Jersey through in-depth conversations with the state's top legislative leaders, political pundits, and "movers and shakers." Gibbons is the sole law firm sponsoring those programs. The firm is not only highlighted with its name and logo on the air and through print and Internet advertising for these programs, but it also aggressively cross-promotes its sponsorship of these programs through its own Web site, highlighting its commitment to staying on the leading edge of the state's business and public affairs.

Gibbons is also the sole law firm sponsor of a PBS series called *Enterprising Women*, which celebrates the country's most successful women in various professions. The sponsorship was strategically linked to the Gibbons Women's Initiative that earned Gibbons the prestigious Catalyst Award and a place on *Working Mother* magazine's list of the nation's best law firms for women. Innovative programs, coupled with the firm's commitment to promoting women, have made the Gibbons brand synonymous with the retention and advancement of women in the legal industry. For example, the firm's part-time and full-time flexible work arrangements allow women attorneys to transition back to work after the birth of a child (or for any other reason). Moreover, in 2006 the firm promoted only women to director and counsel positions, many of whom were part-time employees.

Meanwhile, the Gibbons Diversity Initiative was also being recognized as a leader in the legal profession. In order to further enhance this program and continue to develop a diverse attorney workforce best positioned to most effectively solve client issues, Dunican hired the firm's first Chief Diversity Officer in 2007.

Again . . . It's About Your People

Beyond the media, PR, and marketing initiatives, Dunican and Afanador argue that all these efforts to build a brand mean nothing if the people on your team are not top-notch professionals who are totally committed to representing the firm and its brand in a most positive way on a daily basis.

When I asked Dunican how much of him was in the firm's brand, Dunican said: "I am not the brand. I am simply a leader of the firm that is the brand and one of the faces of that firm. Each of our lawyers is the brand, because a client hires an individual attorney; without quality lawyers, there is no firm. The individual lawyers are the identity of the firm. We are 230 lawyers, but with Judge Gibbons as our standard bearer, the Gibbons name implies a consistent, exceptional standard of service, skill, dedication, and dignity, and that is the brand that each one of us carries out there into the community. There are a number of law firms that have had to deal with the rogue lawyer, and the brand is tarnished when something like that happens."

Says Afanador: "A company must employ people who are really strong leaders, who believe in the brand and believe in what it's saying—the instinct has to be there. People who are leaders need to know how to push forward. Patrick [Dunican] was a bit afraid of changing the firm's name, so that fear inspired him to work even harder to let people know that the brand is the same, even if the name has changed. He was hesitant to let our lawyers engage in social media—Facebook and Twitter—because he worried about inappropriate postings, but he recognizes the unique value of those outlets to branding, and so he is now encouraging us to experiment with the formats that work best for us. That is why he is an innovator."

The other thing that has become clear as I've gotten to know the Gibbons firm is that Patrick Dunican and Dawn Afanador's passion for building and promoting the Gibbons brand has been essential to the firm's success. Successful branding is not simply an organizational activity or function. It is a way of life. Leaders of the company have to live it every day. It has to be an integral part of the culture. In order for that to happen successfully, those leading the effort must be the number-one cheerleaders.

Says Afanador: "Patrick and I can be ebullient at times. We get excited about a story or something in the press; we enjoy it. We want our lawyers winning awards. We put our lawyers' names up for acknowledgment. These things make the job more fun and more challenging."

A Risk Worth Taking

Says Afanador's branding partner, Dunican: "Lawyers are trained to be risk-averse. That's what we counsel our clients on every day. Minimization of risk. So in brand building, there is an inherent risk that you will be out there on a limb and doing something that is creative or innovative, and that is not the hallmark of the legal profession."

The bottom line is that whether you are a law firm or a sports figure, an automaker or a small entrepreneur, in order to truly reach your professional potential, successful branding is not an option—it's a must. Dunican and Afanador took several strategic risks to rebuild the firm's name and brand in a very risk-averse industry. But that's what successful branding is all about: bold, decisive decision-making. It takes change, but not simply for the sake of change; the change must be strategic and multifaceted. Sure, it's in the sign outside the building as well as on the logo on your lapel pin. But it's also in the awards you earn and in the way you carry yourself, representing your organization in the community. It's in the passion of the employees and in the day-to-day attitude they bring to work. These aspects of the brand go well beyond advertising and become part of the fabric of the organization and its people.

Gibbons has taken these extra steps to create a brand that is strong and growing. That doesn't mean there won't be challenges and obstacles. In fact, I know there are some who believe that Patrick Dunican has broken some of the unwritten rules in the legal profession about marketing, public relations and, yes, branding. But some of that is professional jealousy. Some of it also is simply a resistance to change that makes certain industries want to hold on to old ways of doing things, whether those ways make sense or not. (See the chapter on JH Cohn for another look at this dilemma.)

Branding Lessons

No matter what industry you're in, your brand must grow and change with you and with the times. Kudos to Gibbons for having the courage to show the rest of us how it's done:

- Don't change your brand just for the sake of change. Do it for a well-defined reason in a way that is strategic, multifaceted, and phased in over time.

- Brands are built on the company name. If the company name is difficult to pronounce (check out the chapter on Blackwater changing its name to Xe. Huh?) or too long, or in any other way getting in the way of successful branding, don't be afraid to revise the name as part of a multifaceted rebranding. Most people can and will make the adjustment over time.

- In order to have a successful brand, those who lead the effort must be passionate about what that brand stands for, and they must pass that passion on to others.

- The brand does not exist only in the logo, sign, or stationary. It is not an activity or a function. It is a way of life. You and all employees must own the brand—wear it; live it . . . every day.

- If your present brand stands for tradition and history, but you realize a need to evolve, it is possible to balance a modern image with that foundation of tradition, but it requires courage and vision.

Governor Chris Christie

When Being "Blunt" Is Your Brand

New Jersey Governor Chris Christie has been called a bully and an intimidator with an "in your face" style of communication. According to Christie, "Listen, I was sent here to bring change. . . . Direct, blunt and honest—that's how I'd describe my style. And candidly, I enjoy it."[1]

I've known Chris Christie for over a decade, and I'd say he's spot on with this self-description of his style, which translates in all areas to his brand. He first grabbed the political spotlight when he was appointed U.S. Attorney in New Jersey by former President George W. Bush. When he was selected, many questioned his credentials for such a lofty post, as he was just a little over thirty-five. But, the one thing about Chris Christie's brand, beyond his direct and, yes, confrontational style of communication, is that like many others in this book, he is supremely confident in his abilities. This confidence has gained him a name—a brand. According to George F. Will in an op-ed in the *Washington Post*, Chris Christie is "the nation's most interesting governor."[2]

Telling It Like It Is

As U.S. Attorney, Chris Christie prosecuted and convicted over 130 elected officials for corruption and related charges. Christie used his platform as a crusading prosecutor to gain national media attention and ultimately to run for governor in 2009 against a beleaguered and brand-challenged Jon Corzine. Christie won that race more because of Corzine's lack of popularity (and a very weak political brand) and the dismal economic climate in the state than anything else.

Once elected, Christie took over the statehouse by storm. He made it clear that he was in charge and that he had been sent to Trenton to dramatically cut the cost of government and hold the line on taxes. (In just six months, Christie spearheaded the successful effort to cut the state budget by $2 billion and cap annual property tax increases at 2 percent.) But, it's not just Christie's policies that have created such a clearly defined brand; it's his style. I've interviewed him on numerous occasions: He is convinced he is right on just about every proposal or idea he puts forward, and therefore, this guy simply doesn't flinch when challenged.

And he's been challenged a lot. He loves the daily fight with the public employee unions and recalcitrant legislators. He loves the battle with the media. In fact, one day, in the statehouse, when my colleague Tom Moran, the *Star-Ledger's* editorial page editor, asked Christie about his "confrontational tone," Christie went off and created a YouTube sensation by saying, "You must be the thinnest-skinned guy in America. Because if you think that's a confrontational tone, then, you know, you should really see me when I'm pissed."[3]

Christie went on to ask Moran and others in the press core whether they would rather he communicate in a fashion similar to Jon Corzine: "Now, I could say it really nicely. We could say it in a way you all would be more comfortable with. Maybe we could go back to the last administration where I could say it in a way that you wouldn't understand it."[4]

Further, he reframed the argument about him being unnecessarily confrontational and blunt by saying, "Blunt, direct, maybe you could just say 'honest and refreshing. . . . ' But the fact of the matter is, this is who I am, and this is who the people elected."[5]

That's right. This is who the people elected, and the irony is that while people say they want honesty and candor in their elected officials, when they get it in spades it can be surprisingly upsetting to some. Chris Christie's popularity hovers around 50 percent at the time of this writing, and I'm not convinced he's ever going to be as "Reaganesque" as the *Wall Street Journal's* William McGurn claimed when he complimented Christie for "offering the voters a dose of Reagan republicanism—with a Jersey twist."[6] But that's not really the point. The fact is, Chris Christie tells it the way he sees it. He tells folks that New Jersey can't afford property tax rebates any more. He proposes massive cuts in state aid to local school districts because he says we can't afford not to. He tells the public employee unions (particularly the teachers union—the NJEA) that they are being greedy and selfish by not agreeing to a pay freeze, thereby causing massive layoffs of teachers and skyrocketing local property taxes. (He also accused the NJEA of using students as "drug mules" in their effort to influence the opinions of parents.)

So, forget about whether you are a Democrat or a Republican, conservative or liberal, you have to agree that Christie is telling people in no uncertain terms, in the most direct and blunt way possible, that the state is about to go bankrupt, and that he is not going to sit by while it happens. Sure, I disagree with his refusal to raise taxes on millionaires in the state, but how could you have a serious problem with a guy whose brand and reputation is based on telling it like it is just because you don't want to hear what he's telling you?

Branding Isn't Always a Popularity Contest

Governor Christie's brand is also bolstered by the fact that he is not dying to be liked. Sure, he wants to succeed as a politician, but unlike so many other elected officials, he is reluctant to pander, and I'm convinced that he is sincere when he says if he serves only one term, he'd be fine with it, as long as he takes the state from the edge of the fiscal abyss.

Successful political branding isn't just about how many people like you or your style at a particular time. Frankly, Christie doesn't get a lot of style points. But, it's in fact the "anti-politician" brand that makes him so unique. The fact that Chris Christie doesn't care what you think in some way makes him oddly appealing. As does the fact that he would like it if you liked him, but he isn't going to tell you what you want to hear in order to get you to do that. That makes his brand stand out in a world dominated by pandering pols.

The dilemma or paradox in this case is that in order to truly lead, you must have followers. So the concern for someone like

Chris Christie, whose basic philosophy is "This is who I am, and I don't care if you like it or not," is that he needs legislators, citizens, interest groups, and the media to be supportive enough to get his policies enacted. Being a governor or a president is not the same as being the emperor. There are other stakeholders. Christie seemed to grasp this concept when he reluctantly compromised with Democratic legislative leaders on key aspects of his effort to cap or limit property tax hikes. There is a fine line between being principled and being stubborn and inflexible.

So, what fascinates me about Christie and his brand is that it represents a stark and graphic example to all of us, regardless of our profession, who too often try to soft-pedal and nuance our message. We are so afraid of offending others that we wind up saying nothing in the effort to get everyone to like us. Being popular has its benefits, but if being popular comes at the price of saying nothing, what's the value?

Pissing People Off

Chris Christie's brand provides this powerful lesson, which General Colin Powell once told me in an interview: "If you're not pissing someone off, maybe you're not doing your job." Christie pisses people off every day, and he doesn't lose sleep over it. I'm not advocating that the rest of us go out and pick a fight just to be in a fight, but we shouldn't be so afraid of the fight itself for fear that someone might be offended or put off. Could Christie soften his tone and therefore his brand just a little bit? Sure. (He did that on the property tax cap fight.) Can you get more flies with honey? Obviously. But this is who the guy is, and being true to himself, regardless of the consequences, has its benefits. Lots of respectable political operatives and commentators have labeled Christie a future national political star.

I don't know whether Christie is going to succeed politically in the long term or not. That's not really the issue here. My takeaway, and I hope yours as well, is that being in someone's face over something you really believe in is pretty damn refreshing in a world dominated by so many of us who measure every word, every action in an effort to stay in the middle of the road and not veer too much to one side or the other. Like him or not, Chris Christie is coming right at you, like a bull in a china shop. And, when he's gone, you'll know he was there. I kind of like it.

Branding Lessons

Although, unlike Governor Christie, we can't always use our official position to make people do what we feel strongly is the right thing, we can still learn a thing or two from his leadership style:

- Above all, be confident in who you are and what you believe. It will help you communicate effectively when the heat is on.
- Your style is the brand, so stay strong when you know you're right. But, remember, sometimes compromising is the best way to get half a loaf instead of coming up empty.
- Candor counts . . . a lot. Be honest with your beliefs, even when that honesty is not popular.
- Sometimes, it's okay to piss people off if that's the only way to deal with a difficult situation or challenge.

Lebron James

When Your "Decision" Hurts Your Brand

Lebron James is a superstar and an American sports icon. He is a marketing machine and a huge money maker for the NBA. Together with Kobe Bryant, James is clearly one of the heirs apparent to the Michael Jordan legacy of being the greatest basketball player around. No doubt, Lebron James is also a huge brand. In fact, in the summer of 2010, James's brand was so big that he, together with his PR advisors, were convinced that it was a smart idea to do a primetime ESPN special called "The Decision" in which James would announce which NBA team he would be joining after his much-publicized free agency.

James had played for the Cleveland Cavaliers for seven years. He was a product of Cleveland, a hometown hero. He was the franchise of the Cavaliers, and outside its basketball arena, which was packed for virtually every home game, the city had placed a large poster of James. But here's the catch: sometimes your brand and in fact your britches can simply get too big for your own good. That is a branding disaster.

Playing Hard to Get

Lebron James, together with his media and entourage, allowed a very public courting by numerous NBA teams during his free agency. These teams publicly kissed Lebron's butt and offered him the sun, the moon, and any star they could get their hands on. This went on for months and months until it started to feel like a bad episode of The Bachelor, in which some creepy guy goes on all these awkward "dates" with women who allegedly will do anything to be with him. In the end, when the Bachelor makes "the decision" as to which woman he will be with, it's even creepier.

Creepy is a good way to describe this hour of primetime modern media insanity when Lebron James sat with broadcaster Jim Gray (who in fact has a direct business relationship with some of Lebron James's ventures). James finally announced that he would play for the Miami Heat, but that's not really the point of this story. Rather, it's the fact that James looks so good on the basketball court, but looked so bad on television during that ESPN special. It was a terribly dumb and ill-conceived branding and marketing idea that overplayed James's hand. It made him look trivial, egocentric, and narcissistic. He is an amazing player, but the circus atmosphere that surrounded the announcement of his decision made it look like James saw himself as bigger than the game, and no one, not even Lebron James, is bigger than the game (just ask Tiger Woods).

To many, it looked like he was totally insensitive and unfeeling toward the city and the team who had been so loyal to him—Cleveland, Ohio. The problem is not that he didn't pick Cleveland. He had a right to make the best decision for himself, his family, and his future. The problem is that he didn't have the decency to let the city and the team know that he wasn't picking them. That's a classless move—which is always bad for your brand. According to Peter Vecsey of the New York Post: "It was an awful idea from the gitgo and only got more discomforting as the hour and Jim Gray's repetitive, scripted, no follow-up line of questioning dragged on."[1]

Further, James made a tactical PR mistake when he tried to position his decision to join the Miami Heat as an effort to show that money wasn't important to him, but rather that joining a team where he could win a championship and be part of an ensemble was most important. Let's get this straight—either way, Lebron James was signing a deal to make tens, in fact hundreds, of millions of dollars, whether it was with the Heat, or the Cavaliers, or the New York Knicks. So, to try to come off as if money didn't matter while millions of Americans are out of work and struggling to pay their mortgages and keep their homes made Lebron James look disingenuous and insensitive, not to mention an out-of-touch and grossly overpaid professional jock.

Sure, the ratings were huge for this ESPN special. According to the Nielson Company, more than 7 of every 100 homes with TV sets watched the James program.[2] But ratings alone for one particular program don't build or foster a brand. In fact, sometimes playing it low-key or not drawing so much attention to yourself is the smarter, more prudent branding move, even if you are the top dog in a professional sport or any other line of business.

Lebron James did everything he could to raise interest and speculation abut which team he would chose. He intimated that it might be the Knicks by wearing a Yankee hat on certain occasions, but also talked about his loyalty to Cleveland. The speculation and media manipulation went on and on. Up to a point, this approach is smart; the problem occurs when you don't know when enough is enough.

The Chosen One: Really?

This entire marketing effort was apparently intended to make Lebron James bigger than life. In fact, in a July 8, 2010, article titled "Is Lebron James More Popular than Jesus?" James Kirk Wall compared the way Lebron James played his free agency and "The Decision" special on ESPN to how John Lennon not only shocked but also turned off many in the mid-1960s when he said of the Beatles, "We're more popular than Jesus now; I don't know which will go first, rock and roll or Christianity."[3]

Further, according to an August 7, 2010, New York Times story entitled "Epic Confusion: The Narrative of a Superathlete": "The travails of these athletes illustrate the ancient wisdom: Hubris and temptation, gentlemen, have laid low many a would-be hero. James goes by the nickname King James, which maybe should have been a tip-off to trouble ahead. Woods gave in to so much temptation that the tabloids fought to come up with the best annotated count of other women.

"There is an ancient lesson, as well, to be understood in modern sports culture. The status of sports hero, to the extent that it existed, was conferred, not proclaimed. The greats of the past—Joe DiMaggio, Sandy Koufax, Johnny Unitas, Bill Russell, Hank Aaron—did not declare their own greatness; in their time, that was unseemly.

"But LeBron James has a tattoo on his back that says 'Chosen 1,' which, coincidentally or not, is what Tiger Woods's father called his golfing prodigy of a son. Both athletes, awash in their own hype, seemed to lose sight of how the world of mere mortals might regard them."[4]

So there you have it. Just like Tiger Woods, who was pictured "walking on water" in that ill-conceived video game, Lebron James and his handlers tried to create the image of him as a deity or god-like figure. In fact, the picture of Lebron that was used to promote the ESPN special shows him, arms stretched out, head back, looking up to the sky. It looks Jesus-like, almost as if he was hanging on the cross. You think I'm kidding? Google it and you will see what I mean. It's weird and kind of freaky, and it is definitely bad for the brand. That's coming from someone who loves the way Lebron James plays basketball.

Too Little Too Late

In early August 2010, Lebron James and his so-called branding advisors attempted to soften some of the damage he had done to his public reputation, particularly in Ohio. He took out an ad in the *Akron Beacon Journal* filled with photos of himself at a variety of local charity events; the copy read: "Akron is my home, and the central focus of my life. It's where I started, it's where I will always come back to. . . . Thank you for your love and support. You mean everything to me."[5]

Can you say too little, way too late? This ad was a lame attempt by Lebron James to soften some of the resentment felt toward him for not having the common decency to let the people "who mean everything to me" know, before his prime time ESPN special, that he wasn't coming back to the Cleveland Cavaliers. The backlash to the ad was intense. Some fans criticized James for not even mentioning the city of Cleveland, the place where he played for all those years. In addition, t-shirts with the expression "We are all Quitnesses" were selling like hotcakes in stores throughout Ohio. The quote was a reference to a mural that was prominently displayed in Cleveland for years (before it was removed immediately after the

EPSN special) in which Lebron James had his arms stretched out with the words "We are all Witnesses" prominently displayed. This again seems like another divine reference. Witness to what? An extraordinary basketball player or a godlike figure who has been sent here to save us all? These marketing and branding techniques may seem harmless when conceived by so-called advertising and marketing "geniuses," yet, as we've seen, attempting to place yourself so far above the masses can be risky branding business indeed.

No one is bigger than God (no matter who your "god" is), and it's never a good idea to compare yourself to Jesus—no matter how great a player, entertainer, or brand you are. I say Lebron James blew it with how he handled his free agency and his "The Decision" special on ESPN. Sure, he may recover, and if he wins an NBA championship with the Miami Heat, a lot of his stupidity will be forgotten. But, his once largely untarnished image and brand has been burned big time. Where he was cheered in NBA cities across the country I'm betting he's going to get a very different reaction, particularly in those cities he courted so shamelessly. I can hear the boos now. He will never go broke because he has more money than he'll ever know what to do with, but his brand will never be the same because it's now tainted with labels such as "out-of-touch" and "unbearably narcissistic." I'm convinced that was not his intent, but that's what happens when you don't think through the potential ramifications and reactions to such a bold and risky media venture, which turned this basketball superstar into a not-so-likable spectacle, not just for one night, but possibly for many, many years to come.

Branding Lessons

You and I will never be in a position to make decisions about how to protect our brand while publicly announcing which NBA team we will play for, but still, there are branding lessons to remember from the Lebron James case:

- No matter how big or successful you are in your industry, never position yourself as bigger than the "game" itself.

- Sometimes playing it low-key and not drawing so much attention to yourself is the smartest branding move you can make.

- Often, media and marketing advisors are not willing to be candid and honest enough with their clients to tell them when something just doesn't make sense; instead they tell them what they want to hear.

- Remember who brought you to the dance and be loyal to your supporters and customers who helped you succeed in the first place.

Newsweek

Times They Are a-Changing

Sometimes even the strongest brands just run their course. No matter how successful a brand is, sometimes demographics, technology, market forces, and the inability and/or unwillingness to respond to sweeping changes can erode a brand. Consider the case of *Newsweek* magazine.

For decades, being on the cover of *Newsweek* or TIME magazine was a very big deal in American culture. These two media giants competed head to head, week by week, for the best, most compelling news stories.

Personally, *Newsweek* was my magazine of choice. I found it to be thoughtful, easy-to-read, fair, balanced, and nicely packaged. Then, after seventy-seven years of publication, in the spring of 2010 the Washington Post Company announced that it was selling *Newsweek* because it just couldn't make enough money with what once was one of the greatest American media brands.

This brand and case study of *Newsweek* is not unique. It happens to other highly successful organizations all the time. Let's consider how the *Newsweek* brand was weakened by several powerful forces and factors, by a thousand small cuts—one at a time.

Changing Demographics

For years, *Newsweek* was seen as a countervailing force to what was perceived to be a more right-leaning, conservative TIME magazine. *Newsweek* was trying to appeal to a younger, hipper audience that would be as interested in pop culture and music entertainment as they would be in a detailed analytical piece about the Middle East. But successful branding is about effectively matching up your product to the marketplace demands.

For many of these younger, hipper consumers, magazines like *Newsweek* seemed archaic, obsolete, and increasingly irrelevant. My own eighteen-year-old son consumes news and information on a regular basis, and he knows that there is a magazine called *Newsweek*. However, I doubt he has ever read it. Why would he? Why deal with a not so cheap, cumbersome magazine with messy newsprint when you can get convenient, real-time information on your iPhone in the palm of your hand? FREE!

What happens when you lose the niche group you've targeted to sustain your brand? Advertising dollars drop. As *Newsweek* lost readers, it became increasingly difficult for its sales team to sell the magazine. Over time, like many other print publications (including several that publish my columns), there were fewer and fewer ads, and the publication became thinner and thinner. It's a matter of simple mathematics and economics. If fewer people are reading your content, how are you going to convince other companies who want to promote their own brands via print ads that you are the place to be? It's a very tough sell.

And so the numbers dropped. According to the *New York Times*, *Newsweek* had operating losses of $28.1 million in 2009, and $15.4 million the previous year. Its revenue declined from $227.4 million in 2008 to $165.5 million in 2009, a decline of 27.2 percent.[1] Its targeted readers were fleeing in droves and there was no one lined up to take their place.

Encroaching Technology

Sometimes, brands succeed or fail because of the times they live in. Edward Costner, who created *Newsweek* in 1963 and was later its editor, said, "Those magazines [*Newsweek* and TIME] had much more stature in those days. . . . It was really important what was on the cover of *Newsweek* and what was on the cover of TIME because it was what passed for the national press. They helped set the agenda; they helped make reputations."[2]

Unfortunately, according to Charles Whitaker, research chairman in magazine journalism at Northwestern's Medill School of Journalism: "The era of mass media is over, in some respect . . . the newsweeklies, for so long, have tried to be all things to all people, and that's just not going to cut it in this highly niched, politically polarized, media-stratified environment that we live in today."[3]

This new world, of course, includes the Internet, which has played a major role in hurting Newsweek's brand and its market share. Before the Worldwide Web, Newsweek was a must-read for many who wanted to be in the know. But in the age of instant information and analysis (no matter how accurate), why would an information consumer wait for a weekly news magazine? In the process, why pay $5.95 for it?

While the Internet was stealing customers from newsprint, so was cable news. Someone could watch MSNBC, FOX News, or CNN any time of the day, seven days a week. Why wait for Newsweek to come out every week? Each day, less and less people have that kind of patience.

My two youngest sons are six and eight years old. When they get to college, it's possible that they will not even recognize a magazine or a newspaper, which I personally find really sad. The time you live in certainly can make or break your brand.

Leaders Must Respond . . . or Your Brand Suffers

While much of Newsweek's brand demise is a product of changing demographics, market efforts, and technology, some of the fault lies with the key decision makers at Newsweek, who either refused or were unable to adjust to the changes around them.

According to Jon Meacham, Newsweek's editor at the time of its sale, "You would have to have been hopelessly Pollyannaish not to have suspected that there were fundamental shifts ahead . . . I decline to accept that Newsweek in some form does not have a role to play going forward."[4]

That positive attitude may sound fine, except for the fact that brands don't succeed or grow just because those who are in control of them think that they have some right to exist. It is a competitive marketplace, with intense market forces and cutthroat competition. Just being thoughtful and analytical isn't enough to succeed as a brand. You have to consistently appeal to your audience/customer.

If your customers change, you have to change, too, or help them understand that what you are offering (whether they realize it or not) is something they really want and/or need. *Newsweek* never did that to the degree it needed to. In this regard, *Newsweek* is not alone. Countless magazines and newspapers made the same mistakes. Over time *Newsweek* never made the sale. It never adjusted. It never found a way to create the kind of exciting, Web-based video content that would draw younger consumers to its brand.

On one level, as a journalist, I respect *Newsweek*'s decision to stick to its knitting and be true to itself. But there has got to be a more realistic and practical balance between being who you think you ought to be and appealing to enough customers and consumers to pay your bills and make a profit. *Newsweek* never found that balance. So circulation dropped: It was 3.14 million in the first half of 2000 but only 1.97 million by the second half of 2009.[5]

That's too bad, because *Newsweek* was damn good. But in the world of branding, being good when it comes to substance isn't nearly enough. It's just a start, and those who stop there and ignore changing market forces risk becoming obsolete.

Branding Lessons

Whether you're in the news/information business, or you sell popsicles and widgets, the demise of a strong brand such as *Newsweek* speaks volumes:

- When the market around you changes, either change with it or die.
- You'll know that your brand history and reputation are becoming increasingly irrelevant if you can't answer this question in a compelling and credible fashion: What makes my brand distinctive?
- Always measure how you stand in the marketplace. If you're losing market share, take steps to respond to market forces and reposition your brand.
- In certain arenas, like publishing, no one cares what you did yesterday, because that is yesterday's news. Rather, focus on what you can do for your customers today and tomorrow.

Daniela Costanzo

Spinning Her Magic

Several years ago, I was looking for a different kind of workout when I heard about a spin class offered at the New York Sports Club (NYSC). Word around town was that the class was intense and challenging and that the instructor was great, but definitely demanding.

After looking over the weekly schedule of Daniela Costanzo's eight spin classes, I decided I'd drop by the Sunday 9 A.M. class. I had no reason to think my plan wouldn't work, but when I got there, all twenty-four bikes were occupied, and there was a line out the door. When I asked at the front desk what the deal was, I was told: "If you want to take Daniela's class, you have to sign up way in advance." I then learned that there was a special call-in procedure established for Costanzo's cycling classes: During a narrow window starting at 7 A.M. on Saturday, I could call in to get one of the 24 bikes. Okay, so the next Saturday, I called at 7 A.M., but the phone line was jammed, and when I actually got through at 7:07 . . . well, you can guess the rest of the story.

The question that then had to be answered was: How has Costanzo, otherwise known as "D," built her brand from scratch in a way that makes her stand out as one of the most effective and popular fitness instructors around? When I finally got a spot in her class several weeks later, it became clear to me what made "D" so special.

Know Yourself

Costanzo isn't a spin instructor biding time waiting for her real career to take off. Fitness is her love, her passion. During our informal interview, she was very clear about where she's going: "I've always been active. I played basketball and did gymnastics competitively. For me, physical fitness comes easy because it's something I truly love."

180

In 2009, Costanzo made the decision to make something bigger out of her love of fitness and cycling by getting her personal trainer certification. Shortly afterward, she had a thriving personal training business, and clients lined up for her spinning classes. That didn't happen just because she got certified; that happened because she's really good and she's passionate about her career. "Everybody has a gift," she says. "It's just a matter of figuring out what it is. I've always had the ability to connect with people, and I think that connection draws people to my classes. Anybody can go to a job every day and be successful, but that doesn't necessarily make them feel fulfilled. Real success comes when you look within and find your true path."

"I'm not exactly where I want to be in this field yet," she says. "But I know the fitness world is where I need to be. I know me. I know what I love. And I know that eventually [maybe even by the time this book comes out!] I'll have my own studio where I can make a real difference in the lives of a lot of people."

I'm betting she is going to do it.

Know Your Customers

Often, people come up with a formula for how to meet the needs of their customers, and when it's successful, they stick with the formula. Unfortunately, that method will only go so far in maximizing a brand. Your customers are always changing and therefore you must be open to shaking things up on a regular basis if you intend to continue to meet their needs.

As this book goes to print, Costanzo is actually pursuing opening up her own all-purpose fitness facility, which has been her professional dream. I'm convinced that Costanzo's brand is solid in a tough-to-survive field because she connects with her customers and keeps them engaged and energized. "I know that my clients are people struggling with careers, children, and home life," she says, "but when they walk into my spin studio or meet with me for one-on-one personal training, it's my job to help them forget all that, put themselves first for just a little while, and have some fun."

"Fun" to Costanzo is all about energy. That's where the mystery and magic of her personal connection spring from. First, the music she uses is the best—it's a mix of Motown, hard rock, hip-hop, and such, so I never know what I'll be spinning to when I arrive for a session—It could be Mary J. Blige, Amy Winehouse, and U2 back to back.

Costanzo also is constantly changing up the cycling routines. The core remains the same—you're going to work harder in her class than in any other, and the routines will be more impressive— but she doesn't lead you through the routine the same way twice. Wondering, "What's Daniela bringing to the studio today?" takes away the monotony of spinning that had bothered me for years. It also makes Costanzo stand out from all the other instructors.

Be a Role Model

Daniela Costanzo is her brand—she is a model of fitness. You would think this would be a no-brainer for anyone hoping to build a fitness brand, but I've seen plenty of out-of-shape and lazy instructors strolling around the room, yelling out instructions and then getting annoyed when the class members are slacking off. Not Costanzo. Not ever.

Costanzo shows us all how it's done and what the results can look like. Her arms and shoulders are impressively muscled without being bulky. She is long and lean and strong. She's in great shape, and it shows. When I see her spinning, perfectly positioned with her back straight and her shoulders high, I want to model that. Costanzo never cheats. She never slacks off. She is always modeling what she expects from her customers—and that often involves a lot of shared sweat.

I'm impressed that Costanzo sweats more than anyone else in the class because I know how hard it can be to place yourself in front of the room and practice what you preach. As a communication coach, I can't talk about the importance of being concise in presentations or of being a great listener, and then lead a discussion in which I am long-winded and I cut people off without hearing what they have to say. I know that when I do that I am breaking my own rules, and that makes it harder to be the authentic brand I want to be.

Whether it is leading a seminar on communication or teaching a cycling class, to be a successful brand, you have to practice what you preach and live it every day.

Give It Back

You are the brand, but that doesn't mean it's all about you. While Costanzo has certainly worked hard to make herself stand out, and she has benefited financially from her successful branding as a fitness trainer, she adds to her reputation by giving back. A few months ago, for example, I signed up for one of her fundraising spin classes after receiving an e-mail from her personally. The e-mail, labeled "Sunday Spin for Haiti Relief," explained that she was raising money for the Red Cross to help people in Haiti who were victims of the terrible earthquake. People signing up for the class would contribute anything they wanted to the relief fund. That Haiti relief spin class was quickly oversubscribed, so she held more than one. Afterward, Costanzo posted flyers around NYSC saying: "Thank you to all our generous riders who raised $1,500 for Haiti relief in two hours of sweat and hope." The fliers featured a logo of the American Red Cross with D's Web site. Costanzo raised money, we all felt good about it, and she strengthened the power of her brand. Doing well by doing good!

Branding Lessons

Sometimes people wonder whether building a personal brand is only for an entrepreneur like Costanzo—someone whose career is directly connected to a professional identity. That's just not true. Clearly D has a unique type of brand, but the lessons that she offers are relevant for anyone regardless of his or her profession:

- To build a successful brand, you must know who you are and where you're going. With an eye on the target, you must feel the passion of your work and show that passion to your client/customers every single day.

- You can't do the same thing the same way every time—even if that way is quite successful. Yes, you have to have a core approach and methodology for what you do, but you must vary it. You have to read your customers/clients and see what they are responding to and what they are turned off by. Remember, going on "autopilot" or going through the motions is a brand killer.

- Model the trait you're selling—whether that is reliability, dependability, honesty, proficiency, intelligence, or even physical fitness. Your level of excellence will motivate your client base to kick it up a notch.

- Take and give back. Use your success to position yourself as a community leader and philanthropist who cares about the well-being of others. Your brand is built on an image; work to make that image a generous and thoughtful one.

Sarah Palin

So You Want to Be Taken Seriously?

Political brands can be hard to figure out. There have been some names and brands associated with great leaders throughout American history—names such as Washington, Lincoln, Jefferson, JFK, Roosevelt. You get the idea. But in the modern, media-obsessed, Internet-driven blogosphere, building and sustaining a successful political brand requires an understanding of a far more complicated equation. Consider the case of Sarah Palin.

Until August 2008, who really knew who Sarah Palin was? I didn't, and a big part of my professional life involves doing political commentary. Within minutes of the announcement that GOP presidential candidate John McCain had picked Palin to be his vice presidential running mate, the name "Sarah Palin" exploded on the national political landscape.

Since then it's been a branding roller coaster for Palin. So much of how she is viewed is a product of the way she looks, what she says, how she says it, and who she blames when she says it. Palin offers a unique look at the modern-day branding process for anyone hoping to rise into a leadership position or to understand the creation of an instant celebrity.

Looks Matter

The fact that an attractive, forty-five-year-old woman from Alaska stands out among the countless white, middle-aged and older, men who dominate politics in our country says something about the role of one's appearance in the political branding process. It's been said that if Sarah Palin looked like Susan Boyle (the Internet-created singer from England), she would never be the political star she is today. Let's face it—to a lot of people, particularly men, Sarah Palin is hot. (And don't kid yourself, this isn't a sexist comment. A big part of Barack Obama's appeal is that he's a good-looking and physically fit younger guy; in 2008 when *People* magazine featured him without his shirt on, all of a sudden Obama's pecs became part of his brand.)

I know it sounds trivial to consider how somebody looks when you're talking about electing national leaders to solve problems of world peace, terrorism, environmental catastrophes, a fiscal crisis, etc., but when you're building a political brand, looks do matter. How do you think John Kennedy beat Richard Nixon in the 1960 presidential race? The JFK brand, while greatly influenced in later years by his assassination in November 1963, was to a large extent the product of the fact that he was a great-looking guy running against a not-at-all-so-good-looking Richard Nixon in the first televised debates in our country. Those who listened to the debate thought that Nixon won, while those who watched the debate on television thought that Kennedy won. (Could it be related to the fact that Nixon refused to wear makeup during the debate?) Looks matter a whole lot. Sarah Palin has been on the lucky side of this line.

The Power of Words

Beyond being physically attractive, Palin's brand is a product of her tendency to say pretty outrageous things. Part of her appeal is that she's unpredictable. (She likes to call it "going rogue.") The media realized very quickly that she's good TV—even if what she says often doesn't make any sense or, as was the case in the 2008 campaign, demonstrates a shocking lack of knowledge. In the book *Game Change: Obama and the Clintons, McCain and Palin, and the Race of a Lifetime*, authors John Heilemann and Mark Halperin note the following:

There was the matter of Palin's substantive deficiencies. On September 10, she was preparing to fly back to Alaska to see her son Track ship off to Iraq and to tape her first network interview with ABC News's Charlie Gibson. Before the flight to Anchorage, [McCain advisors Steve] Schmidt, [Nicole] Wallace, and other

members of her traveling party met Palin at the Ritz-Carlton
near Reagan airport, in Pentagon City, Virginia—and found that,
although she'd made some progress with her memorization
and studies, her grasp of rudimentary facts and concepts was
minimal.[1]

Apparently, this is a kind way of saying "atrociously unaware." The authors of *Game Change* go on to give specific examples that illustrate the extent of Palin's lack of knowledge regarding the most basic aspects of U.S. government:

Palin couldn't explain why North and South Korea were separate
nations. She didn't know what the Fed did. Asked who attacked
America on 9/11, she suggested several times that it was
Saddam Hussein. Asked to identify the enemy that her son would
be fighting in Iraq, she drew a blank. (Palin's horrified advisers
provided her with scripted replies, which she memorized.)
Later, on the plane, Palin said to her team, "I wish I'd paid
more attention to this stuff." But after cramming furiously,
Palin managed to emerge intact from the Gibson interview—
stumbling only over whether she agreed with the "Bush doctrine"
("In what respect, Charlie?') and in discussing why the proximity
of Alaska to Russia afforded her insight into its behavior on the
world stage ("They're our next door neighbors, and you can
actually see Russia from land here in Alaska.").[2]

Branded as Damaged Goods

Once Sarah Palin lost the race for vice president and was no longer the governor of Alaska, one might think that she'd become a political has-been without a salable brand. But no. She's still very much out there on the media landscape as a well-paid "talking head" on FOX, as well as on a variety of other media venues. She gets $100,000 or more to speak. She wrote a bestselling book and enjoyed the accompanying media tour on TV, radio, and book signings. So, what, we all must wonder, is her brand now?

I believe Sarah Palin's still figuring out for herself exactly who she is and how she wants to be portrayed in the public eye. If she doesn't choose to run for president (which I predict she won't), she'll be just fine because she is attractive, she is recognized, she does have loyal followers, and apparently, whether you love her or hate her, most of us are curious as to what she has to say. However, if I'm wrong and Palin runs for president in 2012, her brand as a credible leader is a very badly damaged commodity. And here's why:

She's a quitter. How could Sarah Palin ask people to elect her to the position of President of the United States when she quit as governor in Alaska without any reasonable explanation? She just quit in the middle of her term. If she did that because she wanted to make some money as a private citizen, that's fine. But that's not what she said. Instead, she blamed the media and her "enemies" for creating an environment that made it impossible for her to govern Alaska. Well, I don't get it. How would that circumstance be any different if she were president? (Ask President Obama or George W. Bush.) It would just be a thousand times worse. So now the American people have reason to distrust her—that's a brand killer in any profession.

You see, the branding game works both ways: it's a way to shape the public image you'd like to portray, but it's also a way for the public to label you. Palin has made decisions that set her up to be perceived as someone who isn't serious about governing, but is very serious about building the celebrity factor. (In fact, in the summer of 2010, her daughter Bristol got together again with her baby's father Levi Johnston for what many believed was a publicity stunt in order to star in a "reality show" about the two of them and their child. Clearly, Sarah Palin and her PR folks had to sign off on such a branding strategy.)

The concept speaks for itself. She appears to like the idea of branding herself as a national public figure (accompanied by all the trappings of celebrity that include massive media attention and big money), but does not want any of the responsibility that goes along with being a true leader in an elected office. You can't quit as governor of Alaska and then ask people to trust that you're serious enough to go through the rigors of a presidential campaign. She has branded herself as someone who quits when things get too tough. Her actions have far more influence on her brand than anything she might say from this point on.

She's a finger-pointer. Another major problem with Sarah Palin's political brand is that she blames way too much on other people. (It doesn't help President Obama's brand either when he blames former President George W. Bush for the problems Obama inherited—it's part of the job.) Great leaders brand themselves by taking responsibility for their actions even if others could rightly be blamed. Harry Truman, for example, set his presidential brand in stone when he put a sign on his desk that said "The buck stops here." But with Sarah Palin, the buck never stops here.

Palin has accused McCain campaign operatives of contributing to many of her shortcomings in the 2008 race. She has publicly stated that they didn't understand her, they mismanaged her, they interfered with her wardrobe choices, and they didn't prep her for the now-infamous interview debacle with CBS's Katie Couric. When Couric had the audacity to ask Palin what she read to form her opinions, Palin couldn't or wouldn't answer. She kept repeating, "I read everything." When pressed by Couric, Palin came up with nothing, but later when interviewed by Oprah while promoting her book *Going Rogue*, Palin said that she didn't want to answer Couric's question about what she read because of Katie's attitude. Huh? Blame the interviewer? That's not what serious professional people do. That's what children do. Immature and petty children.

She's not that bright. What bothers me most about Sarah Palin is that she seems so convinced that she's so right about so many things despite the fact that she has little evidence to back up her claims. What does this have to do with branding? A lot, because it affects the image that's portrayed to the public regarding a leader's level of intellect.

One of the adjectives that some people use in describing the Sarah Palin brand is: "clueless." Those willing to be less harsh feel she's not intellectually curious. She's not well-read. She's not that well-informed. When Palin was caught on camera with a few hand-written and simplistic "talking points" on the palm of her hand, it further perpetuated the image of her as intellectually challenged. This perception is an obstacle for someone hoping to be branded in a serious way as a national political figure.

Consider why the Tina Fey *Saturday Night Live* series of Palin spoofs was so powerful. It was because Tina Fey nailed it. Every time Fey said something stupid or off the wall while looking quite attractive in Palinesque attire, it was spot on. Fey's skits didn't seem like some exaggerated version of Sarah Palin—it was Sarah Palin! To her credit, Palin went on *Saturday Night Live* with Tina Fey and did a series of funny skits that were self-deprecating and entertaining. (Palin may not be an expert on the issues, but she is very smart when it comes to promoting her "celebrity.") But being entertaining is not going to build a legitimate, national political brand that will encourage the majority of Americans to vote for her as the leader of the free world.

I don't know exactly how Sarah Palin hopes to mold her future brand, but I do know that for now she has successfully branded herself as a cultlike celebrity performer, and that reputation is bound to limit her opportunities to succeed as a serious national figure prepared to lead.

Branding Lessons

I've never seen a political figure explode on the scene so quickly from virtual obscurity and establish such a recognizable and riveting brand as Sarah Palin. But being known, recognized, and talked about isn't enough to be a successful, enduring, and serious brand if you want to rise as a national leader. A few lessons from the Palin experience include:

- Looks do matter. Being attractive and telegenic count for a lot in our media-obsessed world, but don't base all your branding strategies on this one attribute.

- Go rogue with caution. Being unpredictable isn't necessarily a bad thing. Speaking your mind as a "rogue" personality can actually be a part of the brand of a person on the rise. However, if those unpredictable actions and rogue comments are outlandish and/or nonsensical in an arena where you are expected to conduct yourself in a professional and well-prepared fashion, that's exactly how you'll be branded.

- Leaders don't quit in the middle of the game. A brand built on leadership qualities must have a foundation grounded in responsibility and dependability. If you cut and run, leaving behind those you pledged to lead, your brand can be irrevocably tarnished.

- Take responsibility for your mistakes and shortcomings. If you want to build a reputation as a strong leader, you can't point the finger of blame at others beneath you. The buck stops with you, and on that promise you build a brand.

- Know what you're talking about. Those who want to be viewed as credible or professional leaders must be more informed, more well-read, and more intellectually curious than those they want to lead. Know your stuff before you open your mouth.

Rutgers University

The Block R Success Story

I have three college degrees from New Jersey schools. Of course, the most notable school in this state is Princeton University—but that's not where I got my education. I got my master's and doctoral degrees from Rutgers University, which, to many, is of Ivy League caliber. I mention these two schools in this opening paragraph because name identity is a big part of branding. Have you heard of Princeton? Of course. Have you heard of Rutgers? Yes, especially if you follow college football.

While Rutgers gets big academic points and has become quite selective in its admissions process,* if we are going to be totally honest here, the Rutgers brand has been enhanced more by its much-publicized football program than anything else in the last decade. The decision to pour big money and attention into one sport in order to build a university brand has a lot to show us about bold, creative, and yet controversial branding.

The Coach

The person most responsible for building the Rutgers brand and creating a buzz about the Rutgers "Block R" logo is its football coach, Greg Schiano. Schiano, as far as I know, didn't study advertising or branding, but he is a Rutgers guy. Born and bred in New Jersey, he understands Rutgers, and he knows better than most how challenging it is to market, promote, and, yes, brand, Rutgers as an elite, top-of-the-line school, particularly after years of losing and being a laughing stock in Division I sports.

No doubt, there is an internal debate going on within the university community as to whether Rutgers is doing the right thing,

---

* Full disclosure: I have taught numerous courses and seminars at Rutgers University.

spending millions to promote the football program as the way to build its national brand, while at the same time cutting back on classes, eliminating other athletic programs for now, offering buy-outs for professors to save money, and dealing with a fiscal crisis of epic proportions. But putting that debate aside, the story of how Greg Schiano has helped build the Rutgers football brand, and in turn the university's reputation in the national media landscape as well as with prospective students, is a case study of what's possible when a hard-charging visionary/salesman takes the reins and makes believers out of many. That's who Greg Schiano is, and without him, there is no way I'd be writing a chapter on the Rutgers University football program in this book about branding, no matter how many degrees I have from the school.

The Logo

Part of the problem with the Rutgers brand was that it was diluted and confused. There was no one logo that stood out. Ad agencies and internal marketing folks at Rutgers kept trying to put the word "New Jersey" in the name. It didn't work. "New Jersey" complicated the Rutgers brand; when trying to recruit and attract students and athletes from all over the country, let's not kid ourselves, "New Jersey" is not a universally great sell.

It was Schiano who came up with the Block R logo that changed everything. According to TJ Nelligan, founder and CEO of Nelligan Sports Marketing—one of the top firms in the country when it comes to branding athletic programs in higher education—"Greg Schiano came up with the Block R. People try to make logos too complicated. The Rutgers 'R' is now known nationally, and you know that R stands for Rutgers' athletics. In 2006, Schiano took a program that has floundered for 139 years and put it in the top five in the country, and he did it the right way with good kids who go to class, who are in the top five in the academic numbers, who score a touchdown and hand the ball to the ref. Greg is one of the smartest guys in the country when it comes to branding. Rutgers' sports brand is tied to Schiano. I grew up in New Jersey, and I never thought to go to Rutgers to watch a football or basketball game. [Nelligan is not alone on that.] But the year after the team had its great run, donations, applications, and incoming visits significantly increased. It gets people excited to say, 'I am in a good school where there is something exciting to do.'"

According to Steve Jones, president and CEO of Robert Wood Johnson University Hospital, a long-time Rutgers booster who was there during the lean days when the Rutgers brand was struggling mightily: "I tell people the story about how ten years ago, I was the only person on a Monday morning who talked about Rutgers football. But then there came a time when the water cooler Rutgers conversation was a huge buzz. As you drive around the community, not just New Brunswick, but North and South Jersey too, you see the Block R, and I'm told you will see a white t-shirt and see the Block R and immediately know what it stands for. It is huge; it is a visual identity. Compare it to the 'M' of Michigan and the burgundy of UFC. Or, the Nike swoosh."

None of this branding success would have been possible if Rutgers had not created the Block R, because people wouldn't have been sure what exactly the brand was, or what they were rooting for. To that end, the Rutgers Block R is everywhere and on everything. It is on a hat that I wear when I work out; it's on the side of a helmet I bought for my young son Nick. It's on jerseys and stickers. It's everywhere. Consistency is a key to effective branding. It doesn't even have to say "Rutgers University." You know what the Block R means.

The Players R the Brand

Beyond the Block R, Schiano knew that to improve the Rutgers athletic brand, he needed to attract legitimate student athletes. He did just that. He recruited kids who could compete academically at Rutgers, and he made sure his players got a lot of help from tutors. His graduation rate was exceedingly high, and in turn, these Rutgers grads, whether they play professional football or not, become ambassadors of the Rutgers brand. When people meet them and see how smart, articulate, and successful they are, and then find out that they are part of the RU football program, it speaks volumes about the academic quality of the school. No matter what the logo or slogan is, word of mouth remains one of the most successful branding tools around.

Consider the case of Ray Rice, who was #27 when he played for Rutgers, which was a brand in itself. He was not only a star running back, but a terrific guy who did make it to the NFL. This is a great accomplishment that reflects well on Rutgers, but Rice is also involved in countless charities, and that, too, makes a positive impression about the player and the school that groomed him. According to TJ Nelligan, who deals with athletes from colleges all the time: "All you hear about Ray Rice is what a great person he is. People talk about him being a good human being. Ray Rice is carrying on the RU brand, which dramatically affects the perception of Rutgers."

Media Savvy

Schiano also made sure that he cut smart and strategic television and other media deals that would provide Rutgers with national exposure. Nelligan Sports Marketing was a key part of that effort, but Rutgers needed to get into bowl games in order to keep interest high. Easier said than done. However, even though Rutgers has struggled at times on the field, the team made it into numerous bowl games.

Beyond that, Schiano himself became a media darling of sorts. Not only does RU football have its own program on various sports-related networks, Schiano also made sure that he had a strong presence in key recruiting states like Florida. Also, it doesn't hurt that Schiano is good on TV. He makes a strong appearance; he is dynamic and forceful. He is the RU football brand, and he's not shy about selling himself, thereby selling the program.

That image is further developed by Schiano's personal appearances. He is a dynamic motivator, not just of his players, but of contributors and sponsors of the program. He is constantly out speaking at events and talking about Rutgers football. He is a huge supporter of causes like Special Olympics and encourages his players to participate as well. Again, he is the brand, so if you are in an audience where Schiano is speaking, and he makes a positive impression, in turn, you can't help but have a better feeling about Rutgers.

Further, like many of the brand experts profiled in this book, Schiano and his team understand the importance of social media. According to Jon Newman, a partner of the Hodges Partnership, a public relations firm in Richmond, Virginia, one of the keys to building a brand is to use all the platforms: "Text messaging, expanded websites and streaming video, Facebook pages and, yes, even Twitter updates, the Schiano marketing machine continues to build the brand. Now however, after four straight winning seasons, the next generation of New Jersey and even national high school recruits, don't remember the old tainted brand, but only the new Block-R winners who have gone to four straight Bowl games. The sell is now easier because the brand has been elevated."[1]

Make the Investment

The rebranding of Rutgers based on its football program did not come cheap. Schiano convinced the Rutgers leadership that in order to build the program and ultimately build the brand, it was absolutely necessary to spend money on recruits, advertising, and social media, but also to expand the football stadium. Some people felt it was a mistake, but he persisted.

The lesson here is that when you are bold, creative, and willing to articulate in a very public way what your vision is, expect to be criticized; if you have thin skin and you can't handle it, you are never going to succeed in reaching your brand equity potential.

Schiano heard the criticism and understood it, but he was committed to the direction that he felt needed to be taken. That doesn't make him 100 percent right all the time, but it does make him a very strong leader, and, right now, it does make him the face of the RU brand.

Branding Lessons

Whether you're working on the gridiron or behind a desk, the branding of a football team has relevant lessons:

- When building a company's reputation, almost anything is possible when a hard-charging visionary/salesman takes the reins and makes believers out of doubters.

- A logo has to make a quick visual impact. Complicated, confusing, and inconsistent images are not the way to go. Be simple, bold, and memorable.

- The members/employees/teammates are the true public face of a brand. Make sure they know how, at all times, to represent the message you want to convey to the public.

- Although you are the brand, you can't do it alone. Brands are often built on savvy use of the media to spread the word, the image, and the reputation of good businesses.

- Dream big, even if some people don't agree with what you see.

TJ Nelligan

Doing Well by Doing Good

TJ Nelligan is a character. Any way you look at it, he stands out in the marketplace as one of the most creative, aggressive, and entrepreneurial sports marketers in the country. His firm, Nelligan Sports Marketing, was created on June 4, 1999, after Nelligan spent nine years at industry leader Host Communications, learning the trade.

Frankly, I've been struggling for months about how to approach this chapter because ultimately the question comes down to figuring out exactly who and what represents the brand. Is it Nelligan Sports Marketing? Is it the company's close association with the Special Olympics organization? Or, is the brand TJ Nelligan himself?

These are the kind of questions each one of us has to consider and answer as we strive to build our brands in a world where relationships rule. I've come to the conclusion that TJ Nelligan himself is the brand, not in a narcissistic or egocentric way, but from a practical point of view. There is a reason why Nelligan Sports Marketing (where I have provided communication and sales coaching for its top executives) isn't called "National Sports Marketing." It needed Nelligan's name, his reputation, his track record, his passion, his relationships, and yes . . . his personal brand.

As I explored the power of Nelligan's brand, I saw that it is rooted in his character and drive—but I also saw that those strengths came to be his brand through his work with the Special Olympics, an organization I volunteered for in college and reconnected with through Nelligan. Nelligan's story gives all of us an excellent opportunity to look at our own lives and see how the decisions we make each day become part of who we are—and don't kid yourself: who we are is inextricably connected to our business success.

What "Road" Are You Going to Take?

The work of the Special Olympics is recognized by millions around the globe, but when Special Olympics New Jersey was trying to decide if it could build a sports complex in the Princeton area, in which it could hold statewide, national, and international events, it turned to Nelligan. As chairman of the board of Special Olympics New Jersey at the time, he became the point person who worked with Marc Edenzon (president of Special Olympics) and helped raise over $8 million of private money to get the project done.

Why? Virtually everyone in the sports marketing world knows Nelligan, and so he can trade in on those relationships in a smart, strategic, and consistent fashion. It's also why he can raise money by picking up the phone and calling friends and associates from his Rolodex (or should I say BlackBerry) and telling them that he is personally involved in an important project and needs their help. The overwhelmingly positive result of those kinds of phone calls is clear evidence of a powerful brand.

When I spoke with Nelligan about how he uses his name to help Special Olympics do things that it otherwise wouldn't be able to do, he had the following to say: "Philanthropy is a huge business in itself, even in this economy—from Bill Gates to the people who volunteer their time to multiple charities that are so worthwhile. However, I didn't seek out to do good things for people. And I certainly didn't choose Special Olympics, Special Olympics chose me through my son Sean. He was born in 1990, and although I was at first in denial about the cause and serious nature of his many health difficulties, by the time he was about eighteen months old, I realized that Sean was not going to be okay, that I wasn't going to coach him in Little League, and that he wasn't going to go to college. It was at that time I had to decide what road to take."

Lots of people in Nelligan's shoes choose the difficult and winding road that leads to thoughts like, "Poor me. My poor kid. What did I do to deserve this? I got cheated. Why did this happen?" But not Nelligan. He says that it didn't take him long to choose the road that would show him how to make his boy's life the best it could possibly be. "Everyone deserves the chance to maximize his or her full potential," says Nelligan with the kind of conviction that is bound to lead to good things.

When Sean was about four or five years old, Nelligan ran into a college fraternity brother from the University of Richmond, who told him about Special Olympics and introduced him to Marc Edenzon, president of Special Olympics New Jersey. Nelligan attended the Special Olympics Summer Games with his son that year, and he was inspired by the athletes and the unbelievable competitiveness, along with their pride and their smiles. Nelligan recalls: "For the first few years of Sean's life I saw only the agony of miserable people who didn't have any hope. But when I went to the Special Olympics event, I saw the exact opposite. Something just clicked. I said to myself, 'This is going to be okay.'"

Things have been better than "okay" for Nelligan and his son Sean since that life-changing day. In fact, Nelligan believes, "If Sean was a 'normal' kid, I would not be as successful as I am today. I look at Sean, who is now twenty years old, as my role model. He shows me every day how to live. He's never had a bad day. He gets out of bed and shouts 'Good morning! It's going to be a great day!' [I've been with Sean on many occasions and can confirm everything his proud father says about him.] I didn't choose the Special Olympics on which to build my name, reputation, and my view of life; it chose me through Sean."

What Is the Brand Connection?

Some of you might be saying, "This is a nice story, but what does this teach us about branding?" For an answer to that question, I went directly to Nelligan and asked him how his experience with Special Olympics impacts how he brands himself. Said Nelligan: "I think my work with Special Olympics and with my son Sean has changed how I perceive what a brand really is. When I worked on Wall Street, I had a more aggressive personality and killer instinct. Today, we have a company that is full of people who believe as I do that we have an obligation to do things for people who can't do things for themselves. We don't go out of our way to put up billboards or to tell people that we are doing good for others; it is intertwined in what we do as a company every day. Our annual sales meetings are held around the Sean Nelligan Foundation Golf Classic to benefit Special Olympics New Jersey and we have managed to raise almost $500,000 over the years for the Special Olympics Tribute Patio at the Sports Complex—which has Sean's name on it. We have been able to encourage others to join us—in fact, we even got Rutgers football coach Greg Schiano to serve as the honorary coach of Special Olympics and have his players attend the opening ceremonies at the Summer Games each year and march in with the athletes of Special Olympics. I'm not sure who has bigger smiles walking into the stadium—the Rutgers football players or the Special Olympic athletes. Our employees all participate in the golf outing and many have become volunteers and even board members for Special Olympics. This gives our employees the opportunity to see that our company is a compassionate organization. We chose this particular charitable cause, and we have wrapped our name and our reputation around it."

We all have heard that it's better to give than to receive. But sometimes it sounds like a trite cliché. But as the story of Nelligan shows, when you actually give without caring what the consequences are, it comes back to you. It just works. The more you give away, the more you get back.

So what exactly is Nelligan Sports Marketing? How does it stand out in the marketplace and how did it start? Says Nelligan: "I was given an unbelievable opportunity by Jim Host (the real pioneer of college sports marketing) to be the first employee of Host Communications in New York City. The company didn't have a presence in the Northeast and when I started, there were two people— me and Jim Host—selling the NCAA Corporate Sponsorship Program to a handful of companies. When I left in 1999, I was managing thirty-five people in eight offices around the country. We built the best sales force in the country, putting together the largest college sports marketing sponsorships at the time with some of the most recognizable Fortune 100 companies. Imagine learning a business from a guy who basically invented it—that's what working for Jim Host was like—it was a great experience—except for the 5:30 A.M. breakfast meetings!"

"When I left Host, I knew most of the athletic directors, conference commissioners, and key marketing people across the country. My theory was, if they already know who I am, why would I call my new company XYZ? If I call and say 'Nelligan Sports Marketing,' they say, 'Hey, TJ.' I already had a great track record and name recognition—so I figured that is what I should name the company."

Rolling the Dice

Sometimes in business, you've got to take a risk, and I'm talking about a big risk, like rolling the dice, putting everything you have on the line, mortgaging your future and that of your family. That's exactly what TJ Nelligan did in 1999. Here's how he tells it: "When I started the company in 1999, I signed over all my assets and if I blew the company up, I would have lost everything. Within the first sixty days, using my equity and goodwill, I was able to sign five big properties, St. Johns University, Seton Hall University, Georgetown University, the Big East Conference, as well as some college events at MSG and the Meadowlands Sports Complex. Much of that was a product of my relationships and my track record of being able to maximize revenue from corporate sponsorships. One hundred percent of those people knew who I was and what I did. What I brought them was the ability to get in and maximize their revenue with our relationships in corporate America. We started the company with five people in Little Falls, New Jersey, and a decade later we have twenty-four offices nationwide, 120 employees, and represent thirty-plus colleges, universities, conferences, and Bowl Games."

Relationships Matter When the Chips Are Down

When I asked Nelligan exactly how the whole relationship game works, here's what he told me: "The ability to maximize and keep the revenue in place is based on relationships. Say, for example, when you are in a recession and the guy at Deans Milk tells his team to cut the budget by 30 percent. We hope we are in the 70 percent that does not get cut. People in our industry, our competitors, hire the guys that couldn't make it in our company. They are not at a high enough experience level, with fire, ambition, and knowledge to be able to get the job done. When our people sit down with a client, they know that they will know about the client's business, what their objectives are, and will tell them, 'here is how we are going to deliver to you something that will help to move the needle and sell your products and services.' I get calls saying how great my people are. That is all because of relationships."

Nelligan cautions, however, that having a successful brand and accomplishing your goals can happen only if you are doing something you love and keep a positive attitude. Says Nelligan, "The most successful people love what they do. They don't get out of bed and say, 'I'm going to work.' They live a lifestyle, not a job. They also understand that it's not what happens to you in life, but rather how you deal with it that matters most. If I didn't have Sean, I don't believe there would be a Nelligan Sports Marketing. He helped me choose that road that led to positive action rather than the one that cried 'Why me?'"

One of the ways to find out about someone's brand reputation is by asking those who know these people best. Andy Duke has known TJ Nelligan for many years and is a successful entrepreneur in his own right, heading up Metrographics, a full-service commercial printing company that is known for its quality work with business forms, specialty items, and print management and distribution. His company is a vendor of Nelligan Sports Marketing, and Andy is part of a group of us who have played golf and socialized together for many years. Here's his take on the TJ Nelligan brand: "When you are dealing with any representative of Nelligan Sports Marketing, you feel like you are dealing with TJ. He doesn't need to be directly involved to still give customers that one-on-one feeling. His personality and the way he has made these personal business contact relationships have carried over into the day-to-day business operations through his team. It all has his blessing."

"With TJ, it's personal," continues Duke. "TJ's success in his business and in the fundraising for Special Olympics is not due to his business skills, but rather due to his personal skills. It all translates to his business success. At a golf outing, special event, meeting or wherever, you always know that TJ is there. It is that larger-than-life personality. You cannot say TJ Nelligan's name and not smile. Not many names can do that! He was a successful person, and then became a successful business person. He would be successful no matter what field he went into."

Your brand, too, has a tone, an attitude, a view of life that grows from who you are as a person. If you want it to be truly successful, consider the advice of TJ Nelligan and find ways to make your brand sing with the joy of life.

Branding Lessons

Difficult challenges often offer the greatest opportunity for growth and happiness. Take advantage of that fact by remembering:

- When life places you at a fork in the road, choose the one that offers the opportunity for positive action. Successful professionals, and in turn their brand, cannot afford to be stalled by whining and complaining.

- It isn't just what happens to you that dictates your brand's reputation . . . it's what you do about it.

- Philanthropy as a business asset cannot be limited to the "good times." If your brand can benefit from association with a nonprofit charity, then you must give your enthusiastic support even in bad times. Ultimately, the more you give away, the more you get back.

- If you employ others, bolster your brand by giving those employees opportunities to actively participate in the company's philanthropic and volunteer activities.

- Tomorrow, think of Sean Nelligan and get out of bed and say "Good morning! It's going to be a great day!"

- Even in a bad economy, it is your strong and consistently built relationships that will sustain your business and, yes, your brand.

Eliot Spitzer

Go Figure

Eliot Spitzer's story proves that in America, no matter how embarrassed or ridiculed public figures may be, there is almost always the opportunity for a "second act." Let's recap Spitzer's story: Eliot Spitzer had built a damn good brand as the "sheriff of Wall Street" when he served as New York attorney general. Spitzer was also the guy who went after prostitutes. He actually wanted to make the penalties for prostitution tougher. He never gave anyone an inch. He was a hard ass who prosecuted everyone and everything he could in order to build his brand as the tough and honest prosecutor who was just what the American political scene needed to clean it up.

He than became governor of New York, where he didn't really accomplish a great deal. He was constantly in the tabloids for one embarrassing incident after another. He actually got caught using New York state troopers to investigate some of his political enemies, including, at the time, the Senate majority leader Joseph Bruno. The incident became known as "troopergate." Spitzer was seen as petty, vindictive, and frankly not very effective as the state's chief executive.

Then, in 2008, Spitzer was forced from office in a much-publicized sex scandal. It was revealed that he not only was paying $3,500 a pop (excuse the pun) to be with top-of-the-line prostitutes, but that he was going out of his way to wire money across state lines in order to get it done. (He became known in the media as "client number 9.") We're talking about a guy who many saw as a hypocrite for breaking laws while he was enforcing them as attorney general.

Not a lot of people felt bad for Spitzer when the end came later that year. In fact, many on Wall Street—a target of Spitzer's prosecutorial ire—celebrated when it was revealed that the feds had nabbed Spitzer as part of an investigation into one of the most lucrative prostitution rings in the country.

If you would have asked me at that time if the less-than-congenial New Yorker would have wound up cohosting a prime-time program on CNN, I would have told you that you were nuts.

The Spitzer case gives us an up-close look at the reasons why branding is not an exact science that works the same way for everyone. Spitzer does everything that should ordinarily kill a brand, and yet comes out like nothing happened. Go figure.

Embarrassed . . . Are You Kidding?

What's so amazing about Spitzer's reemergence in the public eye, after one of the most sensational and lurid sex scandals involving a public official, is that in many ways, Spitzer's actions often contradicted what I have always felt would be the smartest and most appropriate course of action for someone in such a position.

I don't know what I would have done if I had been in his position, but I'm pretty sure I would have been more embarrassed to show my face so soon. I think I would have kept a very low profile, stayed below the radar of news events, and waited for people to forget about me. But, within months of the scandal heard round the world, Spitzer was back on television as an expert commentator on the top cable news networks, talking about financial reform of Wall Street. He quickly became a "go to" talking head as to how to deal with the Goldman Sachs of the world.

Spitzer may be the ultimate opportunist, and I don't necessarily mean that in a negative way. He understood that the fiscal chaos on Wall Street, along with the sub prime debacle, created an opportunity for him to be "out there" in the public eye on countless cable news programs, talking about what went wrong and why. And he also understood that the window of opportunity was a narrow one that might be closed by the time his reputation was ready for rebuilding.

At the same time, he attempted to remind people of what he did as attorney general in New York State, fighting against the excesses in the financial industry and the scandalous actions of greedy Wall Street bankers. In some ways, it's like the classic bait and switch. It is a shell game. It is three-card monte on the streets of New York. The goal is to take people's eye off of one target by diverting their attention to another. Spitzer's goal was to reframe the public dialogue about him by focusing more on what needed to be done to clean up the situation on Wall Street in the hopes that people would focus less on how much he paid for a hooker when he was governor or whether he was client number 8, 9, or 10.

When You Have Nothing to Lose

Amazingly, Spitzer's strategy worked to some extent. The more he was out there talking in the media, the more requests he received to appear as an expert on regulating the financial markets. Interestingly, in 2009, I was approached by a television network in the New York metropolitan area about cohosting a show about politics that would include Spitzer and former New Jersey governor Jim McGreevey (who also resigned in disgrace after his famous "I am a gay American" speech). I declined the offer, thinking that being affiliated with Spitzer in such a public way would hurt my brand as a broadcaster. Then, within a year, Spitzer got a deal to host his own show in prime time on CNN. Hmmm. I worried that his negative image would rub off on me, and he ends up sitting pretty in a prime-time slot. CNN didn't ask me to take over the 8 P.M. slot when they dumped Campbell Brown. What just happened there? The way branding works, I have to assume Spitzer had something CNN needed that wasn't immediately apparent to me or to lots of other media and communication professionals.

What could Spitzer really give CNN? Apparently, he is a brand that CNN very much wanted to affiliate themselves with. In fact, I'm not convinced that Eliot Spitzer would have gotten this opportunity to cohost a program on CNN with political columnist Kathleen Parker if he hadn't been caught up in the sex scandal. On his own, without all the notoriety, Spitzer is the last person you would think who could pull off such a gig. He doesn't have the skills, the look, the persona, or, in my way of thinking, the brand. I'm convinced CNN (whose brand has its own set of serious challenges in the cable news world, as its prime-time ratings have tumbled) picked Spitzer because of the attention, publicity, and potential buzz his selection would create for them. The CNN brass had to know that picking Spitzer would create a sideshow of sorts, which I see as an embarrassment for a network trying to brand itself (unsuccessfully) as a source for serious news and information as opposed to FOX News, which clearly is a conservative media brand, and MSNBC, which unapologetically leans to the left on prime time.[*]

My feeling is that Spitzer's selection will, in fact, hurt CNN's brand over time if its goal is to be seen as a serious source for meaningful news and information. However, if its branding objective is simply to keep people talking about CNN, as opposed to being somewhat forgotten in the media landscape, then it may succeed.

As for Spitzer, he's got nothing to lose. This opportunity to host his own prime-time show on CNN clearly proves that the American dream is alive and well. It also proves that Spitzer knows how to make a comeback, that he is no quitter, and that (even though I may not get it and many others also see him as someone whose credibility is shot) as long as you believe in yourself and are willing to put yourself out there consistently, someone, somewhere, is likely to give you a chance to repackage yourself and improve your brand equity.

I don't know how the Spitzer story is going to end. In fact, by the time this book is published, Eliot Spitzer's gig at CNN may be history. Then again, the opposite could be true. Who knows? If Spitzer is able to poke fun at himself and his world-famous sex scandal, maybe he will begin to be seen as a more likeable and sympathetic figure. If Spitzer succeeds at CNN, and it helps improve the ratings, I wouldn't be surprised if he tried to reenter the political arena and test his new and improved brand with voters. Stranger things have happened.

Branding Lessons

I may not appreciate Eliot Spitzer, I may not get how he can so quickly rebrand himself after his scandal, and I may think he is the ultimate hypocrite, but his story has lessons we can all learn from:

---

[*]Full disclosure: I am an unpaid contributor to MSNBC.com as a media expert.

- A personal crisis is not necessarily the end of your brand. Anything is possible with the American public, whose attention span becomes shorter and shorter each day. Our memories fade, new scandals emerge, other villains take center stage, and the fallen brand can reemerge.

- In this celebrity-obsessed, media/Internet environment, sometimes notoriety comes in many forms, including "negative publicity."

- Usually I disagree with the premise "any publicity is good publicity," but if negative publicity is all you have, there is no harm in trying to make it work for you and your brand.

- If you believe in yourself and are convinced that you have something to offer, being the ultimate opportunist isn't a particularly bad branding strategy.

Wells Fargo/Wachovia

Two Banks into One . . . the Bottom Line

Sometimes it isn't just your organization or your individual brand that needs to be strengthened. Often, a brand needs to be bolstered when an entire industry is being seriously questioned and/or challenged because of recent events that call into question the integrity, character, and behavior of everyone involved. Consider the case of the entire financial services industry, whose reputation took a huge hit in the sub-prime fiasco of 2008/2009. A Gallup poll from October 2009 found that "the percentage of Americans saying they have a 'great deal' or 'quite a lot' of confidence in American banks has dropped to 18 percent, compared to 32 percent in July 2008."[1]

When a brand's customer base takes that kind of hit, efforts to keep a brand strong require a handle-with-care approach.

Combining Brands

The economic meltdown in 2009 is the backdrop and climate in which two American banking giants, Wachovia and Wells Fargo, LLP, came together in one of the most-talked-about and newsworthy merges in banking history. Ultimately, the merged organization will become known as Wells Fargo, but as of this writing the two bank names are working to coexist. According to Sylvia Reynolds, the chief marketing officer for Wells Fargo, "Our strategy is essentially to combine these brands respectfully and honor what's strong about the Wachovia brand: many strengths are common to Wells Fargo . . . our biggest challenge in bringing the brands together is to reassure Wachovia customers that the things they love about Wachovia will remain part of the new company, in particular the brand's focus on outstanding customer service. Our other challenge

210

is building Wells Fargo's brand recognition in areas where Wachovia is very strong but Wells Fargo has not traditionally had a strong presence."[2]

The brand recognition of Wells Fargo will certainly be strengthened by the increased exposure. According to the *Phoenix Business Journal*, "The merger gives Wells Fargo a first-time presence in Alabama, Connecticut, Delaware, Florida, Georgia, Kansas, Maryland, Mississippi, New Jersey, New York, North Carolina, Pennsylvania, South Carolina, Tennessee, Virginia and Washington, D.C."[3] That kind of opportunity growth is priceless, but must be handled carefully.

Bringing or merging two well-known brands together is never easy, but in an interview with Lucia Gibbons, regional president, Northern New Jersey Wachovia, she explained: "Having the two names is a challenge, but we have chosen to view this as an opportunity. We are proactive in talking about the two names and telling the stories 'of success' and talking about the exciting things that are coming with employees, customers, and centers of influence to minimize confusion. . . . In New York and in New Jersey, leading up to the official name change, we are changing the look of the stores—we are painting, adding new furniture and murals, and changing signs that will be covered until the conversion is finalized, which will add to the excitement and present more opportunities to engage customers about the name change."

Making It Personal

Gibbons, who is one of the most recognizable banking executives on the East Coast, has spent many years building relationships and partnerships with individuals and organizations. With the Wells Fargo merger, Gibbons is even more aware of the need to be "out there" with many key stakeholders and audiences. She explains: "I have had heightened sensitivity for the past twelve to eighteen months regarding the name change. I try to be out there even more with employees and centers of influence so that they don't draw conclusions such as 'Lucia has not been visible; she must be too busy with the merger.' It is more important that I am engaged now more than ever because it is a critical time when people draw inaccurate conclusions if you are absent."

Gibbons makes an excellent point about the importance of personal communication. Too many professionals assume that everything will work out smoothly if they send updates about a merger via memos and e-mails to employees and key customers and stakeholders. That's not how it works. In a brand merger, personal, direct, and engaging involvement is critical to the ultimate success. In order to increase the comfort level of all people involved, those people need to see, hear, and engage a company representative in order to ask questions, express concerns, and voice any fears about the merger. When a brand relies on customer and stakeholder confidence and comfort, nothing less will do.

24/7 Branding . . . Getting Your People "Out There"

According to Gibbons's associate Fran Durst, a long-time public relations and communication executive at Wachovia: "Branding is not a one-time experience. It is every day, 24/7. You have to continually build it. It is not something you do because you are changing your name. It's something you have to live every day." To that end, Durst argues that beyond all the advertising and marketing involved in bringing Wells Fargo and Wachovia together under one roof, success again comes down to the people who must lead this effort by putting themselves in strategic positions in the marketplace to tell the story. Says Durst, "We've branded our leaders. People with integrity. Those who tell the truth. They have developed a reputation so that when they do talk about the merger our customers believe them because they trust what they're saying."

Fran Durst's comments regarding promoting the bank's "people" is right on target. As you've seen throughout this book, an organization or corporation's brand is only as strong as the people it puts "out there," as Gibbons argues. This is as true for a bank as it is for a corporation like Hewlett Packard, whose brand took a hit when highly successful CEO Mark Hurd was forced to resign in August 2010 in the midst of a scandal involving his expense reports and a personal relationship he had with a female consultant to HP.

Or, for an airline like JetBlue, whose then-CEO David Neeleman put a nick in the brand when he botched a public appearance on the *Late Show with David Letterman* after the February 2007 fiasco that left flight passengers on the tarmac for more than ten hours.

Whether it's Wachovia/Wells Fargo or any other organization, the best marketing and branding campaigns are only as good as the personnel who represent the name and reputation of the company. According to Sylvia Reynolds, the chief marketing officer for Wells Fargo: "Marketing is not the main way to maintain public confidence. Yes, our advertising should speak to the current environment and the pain consumers and businesses are feeling. But ultimately, how we treat our customers will determine whether they continue to place their trust in us. So certainly it's about more than marketing. Ultimately, we have to show our strength and stability and earn our customers' trust every day through what we do, whether that's continuing to make credit available, changing some of our overdraft policies, or helping our customers with a mortgage modification when they need it."[4]

As is so often the case, again, good branding is not about a huge advertising budget—it is all about quality customer service and the fact that no matter what an organization says it is going to do, it is what it does that matters most. In fact, many argue that poor customer service is the number-one reason most customers change their primary bank. As was the case with TD Bank (see my earlier chapter), Wells Fargo is committed to making sure that in spite of the one name and new colors, the bank will focus on what many see as the "little things," such as greeting customers when they come into the bank, constantly offering additional services, thanking them on a regular basis, and just trying to make the banking process a little easier.

According to Michael Beird, director of banking at J. D. Power and Associates, "As retail banking customers become considerably less loyal, banks need to focus on getting the fundamentals right. . . . Banks that get back to the basics—such as maintaining a clean branch and greeting customers upon entering—may help to alleviate some of the distress customers are experiencing and increase their overall satisfaction."[5]

Branding Lessons

When a financial institution such as Wells Fargo can keep its brand strong in the midst of a merger during a time of economic crisis, its methods are surely worth noting:

- Branding is not an activity, but rather something you have to live on a 24/7 basis.

- Branding your organization must be seen in the context of how your overall industry or profession is seen by the larger community. Branding is not done in isolation, but rather in a larger context of public opinion and perception.

- Effective branding requires organizational leaders to be "out there" on a regular basis representing the institution and its values with enthusiasm, professionalism, and a smile.

Make-A-Wish Foundation
Granting Lasting Wishes

The Make-A-Wish Foundation is an organization that touches the lives of kids who have life-threatening medical conditions. It brings joy to these children by granting their wishes for things like a trip to Disney World or a meeting with a favorite celebrity or a professional athlete, among so many other wish types. According to Tom Weatherall, president and CEO of the Make-A-Wish Foundation of New Jersey, the organization has granted the wishes of more than 6,700 children in the Garden State since 1983 and more than 200,000 nationally since its inception in 1980. The ability to grant such a wish every forty minutes of every day says a lot about the power of a good, authentic, and assertive branding.

Thriving . . . Even in a Tough Economy

At a time when many nonprofit brands are struggling to maintain their reputations, not to mention their piggy banks, the Make-A-Wish Foundation is thriving. The organization is by no means bulletproof and has to constantly evolve and tweak its brand, but the Make-A-Wish Foundation definitely stands out in a crowded marketplace where charitable organizations ask, and often beg, for money in an economy in which more and more people are struggling and fewer and fewer are giving.

"Everyone is challenged by the economic state that we are in," acknowledges Weatherall, "and that's something I go to bed with at night and wake up with in the morning. As great as our brand is, and how much trust is out there, we are not immune from the economic downfall. However, our donors are loyal. The year-on-year giving rate of past donors is so strong. That is what we count on but we do not take for granted. Proper stewardship of such donors is the key."

So what exactly makes the Make-A-Wish Foundation brand so special even in tough times? According to Weatherall, "We all have a different perception of our own mortality, usually we take it for granted. But the Make-A-Wish Foundation works with kids between the ages of two and a half (because science tells us that that is where children begin to collect memories and have cognitive abilities) and age eighteen who are facing life-threatening medical conditions. The foundation comes into their lives to help them battle through. There was one kid, for instance, who wanted to give up during chemotherapy treatments, and said to his mom and dad he couldn't take it anymore. He lost his hair, kids teased him, he was always nauseated, he was tired of the doctors poking him, and he said, 'I'm done, I can't do it. I'm sorry.' The family turned to us. He wanted to meet his hero, this guy who excels in the X-games and can do magical things on a motorcycle and on the four-wheelers. We grant his wish and just knowing he is going to meet this guy gives him the ability to fight beyond the side effects of the chemotherapy. Following the wish, he said to his parents, 'I'm ready to fight again; I'll go through the chemo again.' That's just one example of the kind of work that keeps our donors coming back. I believe Make-A-Wish donors gain an immediate and deep sense of fulfillment."

Stories Matter

I've been working with the Make-A-Wish Foundation for the past several years, since my friend and long-time business associate Ron Del Mauro introduced me to them back in 2001. Ron was being honored by Make-A-Wish, and I was asked to emcee that year's gala. I was hooked on the organization that night as I met the volunteers and contributors, as well as those granting and receiving wishes. It was a powerful experience.

The stories were amazing. Says Weatherall, "Often, nonprofits and other organizations confuse the dumping of data, a plethora of numbers, an inundation of facts with the art of persuasion. Evidence matters, but the question remains: What kind of evidence moves people? What sticks with them, not just in their head but in their hearts? It is, in fact, the heart and less the head that causes people to buy in, to invest not just their money, but their time in an organization." The Make-A-Wish Foundation understands that when you tell a story about a kid whose life may be short and whose pain may be great, but who has been given a ray of sunshine and happiness, some say "the gift of hope," that is what moves people. That is what people care about. Sometimes it's not how many people you help that solidifies your brand, it's the degree to which you help just one person.

Finding the Right Words

The Make-A-Wish Foundation has had to clarify some brand confusion as to what it is and what it is not. For the longest time, people believed that the mission of the Make-A-Wish Foundation was to grant a final wish to a terminally ill child. Think about that. When offering to fulfill the child's wish, the message received by the child and the family was crystal clear—this is a last hurrah before death. But today, that's not always the case, and so the Make-A-Wish Foundation team decided that they would reposition the brand in a different way.

Says Weatherall, "Back in 1980, we used the language 'terminally ill children.' Now, in 2010 you won't find the word 'terminal' in our language at all. Reality is, sadly, some of the children we serve will succumb to their illness.

"Roughly 25 to 30 percent of the children we serve will not outlive their illnesses. But there is great hope for so many others diagnosed with life-threatening medical conditions. And that's the difference between 1980, when we were founded, and today. Science and medicine has advanced significantly; in a case of leukemia, for example, in 1980 the diagnosis was often seen as a death sentence, but today, with the appropriate treatment, the family can hope for a very different outcome. So today, the foundation is not solely for terminally ill children. And, the medical community greatly respects the role we play in serving their younger patients. We pick up where science and medicine leaves off."

This change from serving only those on death's door to those with life-threatening conditions has been a national branding challenge for the Make-A-Wish Foundation. Weatherall continues: "When we were telling the world about the largest gift to Make-A-Wish from philanthropist Joe Plumeri, the chairman and chief executive of the insurance broker Willis Group Holdings, we found that the press who delivered the story changed the verbiage from our mission statement and instead of saying 'life threatening' said 'terminally ill.' So our national brand manager asked for a correction that would say, 'We regret that we used this terminology instead of the correct term, life-threatening.' In response to our request, an AP employee said that AP would interpret the mission statement however it saw fit, and that AP believed that 'terminally ill' was correct. We were aghast and offended. Two hours later, that person called back and said that in the future, AP would use the tem 'life threatening' when discussing the mission statement of our foundation."

This is not a small issue. Words matter when it comes to branding, and in this case, not just raising money, but sending the right message to the children and families that the Make-A-Wish Foundation serves. According to Robb Sansone, a top executive with Fedway Associates, Inc. and a longtime sponsor, supporter, and former chair of the Honorary Board of the Make-A-Wish Foundation: "We grant lasting wishes, not last wishes. This changes the impact the program has on the child and the family. It is not just a wish for a child, but for the entire family. To have a family vacation, trip, or experience is a benefit to all involved."

Be Accountable

It's tough for any business to get behind just one nonprofit when there are so many charitable organizations asking for financial help. So I asked Sansone why Fedway would dedicate so many dollars to support the Make-A-Wish Foundation. "From the corporate side," he explained, "it's important to have a charitable perspective that you can share with your employees so that becomes part of the culture of the company. The Make-A-Wish name is powerful. It is not something you can walk away from. It is reenergizing to people and creates a very lasting impact and that is why people are committed to giving money and also getting involved through the corporation. Here at Fedway, if you mention Make-A-Wish to anyone in the company, it makes a connection with them and defines the kind of work we want to be doing in the community."

This kind of wholehearted commitment is rooted in trust. A nonprofit or charitable organization could have a great mission, but if donors can't trust that the organization is going to spend the donated money wisely and use it both effectively and efficiently to serve the people it's intended to serve, then the brand equity is seriously challenged. As someone who has raised money for public television and other charitable causes, this reality is quite clear to me. Says Weatherall: "First and foremost, the connection between the brand and raising money is trust. We guard that trust as if it were our baby. Whether personal, corporate, or foundation, donated dollars are so precious to us because they are finite. Make-A-Wish has done well over time, because we do not forsake any of our grassroots beginnings. We can never become too big where we take the donor's money for granted. We keep it simple; we do one thing: grant wishes. If we make it more complicated than that, we do the mission a disservice. We let the donors know exactly where their money goes, which is to the funding of a wish. Sometimes the donors are interested in where their funds are directed, such as to a certain illness or pledged toward a certain family or county that resonates with that person, and we try to honor those kinds of requests."

Branding is all about accountability. One of the major themes in this book is that those who are successful in branding themselves and/or the organization or the cause they serve are those who are responsible for their actions. As I've said before, they follow up and they follow through. They are people of their word. When it comes to the Make-A-Wish Foundation, the leadership understands that actions must match promotional promises and rhetoric.

The Company You Keep

Make-A-Wish Foundation has been quite successful when it comes to co-branding and partnering with other established and respected entities. Says Weatherall: "We have to be very careful who we sidle up next to, and vice versa. We turn away money sometimes because we are not comfortable being part of that particular marketing or co-branding initiative. We want whoever is partnering with us to be a great partner."

The foundation has found such a partner in the New York Jets football team; in particular, having their marquee quarterback Mark Sanchez meet and greet a Make-A-Wish Foundation child. Other Jets are doing the same thing. Says Weatherall: "We looked at the Jets' audience, its fan base, and we feel those people would be proud to have the Jets brand associated with Make-A-Wish." Weatherall also pointed out, "The New York Football Giants have been terrific for decades as well, as have the New Jersey Nets, New Jersey Devils, New York Red Bulls, and all the local professional sports franchises in the greater New York and Philadelphia markets. Another great partner has been Macy's. The retail giant has a Thanks for Sharing campaign, which has driven close to $10 million a year into the Make-A-Wish Foundation nationally for the last several years. Disney has been a major and consummate partner pretty much since our inception. Strong brands partnering with other strong brands is key. With its national presence and solid reputations, Macy's and Disney are great for us." You are judged by the company you keep.

Facebook, Anyone?

Social media, too, has helped the foundation find valuable partnerships. Make-A-Wish wasn't on the bandwagon when Facebook first started, but it certainly made up for lost time when it launched its own page in late 2009. Says Weatherall: "At a board meeting where we were discussing social media, a board member who had a marketing background presented a challenge: 'If you guys could get new friends from a Facebook page, our company will match a dollar per new fan you get on the Facebook page.' Suddenly, the page that had twenty or thirty friends (mostly connected family and friends) had seven thousand friends within a matter of a few weeks and that funded the wish of a young man who wanted to visit grandparents in India whom he had never met before. People wanted to hear more about the powerful stories that Make-A-Wish Foundation is a part of. Now, we also use Twitter to put out the word on wishes, particularly celebrity wishes. Celebrities and their staff tweet as the wish is being granted." That's smart, savvy, and effective brand marketing using a powerful social media outlet.

Branding Lessons

Nonprofit and charitable organizations have unique branding issues and challenges because their success is so closely tied to the goodwill of others. That goodwill is largely dependent on one thing: reputation—that is, brand. Here are a few tips to build on the power of a charitable brand:

- Especially in a tough economy, nonprofits that succeed are those that touch the heart of their donors. Do not overlook the power of personal, heartwarming stories that touch people's lives.

- Choose your words carefully. The difference in meaning between terms such as "life-threatening medical condition" and "terminally ill" can literally be the difference between success and failure.

- Nonprofits live and die on the level of trust they build in their donors and stakeholders. The importance of running effective, efficient, and transparent business operation is especially highlighted in businesses where donors have a right to know that you are spending money wisely.

- No need to go it alone. Look for other companies and services that can co-partner with your idea and increase your brand exposure. Social media like Facebook now offer exceptional opportunities in this area.

Fox News

Love 'em, Hate 'em, Trust 'em . . . Watch 'em

Fox News Channel premiered on October 7, 1996. At the time, there was no compelling reason to believe that with CNN firmly established as the number-one cable news operation, that Fox News would become the cable news brand juggernaut that it is today—a decade and a half later.

When Fox News premiered, it wasn't even being carried in New York City, the number-one media market in the country. Fast forward to January of 2010, when a survey conducted by Public Policy Polling found that Fox News had become "the most trusted television news network in the country."[1] Who would have thought that would happen? Even more important, how did this happen and what are the secrets of success regarding the Fox News Channel brand that so many other cable news and other media organizations have failed to understand or execute?

A Bias Indeed . . . For Ratings

Let's be clear. Fox News does in fact have a point of view. Yes, its slogan is "fair and balanced," but it might as well be "we are going to make you watch." For the moment, forget about whatever partisan or ideological bent you think Fox News has; the more compelling and interesting brand bias is that Fox News president and chairman Roger Ailes, one of the country's most media-savvy executives, has put together an on-air lineup that is compelling, entertaining, and provocative. I can't tell you how many people tell me they "hate" Bill O'Reilly, who is on every night at 8 P.M. on Fox News. But then again, The O'Reilly Factor is the number-one cable news program in his time slot. He crushes Keith Olbermann on MSNBC, and CNN isn't even in the game at that time slot.

I've been a guest on O'Reilly's show many times. His on-air persona is pretty much what he's like in person—only a lot taller. On O'Reilly's show, it's all about Bill, and that's the way he likes it. The formula works from a branding perspective. The guy gets a reaction whether on his own show or on other shows considered "enemy territory," including Jon Stewart's *The Daily Show*, *Late Night with David Letterman*, or *TheView*. It's impossible to ignore Bill O'Reilly.

At 9:00 P.M., Fox News features Sean Hannity, who used to be on with Alan Colmes, but now is on alone. Hannity is telegenic, controversial, and clearly leans politically to the right, but his ratings make it clear that just like O'Reilly (although Sean is more likeable), it isn't only those who "like him" who watch. What's so fascinating about people like O'Reilly and Hannity is that they disprove a long-held belief in the world of business that first one must have people "like you" in order to get them to listen to you. In this case, that's just not true. I'm convinced that hundreds of thousands of liberals and Democrats abhor the things said by O'Reilly, Hannity, and for that matter Glenn Beck (a brand in himself that I'm having a hard time figuring out), but watch Fox anyway.

The collective brand of the Fox News Channel, particularly in prime-time, where "opinion is king," is that while a lot of people like and agree with the on-air talent, there is a large number who love to hate them. We are talking about people who get angry, incensed, talk back to their televisions, and say how wrong these three guys are. But then again, they are watching, which allows Fox not only to build its brand, but to charge more for advertising than its competitors. How many other on-air hosts stand out in this manner or get such a visceral reaction?

Appearance Matters . . . A Lot

Fox News's brand is also fascinating because it puts on a product that is visually appealing. Fox was one of the first to use compelling on-air graphics in the now very well known "Fox News Alert" that pops up on the screen with specially designed, "Hey, you better pay attention" music that signals something important is coming. You may argue that what ultimately appears isn't as important as you thought it would be, but what is important is that you paid attention. Roger Ailes knew exactly what he was doing when he created, designed, and built the Fox News brand.

He knew the kind of talent he wanted on the air, which didn't include only "in your face" hosts like O'Reilly, Hannity, and Beck, but also more "newsy," less-strident hosts like Shepard Smith (I particularly enjoy doing Smith's program) and Greta Van Susteren. It also includes talented and incredibly telegenic women who are disproportionately blond but are always "camera ready." Consider the case of Megyn Kelly. She is a lawyer by background who does a show every day on Fox on the issues of the day. She also goes toe-to-toe when she appears on O'Reilly's program (see what I mean about on-air chemistry). Kelly is good not just for O'Reilly's show but for his brand. Kelly is smart, articulate, opinionated, and extremely attractive. Fox News does not apologize for putting very attractive women on the air. Interestingly, the guys on air aren't nearly as attractive. (Nothing new here.)

However, here is the point: In a business in which your brand is predicated so heavily on the physical appearance of those who appear on air, why do so many television networks act like this isn't hugely important? What would be wrong would be if a network was putting women or men on the air because of their physical appearance who weren't qualified or didn't know what they were talking about. On the Fox News Channel, that's just not the case. Every woman on that channel has something meaningful to contribute. Again, you may disagree with what the women have to say, and you may be convinced that they lean to the right, or worse, are serving as cheerleaders for the Republican Party, but they are very good on camera, and they are also extremely knowledgeable and articulate.

When it comes to branding, the physical package of what you are offering—be it in cable news, real estate, or sales—has a lot to do with your success.

Criticism of Fox Hasn't Hurt Its Brand

What's so interesting about the Fox News Channel brand is that, right from the top with Roger Ailes, all those involved in the production of Fox News make no apologies for who and what they are. They are in your face 24/7. Even when Fox is attacked, its brand is enhanced. According to the article "White House Attacks Fox News" by Jeff Louis, the Obama White House has recently said through top Obama aid David Axelrod: Fox is "not really a news station." Or, as former White House chief of staff Rahm Emmanuel said of Fox: It "is not a news organization so much as it has a perspective." Or, consider Anita Dunn, former White House communications director, who attacked Fox by saying, "Let's not pretend they're a news organization like CNN is."[2]

These attacks give Fox national attention. MSNBC (where I have appeared many times and for whom I write a media column on MSNBC.com) attacks Fox News on a regular basis (and Fox hits back at MSNBC and CNN just as hard). But all these attacks don't seem to hurt Fox; in fact, they draw more attention to the Fox network and to the brand. Consider that according to the Public Policy Poll from early 2010: "49 percent of Americans trusted FOX News, 10 percentage points more than any other network."[3]

Further, in the same article on this fascinating poll, while 37 percent said they didn't trust Fox, 41 percent said they didn't trust CNN.[4] So, here's the point: While CNN can be referred to by Anita Dunn or anyone else as a real "news organization," how do Dunn and other Fox News critics explain the fact that nearly half of all Americans name Fox News as the most "trusted" news source in the country?

Those statistics are undeniable. That's the thing about Fox and its brand. The more you attack them, the better it seems to be for the channel and its bottom line. And as for the Obama White House, its attacks on the Fox News brand seem to have backfired. The Obama brand itself winds up looking weak by attacking Fox for being critical of the president. When your brand is strong (see the President Barack Obama chapter in this book), you don't need to attack those who challenge or criticize you, whether you feel it's fair or not. In many ways, the attacks have made the Obama brand look weak. Further, when it comes to the Fox News brand, there is another undeniable fact: Fox News carries nine of the top ten cable news programs currently on the air. How can anyone argue with success like that?

Only the Fox News Channel can run full-page ads, as it did in the New York Post and other newspapers across the country on January 10, 2010, saying: "Thanks America for making 2009 our best year ever! . . . The 1 and only 1 cable news network on television . . . 8 years and counting . . . Fox News Channel, the most POWERFUL name in news." Facts. Even if you don't like them, or think they're biased, you can't successfully argue against the success of the Fox News brand.

Branding from the Top

According to a January 10, 2010, front-page New York Times story about Roger Ailes, written by David Carr and Tim Arango, entitled "A Fox Chief at the Pinnacle of Media and Politics," Ailes is "the most successful news executive of the last 10 years, and his network exerts a strong influence on the fractured conservative movement."[5]

According to Ailes, "I built this channel from my life experience. . . . My first qualification is I didn't go to Columbia Journalism School. There are no parties in this town [New York City] that I want to go to."[6] While Roger Ailes has a very clear and very simple sense of what he wanted the Fox News Channel to be, it is how others, even those who are competitors and critics, characterize his work at the network that best describe the brand's success.

Roger Ailes's background is fascinating. He started as a producer at the age of twenty-seven on The Mike Douglas Show, where he met a very damaged brand in the form of Richard Nixon. When Nixon appeared on The Mike Douglas Show and didn't come off as particularly appealing, he asked Ailes what he thought might be the reason for this weak appearance. As usual, Ailes didn't hold back; in spite of his youth, he told Nixon "The camera doesn't like you." Nixon then said to Ailes, "It's a shame a man has to use gimmicks like this to get elected." But Ailes wouldn't back down to Nixon, and his response clearly characterized the deep connection between successful branding of personalities and the ubiquitous and expanding role of television in the 1960s: "Television is not a gimmick, and if you think it is, you will lose again."[7] Soon thereafter, Nixon hired Ailes to help him craft his own campaign for the 1968 election. Ailes later went on to consult not just political figures, but corporate execs, as to how best present themselves to the world via the media which, simply put, was largely about their brands.[8]

Ailes wrote a ground-breaking book that had a great influence on me called *You Are the Message,* which I have used in countless branding seminars, workshops, and in my own executive coaching.[9]

Bob Wright, who was the former chief executive at NBC, said of Ailes, "He's got a very good sense of simplicity on air." Mr. Wright added, "Because he had that background of being involved in political campaigns, he could develop a message and deliver it and test it quickly to see if it's effective."[10]

That's exactly what Ailes has done at the Fox News Channel. He and his programming team lead by Bill Shine, senior vice president of programming (and my former director/producer at an upstart, but later canceled, cable news network called "News Talk TV") test on-air talent as well as chemistry, graphics, content, and the production quality of their shows on a daily basis. If it works, they keep it and expand it. If it doesn't, it doesn't take long for them to scrap it. A successful brand must be nimble.

While the Fox News Channel has spun off and created a business channel subsidiary to compete directly with CNBC called "Fox Business Network," the Fox News Channel is still the jewel in the Fox cable news brand. According to James Carville, a CNN contributor as well as a hard-core Democrat who was a top advisor to Bill Clinton (one of many Democrats who have attacked Fox News for its approach): "In terms of the news business, the cable television business, and the political business, there is him [Ailes] and then there is everybody else."[11]

I'm not saying the entire Fox News brand is all about Roger Ailes. But the Fox News brand would not be nearly as successful as it has been if some other chief executive had been leading it for the past fifteen years.

Branding Lessons

Consider some takeaways from the branding of Fox News that all of us need to consider, regardless of our political ideology or whatever cable news program we watch:

- You have to know what you want to be before you attempt to build your brand. That was clearly the case with Fox News back in the fall of 1996. Roger Ailes knew what he wanted. Yes, it has evolved on many levels, but it is true to its mission and, whether people love 'em, hate 'em, or ridicule 'em, the mission has not changed.

- When it comes to building a brand, not wanting to offend people just won't work. You need provocative personalities that stand out and that are memorable. Even if viewers (customers/clients) are yelling at the screen while watching them, these customers are remembering them and talking about them. And if your brand is being talked about, then you are three-quarters of the way to success.

- Successful brands see the void in the market and know what their customers want. The Fox News Channel is acutely aware of what its audience wants and needs.

- No successful brand highlighted in this book has been able to succeed without an extremely strong, dynamic, and often aggressive CEO. In Roger Ailes, Fox News has that in spades.

- To those who have issues with Fox News's journalistic standards: (Full disclosure: As an on-air commentator under contract at the time at MSNBC, I said some pretty harsh things about Fox News.) None of that criticism takes away from the fact that after fifteen years, Fox News is by far the most successful cable news brand in the business. This goes back to the title of this chapter: "Fox News: Love 'em. Hate 'em. Trust 'em" . . . but no matter what, you are going to watch 'em. Need we say more?

NOTES

Tiger Woods: No One Walks on Water

1. Natalie James, "Tiger Woods Loses Another Major Sponsor, Gatorade," *The Money Times*, February 27, 2010. http://www.themoneytimes. com/featured/20100227/tiger-woods-loses-another-major-sponsor-gatorade-id-10101875.html.
2. Corey Dade and Reed Albergotti, "Woods Speaks Out on Crash, Blaming Himself," *Wall Street Journal*, November 30, 2010. http://online.wsj. com/article/SB125943335530168067.html.
3. "Transcript: Tiger's Public Statement," February 19, 2010. http://web. tigerwoods.com/news/article/201002198096934/news/.
4. Mike McAllister, "Glitch in Last Year's Game Morphs into 'the Jesus Shot,'" *PG Tour*, August 28, 2008. www.pgatour.com/2008/r/08/28/ jesus.shot.

Buddy "The Cake Boss" Valastro: Baking Cakes and Living Dreams

1. Carly Baldwin, "Hoboken Baker Is the 'Cake Boss,'" *NJ.com*, April 16, 2009. http://www.nj.com/hobokennow/index.ssf/2009/04/hoboken_ baker_is_the_cake_boss.html.

Toyota: Putting the Brakes on Its Brand

1. "Raft of Toyota Recall Jokes Fill up Cyberspace," *USA Today*, February 15, 2010. http://content.usatoday.com/communities/driveon/post/ 2010/02/jokes/1.
2. Ken Thomas and Larry Margasak, "Toyota Official's E-mail: 'We Need to Come Clean,'" *Msnbc.com*, April 7, 2010. http://www.msnbc.msn.com/ id/36236675.
3. Curt Anderson and Danny Robbins, "Toyota's Legal Tactics: Deception and Evasion," *Msnbc.com*, April 11, 2010. http://www.msnbc.msn. com/id/36391413/ns/business-autos.
4. Ibid.
5. Toyota Corporate, "Toyota Responds to AP Report on Discovery Practices," April 13, 2010. http://pressroom.toyota.com/pr/tms/toyota-responds-to-ap-report-on-156936.aspx.
6. Nick Bunkley and Micheline Maynard, "Toyota Is Expected to Pay $16.4 Million Fine," *New York Times Online*, April 18, 2010. http://www. nytimes.com/2010/04/19/business/19toyota.html?scp=2&sq= toyota&st=cse.
7. Jim Lentz, "Our Pledge to Toyota Drivers," Toyota Motor Sales, 2010. http://pressroom.toyota.com/pr/tms/document/OpenLetterAD_5.pdf.

BlackBerry: The Brand You "Can't Live Without"

1. "Jim Balsillie Quotes," *ThinkExist.com*, 2010. http://thinkexist.com/ quotation/we-made-sure-the-cio-was-happy-the-cio-has-a-veto/ 512144.html.

2. "How BlackBerry Conquered the World," *CNN.com*, March 23, 2005. http://www.cnn.com/2005/BUSINESS/03/23/blackberry.rim/.

Coke: It's the Real Thing

1. Bill Backer, *The Care and Feeding of Ideas* (New York: Three Rivers Press, 1994).
2. Mark Haig, *Brand Failures: The Truth about the 100 Biggest Branding Mistakes of All Time* (London: Kogan Page, 2005).

The Catholic Church: A Brand in Constant Crisis

1. "Pope, in Sermon, Says He Won't be Intimidated," *New York Times*, March 28, 2010. http://www.nytimes.com/2010/03/29/world/europe/29pope.html?scp=1&sq=the%20petty%20gossip%200f%20dominant%200pinion&st=cse.
2. Reuven Fenton, "Defiant Pope Rips 'Chatter,'" *NYPost.com*, April 5, 2010. http://www.nypost.com/p/news/international/defiant_pope_rips_chatter_zIlcORsltqZJ4hn0VRNKKM.
3. William Levada, "The New York Times and Pope Benedict XVI," *Vatican: The Holy See*, March 26, 2010. http://www.vatican.va/resources/resources_card-levada2010_en.html.
4. "Satan Behind Media Attacks on the Pope, Asserts Italian Exorcist," *Catholic News Agency*, March 31, 2010. http://www.catholicnewsagency.com/news/satan_behind_media_attacks_on_the_pope_asserts_italian_exorcist. See also Richard Owen and Roger Boyes, "Attacks on Pope Over Child Abuse Scandal Are 'Akin to Anti-Semitism,'" *Times Online*, April 2, 2010. http://www.timesonline.co.uk/tol/comment/faith/article7086143.ece.
5. David Clohessy, "Clergy Sex Victims Blast NY Archbishop Dolan," *The Survivors Network of Those Abused by Priests* [press statement], March 29, 2010. http://www.snapnetwork.org/snap_statements/2010_statements/032910_clergy_sex_victims_blast_ny_archbishop_dolan.htm.

The Kennedys: The Rise and Fall of America's "Royal Family"

1. "The Kennedy Family: Who Will Carry Legacy?" *Jacksonville Observer*, August 27, 2009. http://www.jaxobserver.com/2009/08/27/the-kennedy-family-who-will-carry-legacy.
2. Ibid.
3. Ibid.
4. Andrea Peyser, "Welcome to Blogo-rama," *New York Post*, July 26, 2010. http://www.nypost.com/f/print/news/local/welcome_to_blago_rama_B6g0H30eRdIrChDTt2zQWP.
5. "The Kennedy Family."
6. Ibid.
7. Wyatt Earp, "Caroline Kennedy: She's, You Know, Qualified," *Support Your Local Gunfighter*, December 29, 2008. http://supportyourlocalgunfighter.com/2008/12/caroline-kennedy-shes-you-know-qualified/.

Starbucks: "Your Usual, Steve?"

1. Howard Schultz, *Pour Your Heart Into It: How Starbucks Built a Company One Cup at a Time* (New York: Hyperion, 1999).

Blackwater: Changing Your Name Doesn't Fix Your Reputation

1. Mike Baker, "Blackwater Sheds Tarnished Name: New Name Is 'Xe,'" *HuffingtonPost.com*, February 13, 2009. http://www.huffingtonpost. com/2009/02/13/blackwater-sheds-tarnishe_n_166739.html.
2. "Blackwater Dumps Tarnished Brand Name," *CBSNews.com*, February 13, 2009. http://www.cbsnews.com/stories/2009/02/13/national/ main4800193.shtml.
3. Mike Baker, "Blackwater to Change Name to 'Xe,'" *Information Liberation*, February 21, 2009. http://www.informationliberation.com/ ?id=26535.
4. "Blackwater Worldwide Changes Its Name to Xe; Same Mercenaries, but Now with More 'Aviation Support,'" *Cryptogon.com*, February 14, 2009. http://cryptogon.com/?p=6904.

Campbell Soup: Engage Your Employees . . . Awaken Your Brand

1. Terry Waghom, "How Employee Engagement Turned Around Campbell's," *Forbes.com*, June 23, 2009. http://www.forbes.com/2009/06/ 23/employee-engagement-conant-leadership-managing-turnaround. html.
2. Ibid.
3. Tom Rath and Barry Conchie, "Saving Campbell Soup Company," *Gallup Management Journal*, February 11, 2010. http://gmj.gallup.com/ content/125687/saving-campbell-soup-company.aspx#1.
4. Ibid.

Bobbi Brown: Keeping It Real

1. Christopher Rosica, *The Authentic Brand* (Paramus, NJ: Noble Press, 2007).
2. Ibid.

Oprah: The "Babe Ruth" of Modern-Day Branding

1. Patricia Sellers, "The Business of Being Oprah," *Fortune*, April 1, 2002. http://money.cnn.com/magazines/fortune/fortune_archive/2002/04/ 01/320634/index.htm.
2. Ibid.
3. David Carr, "Oprah Puts Her Brand on the Line," *New York Times*, December 24, 2007. http://www.nytimes.com/2007/12/24/business/ media/24carr.html?_r=1.
4. "Oprah Responds to School Sex Claims," *National Public Radio* [transcript], November 6, 2007. http://www.npr.org/templates/story/story. php?storyId=16047154.

BP Oil: Total Brand Destruction

1. "BP CEO: We'll Pay Oil Spill Costs," *CBS News/The Early Show*, May 3, 2010. http://www.cbsnews.com/stories/2010/05/03/earlyshow/main 6455577.shtml.
2. "BP CEO Tony Hayward: 'I'd Like My Life Back,'" *The Huffington Post* [video], June 1, 2010. http://www.huffingtonpost.com/2010/06/01/ bp-ceo-tony-hayward-video_n_595906.html.

3. Ravi Somaiva, "What Not to Say When Your Company Is Ruining the World," *Newsweek.com*, June 2, 2010. http://www.newsweek.com/2010/06/02/what-not-to-say-when-your-company-is-ruining-the-world-html#.
4. Heidi Avery, "The Ongoing Administration-Wide Response to the Deepwater BP Oil Spill," *The White House Blog*, June 4, 2010. http://www.whitehouse.gov/blog/2010/06/04/ongoing-administration-wide-response-deepwater-bp-oil-spill-june-4-2010.

Howard Stern: "The King of Media"

1. "How Much Is Howard Stern Worth?" *Hollyworth*, March 11, 2010. http://www.hollyworth.com/howard-sterns-net-worth.
2. David Spade, "Howard Stern," *Time*, April 30, 2006. http://www.time.com/time/magazine/article/0,9171,1187317,00.html.
3. Dorothy Pomerantz and Lacey Rose, "The Celebrity 100," *Forbes*, June 28, 2010. http://www.forbes.com/lists/2010/53/celeb-100-10_Howard-Stern_5S85.html.

E*TRADE: When Your Brand Is a "Baby"

1. Matthew Scott, "E*Trade Ads Deliver a Bouncing New Talking Baby," *Daily Finance*, January 10, 2010. http://www.dailyfinance.com/story/company-news/e-trade-ads-deliver-a-bouncing-new-talking-baby/19318738/?icid=sphere_copyright.
2. Ibid.
3. Ibid.

Governor Chris Christie: When Being "Blunt" Is Your Brand

1. Tom Moran, "Picking Fights, Forcing Change: Gov. Chris Christie's First 100 Days," *NJ.com*, May 2, 2010. http://blog.nj.com/njv_tom_moran/2010/05/picking_fights_forcing_change.html.
2. George Will, "Rringing Thunder-ous Change to New Jersey," *WashingtonPost.com*, April 22, 2010. http://www.washingtonpost.com/wp-dyn/content/article/2010/04/21/AR2010042104451.html.
3. Andy Barr, "Gov. Chris Christie: 'This Is Who I Am,'" *Politico*, May 14, 2010. http://www.politico.com/news/stories/0510/37249.html.
4. Ibid.
5. Ibid.
6. William McGurn, "Reaganism, New Jersey Style," *WSJ.com*, April 13, 2010. http://online.wsj.com/article/SB10001424052702303828304575180270979668714.html.

Lebron James: When Your "Decision" Hurts Your Brand

1. Peter Vecsey, "Uncaring LeBron Turned Back on Cavaliers," *NYPost.com*, July 12, 2010. http://www.nypost.com/p/sports/more_sports/king_of_all_disses_trWpbVf7BYYLUljeLuMP80?CMP=OTC-rss&FEEDNAME.
2. Lisa De Moraes, "NBA Star LeBron James Show on ESPN Posts Huge Ratings," *Washington Post*, July 9, 2010. http://voices.washingtonpost.com/tvblog/2010/07/lebron-james-show-on-espn-post.html.
3. James Kirk Wall, "Is LeBron James More Popular than Jesus?" *Chicago Tribune*, July 8, 2010. http://newsblogs.chicagotribune.com/religion_the-seeker/2010/07/james-kirk-wall-is-lebron-james-more-popular-than-jesus.html.

4. Michael Sokolove, "Epic Confusion: The Narrative of the Superathlete," *New York Times*, August 7, 2010. http://www.nytimes.com/2010/08/08/weekinreview/08sokolove.html.
5. "LeBron James Takes Out Newspaper Ad to Thank Akron," *Cleveland.com*, August 2, 2010. http://www.cleveland.com/cavs/index.ssf/2010/08/lebron_james_takes_out_an_ad_t.html.

Newsweek: Times They Are a-Changing"
1. "With *Newsweek* for Sale, an Era Fades," *New York Times*, May 10, 2010. Fadeshttp://dealbook.blogs.nytimes.com/2010/05/06/with-newsweek-for-sale-an-era-fades/.
2. Stephanie Clifford, "*Newsweek* on Block as Era of the Newsweekly Fades," *New York Times*, May 5, 2010. http://www.nytimes.com/2010/05/06/business/media/06newsweek.html.
3. Ibid.
4. Ibid.
5. Ibid.

Sarah Palin: So You Want to Be Taken Seriously?
1. John Heilemann and Mark Halperin, *Game Change* (New York: HarperCollins, 2010), 396.
2. Ibid., 397.

Rutgers University: The Block R Success Story
1. Jon Newman, "Rutgers Football Coach . . . Brand Expert?" *Jon's PR 1.5*, December 27, 2008. http://jonnewman.typepad.com/jons_bridge/rutgers/.

Wells Fargo/Wachovia: Two Banks into One . . . the Bottom Line
1. Rita Chang, "Wells Fargo Aims to Beat Banking-Biz Woes with Data," *Advertising Age*, October 19, 2009. http://adage.com/cmointerviews/article?article_id=139734.
2. Ibid.
3. "Wells Fargo, Wachovia Complete Merger," *Phoenix Business Journal*, January 2, 2009. http://www.bizjournals.com/phoenix/stories/2008/12/29/daily36.html.
4. Chang, "Wells Fargo."
5. "2010 Retail Banking Satisfaction Study," *JDPower.com*, 2010. http://www.jdpower.com/finance/articles/2010-Retail-Banking-Satisfaction-Study.

Fox News: Love 'em, Hate 'em, Trust 'em . . . Watch 'em
1. Andy Barr, "Poll: Fox Most Trusted Name in News," *Politico*, January 10, 2010. http://www.politico.com/news/stories/0110/32039.html.
2. Jeff Lewis, "White House Attacks Fox News," *Beneath the Brand*, October 25, 2009. http://www.talentzoo.com/beneath-the-brand/news.php/White-House-Attacks-Fox-Newstalentzoo/?articleID=5468.
3. Barr, "Poll."
4. Ibid.
5. David Carr and Tim Arango, "A Fox Chief at the Pinnacle of Media and Politics," *New York Times*, January 9, 2010. http://www.nytimes.com/2010/01/10/business/media/10ailes.html?_r=1.

6. Ibid.

7. Scott Collins, *Crazy Like a Fox: The Inside Story of How Fox News Beat CNN* (New York: Portfolio, 2004).

8. Carr and Arango, "Fox Chief."

9. Roger Ailes, with Jon Kraushar, *You Are the Message: Secrets of the Master Communicators* (Homewood, Ill.: Dow Jones–Irwin, 1988).

10. Carr and Arango, "Fox Chief."

11. Ibid.

ABOUT THE AUTHOR

Steve Adubato, Ph.D., is a broadcaster, author, and motivational speaker. He is a visiting university professor at NYU and Seton Hall University, an Emmy Award-winning anchor for Thirteen/WNET (PBS), and a newspaper columnist. Steve regularly appears on the *TODAY* show, CNN, FOX, and CBS/2 in New York as a media and political analyst. He is the author of *Speak from the Heart, Make the Connection,* and *What Were They Thinking?*